*If These Walls Had Ears*

# IF THESE WALLS
# HAD EARS

*The Biography of
a House*

# JAMES MORGAN

**WARNER BOOKS**

A Time Warner Company

Warner Books, Inc., 1271 Avenue of the Americas, New York, NY 10020
**w** A Time Warner Company

Printed in the United States of America

Book design by Barbara Balch

First Printing: August 1996

10 9 8 7 6 5 4 3 2 1

Library of Congress Cataloging-in-Publication Data
Morgan, James
If these walls had ears : the biography of a house / James Morgan.
p.  cm.
ISBN 0-446-51914-6
1. Dwellings—Arkansas—Little Rock—History. 2. Family—Arkansas—Little
Rock—History. 3. Little Rock (Ark.)—Biography. 4. Little Rock (Ark.)—History.
5. Morgan, James, 1944-  —Homes and haunts—Arkansas—Little Rock. I. Title.
F417.A7M64  1996
976.7'73—dc20                    95-52068
                    CIP

*Photo credits:* The author wishes to thank the following for the use of their photographs.
If not listed below, the photographs are from the author's own collection. Pages xii, 3,
13, 16, 24, 35, 39, 40, 42, 56 Mildred Armour; page 74 Joyce Murphree Stroud; page
4 Ruth Chapin; pages 124, 178, 187 Forrest and Sue Wolfe; pages 90, 105, 108, 116
Ruth Murphree; pages 123, 132, 145, 153 Roy and Rita Grimes; pages 158, 168 Ed and
Sheri Kramer; page 198 Sue Goodman; pages 226, 239 Jack Burney.

*For Beth*

*The history of a nation is not in parliaments and battlefields, but in what the people say to each other on fair days and high days, and in how they farm, and quarrel, and go on pilgrimage.*

—WILLIAM BUTLER YEATS

# Contents

*Here's how 501 Holly looked right after it was built, in the fall of 1923.*

# Prologue

In the middle of the night, a house creaks under the weight of its secrets. This isn't merely the racing imagination of someone startled awake by strange noises; this is a middle-aged man's bone-deep knowledge of the way life bears on living things.

A house is a body, like yours and mine. It's not such a stretch to think of beams as bones, electrical wiring as a nervous system, plaster and brick as the layers of skin that protect us from the elements. And yet uninhabited houses and uninhabited bodies are only compelling to contractors and coroners. It takes a soul to give a body life.

I've always been curious about the houses I've lived in, wondered who lived there before me and what their stories were like. But I never looked into any of their histories. There was always *today's* business to attend to. Besides, as with so many of us in the last half of the twentieth century, I've lived in too many houses—twenty-five, to be exact, counting student apartments and starter town houses, from the time I was born up through today. Until I moved into the house I'm now in, and in which I've lived almost seven years, the longest I had lived in any one place was four years and eight months. That was the house my family moved to in Miami, Florida, where I lived from the middle of eighth grade until

I left for college. They stayed there twenty years, but I never really went home again. In fact, I'm not sure I've been there at all.

The story of America has always been the story of a search for home. It's a restless journey in which we never quite seem to arrive. In my case, five times I've followed jobs toward a goal I thought would make me complete. Probably not coincidentally, I've moved twice from would-be homes exposed by failed marriages, setting out alone again to create in life that ideal home that exists only inside my head. Though home is a spiritual concept, it tends to take on physical weight. For the longest time, I couldn't actually describe the place that pressed so upon me; I would just inch my way toward what felt right.

But somewhere along the journey, a picture began to develop in my consciousness. The house is larger inside than it looks from the street. It has fourteen-foot ceilings and gracefully spacious rooms. Its furnishings are old and elegant and a little bit worn. There are solid tables piled high with books and peopled with photos of loved ones in silver frames; in the hall, still other family photographs cover one wall from floor to ceiling. A hardwood log crackles in the fireplace. In the dining room, a massive table is set for twelve. There's a screened back porch lined with rockers, and a laughing crowd of siblings and cousins flows constantly between that porch and the kitchen, where the family is anchored by a sturdy round oak table set dead in the center. Sometimes, in my daydreams, I'm among that group and sometimes I'm not. Sometimes I'm hidden away in one of the nooks and crannies in this house that's large enough to provide such places to get lost in, and I'm reading a book in an easy chair, with the afternoon sun streaming in through the ceiling-high windows, filtered by the sheers.

Is anyone surprised that Ralph Lauren is a rich man?

But this isn't some ideal I've absorbed from reading magazines. The house is actually my aunt May's house in Hazlehurst, Mississippi.

What does it say about me that this is the first house I ever lived in, when my father was away at war and my mother took me home to her sister's?

As a home, that house turned out far from ideal for those who grew up in it day by day. But for me, that's beside the point. For me, the distance works. The distance spins magic, allowing me to create in my own head the illusion of a life that's comfortable and carefree and *safe*. That's a childish notion, I know, but who believes that grown-ups are anything but vulnerable children at heart? Besides, that's one of the things that the home we all chase *is*—a place, a condition, in which the world can't touch you.

My aunt's house also probed this raw nerve of permanence with me. By the time she died in the spring of 1993, she had lived in that house just shy of seventy years. She knew every square inch of wall, every layer of paint, every scuff on the baseboard, every worn spot on the carpet. In the middle of the night, when she was awakened by creaks, she heard the squeals of her children and the laughter of her friends and, yes, the anguished howls of her own private demons. But at least they were *her* demons.

The house I live in now with my wife and stepdaughters fulfills some of the requirements of the house in my head. It's a bungalow in the Craftsman style, which means it's low-slung and solid. It hugs a hill. And yet the house isn't simple and forthcoming in the usual Craftsman way—there are curlicues under the eaves, and arches that seem to curve slightly skyward, evoking an air of mystery that's almost Oriental. It also has a second story. At 3,200 square feet, with five bedrooms, a studio, and an office, it's larger than it looks from the outside, and many of our furnishings are old and elegant and worn. We have stacks of books and an open-air front porch lined with rockers. But our dining table won't comfortably seat twelve, and we somehow never get all our snapshots framed (or even developed). The ceilings are only ten feet high and the rooms, while generous, aren't as big as the rooms in my mind. There is no sturdy round anchor in the kitchen. The house is complex enough to provide hiding places, if, as at my aunt's house in recent years, there were only one person living in it. But with four of us and a dog here, we can run but we can't very well hide—at least not long enough to enjoy an uninterrupted book bathed in the warmth of the afternoon sun.

In the upstairs hall, we've covered a wall with family photographs, but it's the all-too-new kind of American family photo gallery: spliced history. The center of this grouping is a montage from Beth's and my wedding just over six years ago. Here we are kissing, as her little girls, Blair and Bret, and my lanky boys, David and Matthew, look on—a little glumly, it seems to me. Over here to the left there's a snapshot of the new nuclear family, and, down here, a portrait of the new extended family as well—four generations of Arnolds and three of Morgans, posed on a wide staircase, a hybrid genealogical tree forced by modern life to put down new roots, and to tie off old ones. Some of the people in this picture have just met.

No wonder so many people gravitate to old houses, with their comforting implications about the test of time.

In the summer of 1992, on a night when Beth was out of town and the girls were with their dad, I had supper with our neighbors. One of the couples had lived in their house six years, the other thirteen. They were telling stories about the neighborhood, one of which concerned my house. It seems that during one period back in what the neighbors thought was the 1970s, this house was briefly turned into apartments.

That surprised me. This area, called Hillcrest, isn't what you would think of as an apartment neighborhood. It's an old, tree-lined, church-steepled family ground, developed when people wanted to know their neighbors and so built front porches from which to see and be seen on balmy evenings. This happens to be the neighborhood where Bill and Hillary Clinton moved after he lost the governor's race in 1980. Two days after the defeat, they bought an old house with a big porch about ten blocks from here. I wouldn't be surprised if he ambushed potential voters from the front steps as they strolled by.

The story about my house goes like this: One day a proper neighbor lady, seeing a moving van in front of the house, decided to take the new people a cake. She dressed herself and marched over here to 501 Holly Street and knocked on the door. She knocked again, then again. Apparently, the new people couldn't hear her over the music, which, even out on the front porch, she could *feel* thumping through the thick walls. Finally the door swung open and, to the wails of rock and roll, the astonished matron saw a houseful of "hippies," as she characterized them, roller-skating through the living room. The man who opened the door was wearing a dress.

We all laughed, and I uttered that old cliché, "If the walls had ears." The conversation turned to other things, but for the rest of the evening, I couldn't stop thinking about that notion.

It made me wonder about this house and its secrets. What bizarre scenes have these walls witnessed? What joy, what pain? What human drama has taken place here in this very room where I write? People used to know such things, because people used to stay put. Now we're a nation of strangers, to one another and even to our surroundings.

It's astonishing to me, a former magazine editor who actually reveled in assigning pieces on the topic du jour, that the older I get, the more I find myself interested in history. I don't mean the big, sweeping, official-record version of people, places, and events; what attracts me now are the myriad small ways in which we're connected to the lives that preceded us. The other day I had some work done on the porch roof, and after the workmen had gone I found in the yard a fragment of rotted board with a rusty nail sticking out of it. Instead of tossing it without a thought, I stood there holding this silly artifact in my hand, wondering how old the nail was, and who drove it.

The truth is, I suspect that this kind of curiosity is becoming the topic du jour among the leading edge of the baby-boom generation—whether they've recognized it or not. I was at my aunt's cabin recently with an old friend, a man who once believed so relentlessly in living in the present that he wouldn't allow antiques in his house, and he began studying the way the sloping ceiling boards were fitted together. "Look at this," he said finally, running his fingers over the narrow planks that had aged to a honeyed hue. "You know, it's weird, but I've started noticing stuff like how cabin ceilings were built."

But it's not the boards themselves that compel him, any more than it was the rusty nail that intrigued me. The hidden subject here, I believe, is *connectedness*. It shows up in all sorts of ways. As we slouch toward middle age, we begin to turn inward. I've read that this is true, and I'm now noticing it in myself. Family and home begin to matter more to us. The hot front-page story that Sam Donaldson gets paid to be indignant about becomes less urgent to us, while the small human-interest story touches our souls. Sometimes we become nostalgic, even for eras we never lived in. The past appeals from the point of a nail.

I don't know why this is so—I only know what I and others are feeling. Maybe it has something to do with losing parents and raising children. Maybe we start feeling a need to understand how we fit into the rhythm of life. Maybe as we get closer to the edge, we start realizing that time past is a kind of centrifugal force.

These were the kinds of things I thought about that night at my neighbors' house. As my friends laughed and talked, I scrolled back over the houses I've lived in. Conventional wisdom holds that houses reflect their owners, but for me, it's always gone further than that. You make the best of wherever you live, but when you're in the right place—and this is broader than mere houses—your soul feels in sync.

And vice versa. I had lived a lot of vice versa in those other houses, those other towns. This house felt different, however—had from the very beginning. I discovered it on a sunny Sunday morning in late summer, a couple of months before Beth and I were to be married. It was a pivotal time in my life: After nearly twenty years behind a desk, drawing a steady paycheck, I had decided to quit being a magazine editor in order to try to become a writer. Not only that, but I was head over heels in love with a woman ten years younger than I, a woman who happened to have two young children—children who were soon to become my stepdaughters. At the age of forty-five, I was taking on a new family. There was nothing rational about any of it.

In that situation, I'm sure my aunt May's house, which for so long had whispered to me quietly of peace and safety, was now positively screaming inside my head. I didn't need a house; I needed a *sanctuary*. When the Realtor brought me over here that Sunday morning, I loved the wraparound porch immediately. I loved the massive elm tree in the front yard. I loved the little French-doored study just to the left of the living room—it would make a wonderful office. I loved the hardwood floors and the pink-and-black bathroom and the secluded little garden out back. But the thing that sold me was a human touch. In the kitchen are French doors leading to the side yard. The doors were unlocked, and I opened them and went out. This was the south side of the house, and at this time of day the yard—even with its half dozen old trees—was bathed in sunshine. Then I looked down at the steps I was standing on, and there was a coffee cup that someone had left not too long before. Whoever it was had been sitting out here on these steps off the kitchen, having a cup of coffee in the sunlight of this peaceful Sunday morning. The coffee was still steaming. On the edge of the cup was a perfectly formed red lip print. It brought the whole house to life.

That night at my neighbors', I began to believe that it was somehow important for me to know about the lives that had been lived in this house before me. It occurred to me that this time, in this house, in this city and state in which, to my surprise, I've been *consciously* happy, it wasn't enough just to slap a new layer of paint on the walls. For the first time ever, I felt ready to reverse the process— to strip away the surface and dig in. I wanted to belong here. You can't claim a history you don't have, but maybe you can reclaim one.

And if I did, I might finally come close to touching what's eluded me all these years: continuity, connectedness, permanence.

A few days after that dinner, I drove downtown to the Beach Abstract Company. After 4:00 P.M., they'll let you go in and nose through their books, those oversized volumes that contain the outlines of so many people's lives. The theme of these books is change, the narrative a relentless tale of moving on. The seller of a property is known as the grantor; the buyer is the grantee. I started with the most recent sale of my property, when I was the grantee and Alfred Jack Burney was the grantor. Working back through the years, I reconstructed a loose ownership history of this house: In 1989, I bought it from Burney; in 1981, Burney bought it from Myron and Ellen Sue Landers; the Landerses bought it, in 1980, from Forrest and Sue Wolfe; the Wolfes bought from Ed and Sheri Kramer in 1976; in 1973, the Kramers bought from Roy and Rita Grimes; the Grimeses bought, in 1966, from Billie Lee and Ruth Murphree; the Murphrees bought it all the way back in 1947, from Jessica J. Armour; C. W. L. and Jessica Armour *built* the house in the fall of 1923; earlier that summer, they had bought the land from Melissa Retan, who had owned this and other parcels in the neighborhood since 1892.

An exclusive club, I thought: For an entire century, only nine families have owned this place—eight if you don't count the Retans. Eight families forever linked by having lived part of their lives in this one house, out of all the millions of houses in the world.

For a few minutes, I pondered such big thoughts—and then I found myself squinting at the names on the list. Which one of you, I wondered, built that ridiculous sloping patio in the backyard? Who had the brilliant notion of sticking the heating unit in the closet in the back room? Who ripped out the original Craftsman casement windows and put in picture windows? Who rented the place to the horde of roller-skating hippies, and why?

It's a funny thing about houses—you tend to get personal about them.

I had never been a fan of traditional detective stories—all that shoe leather, those shot-in-the-dark leads, those tedious hours of poring over yellowed documents buried away in dusty files. But, then, I'd never had my own case before. After that initial trip to the abstract company, I began thinking of this as detective work, and I was riveted by it.

When I got home, the first thing I did was look in the phone book. I knew the Burneys were still in Little Rock, and I thought the Wolfes might be. As for the rest of them, I had no idea. I found no Retans listed whatsoever. There was a Joseph Armour in North Little Rock, but what were the odds that he would be related to a family who had built this house sixty-nine years ago? I looked under Murphree, and there was a B. L. Murphree out in west Little Rock. Could this be the Murphree who had bought this house all the way back in 1947? It was a possibility. I found a half column of Grimeses, but no R. L.; a handful of Kramers, but no Ed. Forrest Wolfe was listed, no question. So was A. Jack Burney. As for Myron L. Landers, there was an M. L. Landers in North Little Rock, but was this my man?

As one who has moved all too frequently, I was astonished at how many possibilities I had right here in town. Good thing I was doing this in Little Rock and not in New York City, I thought. But even though I definitely could place two out of three of the previous owners before me, there was a huge gap in the center of the chain, and no leads at the beginning. I had known the recent stories were going to be the easiest to find; it just stands to reason. But what would I have if I had those and didn't have the stories that started it all? I began to see this project less as detective work and more as a classic construction job: You start with the foundation and build up from there.

At neighborhood get-togethers, I shamelessly floated the riddles of this house by anyone who would listen—although, to most people, I didn't mention the word *book* at first; it carries too much potential for humiliation. I simply said I was poking around in the history of my house, trying to learn about the people who had lived here. Most of the neighbors responded immediately to the idea of learning about the past life of a house—they'd all been tempted to do it with their own homes. But as they wandered off to refill their wineglasses, it occurred to me that, on the surface, they didn't have any more interest in my house than I had in theirs. It was a valuable lesson, I later decided. I made a note to myself that if this project was ever going to be more than an exercise for me, I would have to tell a bigger story. At about that time, I ran across the quote from William Butler Yeats that appears as the epigraph of this book: "The history of a nation is not in parliaments and battlefields, but in what the people say to each other on fair days and high days, and in how they farm, and quarrel, and go on pilgrimage." If I could tell about the high days and quarrels of the people who had lived in this one house in this one city in the heart of this country for the major part of a century, maybe it would add up to something.

Fortunately, my next-door neighbors, John and Linda Burnett, responded to this project from the beginning. Having lived within a few yards of four owners of this house, they had more than a passing interest in knowing what had gone on here. We're all voyeurs, given half a chance.

Linda remembered the Wolfes' industriousness and the Burneys' gregariousness. Of the Landerses, she mainly recalled Sue's desperation. Poor Sue Landers was so obsessed with the mortar coming out from between the bricks that she spent all her time frantically trying to patch it. God, I thought, we all have so much of ourselves invested in our houses. I couldn't wait to know Sue Landers's story.

Then John thought of a woman named Ruth Chapin. "You ought to call her," he said. "They moved to Lawrence, Kansas, right before you came. She lived in the house across the street all her life. She must be in her eighties now."

I phoned Ruth Chapin cold, one day late in September, stammering out the reason for my call: I wanted to write "a biography of a house," I said. I wanted to "tell the story of the century through all the people who had lived in this one house." By now, you can see, I had a full-blown epic in mind. She didn't laugh, though she did plead hard of hearing. I told her I'd explain in a letter.

A week later, after she had received my note, we had a long conversation. She was intrigued by the project and would be glad to help as much as possible. In fact, however, she *hadn't* lived in the house across the street from mine all her life, but the house had remained in the family, so she had kept up with the neighborhood. She rattled off a list of names that meant nothing to me—people, she said, who could tell me things about the house and those who'd lived here. Then she told me that C. W. L. and Jessica Armour had had three children, only one of whom she thought was still living. Her name was Jane, and she had married a Mr. McRae from the Scott community, a few miles northeast of Little Rock.

I called directory information for Scott. There were two McRaes. I dialed the first one and an elderly woman answered. I asked if she was Jane Armour McRae, and she said she was. "Well," I said, spanning three-quarters of a century in a single leap, "I live in the house your parents built."

\* \* \*

The people who've owned this house include a soft-drink bottler and a home economist, a mortgage loan officer for the VA and a secretary for a U.S. congressman, a civil engineer and a housewife, a theater director and a medical technologist, a Medicare systems analyst and a teacher, an entrepreneur gone bust and a nurse, an electronics wholesaler and a time-share-company secretary, and two writers. Fifteen children—eleven girls and four boys—have lived here, and for three of them, it was their first home. Hundreds of parties have been held in this house. People have danced here for parts of eight decades, from the Charleston in the twenties to whatever we do to Hootie and the Blowfish in the nineties. Young people—and their parents—have courted on the porch and in other places, and one dad even painted the upstairs windows shut to keep his daughter from climbing out at night. One wedding has been performed here. In addition to the happy times, these walls have witnessed the finality of death and every conceivable level of anguish leading to it. One son disappeared into the hands of the Japanese at the beginning of World War II, not to be heard from for years—and then one day a taxi pulled up in front of this house and he stepped out and walked up this sidewalk in his uniform. There have been bankruptcy, family feud, lawsuits, fire, cancer, horrible accidents, divorce, even the grief of a loved one lost to AIDS. There have been fallings-out between buyer and seller, and in one case the anger has persisted, and festered, for two whole decades.

In other words, life has been lived here. And, in its way, this house has mirrored the wider life that has gone on around it.

That's the story I'm going to tell you now. But beneath the surface, down where we all live our real lives, is the story of every one of us in every house in America—the story of that ongoing search for a place that feels like home.

*If These Walls Had Ears*

# PART ONE

# Fair Days and High Days

*The Armour family in the yard outside their new home. From left, that's Jane, Carolee, Grandma Jackson, Charles, and Jessie. Charlie snapped the picture.*

*This was taken from across the street in about 1927. The girl holding the dog is Ruth Ream (now Ruth Chapin), and just over her shoulder you can see 501 Holly, with Charlie Armour's bizarre little Nu Grape car out in front.*

*Chapter One*

# Beginnings

*1890 ❧ 1923*

The best way to get to know a piece of ground is to mow it. No telling how many miles I've pushed a lawn mower in my life. Well-meaning friends have suggested that I get someone to do that onerous job for me, and for a very brief time I did. It didn't work out. I felt out of touch with my surroundings.

My father, if he were alive, would laugh at that last sentence. When I was a teenager in Miami, Florida, we had an electric mower. I regularly cut the cord so I wouldn't have to finish the job. I think you have to be a homeowner before you understand some of the subtleties of mowing.

One is time for dreaming. For a very short while in a different life, I lived in an old house on the north shore of Chicago. It was a wonderful house, but if I'd had any real money, it could've been so much better. There were two sunrooms that jutted out from the back of the house, and as I mowed the backyard, I would redesign those rooms in my mind. The lower one was going to lose a wall and become part of the kitchen; the upper one was going to become a huge, sunny bathroom. Even then, I was aware that those plans were just fantasies. I already hated my job and knew I was going to have to leave that place, too.

My mowing dreams at 501 Holly mostly concern the dining room. The living and dining areas are now all in one big space, which I would love to turn over totally to the living area. Then, knocking out the south wall, I would extend that area about twenty feet and that would be the new dining room. I figure I might as well add a family room next to it. It would be easy—just a couple of steps down from the kitchen's French doors, with cool tiles imported from Spain.

Or maybe that space would be better as a swimming pool.

Such are the things you ponder as you mow a lawn. It's mindless work, mostly, but you absorb certain information as you go. After nearly seven years, I know this piece of ground pretty well, at least on the surface. From my perspective, the dominant image is *steepness,* what some people choose to call a terrace but which I know is a hill. The land slopes some in the front, which faces west, but it drops off most dramatically on the south, on the side of our house along Lee Street. I have to mow only part of that slope. A third of the way back, the hill is overgrown with hedge and trees and ground cover, providing in the summer a green buffer between our side yard and the whoosh of traffic on Lee.

I have a regimen I follow. I do the steep Lee Street hill first, before the Arkansas humidity has sucked out every ounce of my energy. Standing at the bottom of the hill, I thrust the mower up the incline, left to right, trying to make sure I nudge the mower over at the apex so I can cut an inch or two of grass as the machine rolls back downhill. After the hill, I mow side to side across the front. Three or four swaths into the job, I reach a dip in the ground where a big tree once stood; I have to back the mower over that a couple of times, and even twist it some to make sure I don't leave any long blades of grass. It's at about this latitude that I also have to start edging around the roots of the huge elm near the driveway. Pretty soon, I can cross the brick sidewalk and forget the elm-tree side, which is planted with both lariope, commonly known as monkey grass, *and* ivy. For years, there was nothing but bare dirt under that tree, and in frustration I planted both ground covers. I'll go with whichever wins out.

That's another way you change when you become a homeowner. One of my fondest memories as a child was of just such grassless ground beneath great canopies of tree leaves, raised roots running out from the trunks to form hiding places for toy cowboys or Indians or olive-drab soldiers shouldering bazookas or aiming carbines. Even as a teen, I wasn't embarrassed by bare dirt. Like so many other things—mossy bricks, a rope swing, a cracked sidewalk, a peeling wall—it evoked a certain decadent Southern life that I grew up in and liked the idea of. And yet, as a homeowner, I find myself fretting over bare spots in the yard, not to mention cracked sidewalks and peeling walls. That's one of the tricks houses can play on you. If you grant them enough power, they'll reveal you for the fraud you are.

When I start mowing the side yard, I'm almost home free. Even though this house sits on an oversize lot, there isn't *that* much grass to mow. The north side is all driveway. The back, which faces east, is taken up by the garden and patio and a tacky little storage shed where a garage used to be. Only the front and south sides are mowable lawns, and once I've crossed the fieldstone walk separating front and back, the job is nearly complete. The only hard parts are over by the Lee Street hedge, where I have to mow in and out and around the ancient swing set, and right up near the house where the ground rises and I have to angle the mower if I don't want to leave an uncut sliver. In that spot, the grass also tends to grow over the fieldstone walkway, hiding the scrawls someone left long ago in the wet concrete: J. M. are the initials there. Next to that, there's the word AUSTA.

I had no idea whose marks those were or what they meant when I first walked in this yard almost seven years back. Now I do, of course. But when I would stand on this piece of ground pondering my house's past, I knew that the story had to begin deeper than hieroglyphics in the concrete. An image from another house I once lived in kept coming to mind. Back during the final year of World War II, my mother and I stayed in Verona, Mississippi, with another aunt and uncle, Aunt Gusta and Uncle Wib, who were caretakers in the home of my great-aunt Laura. It was a sprawling, faded old house with an L-shaped front porch from which several doors opened onto shadowy bedrooms. I have many memories of that house, but none stronger than the memory of the seashells.

Pearly and luminescent, they lined the long brick sidewalk that stretched some thirty yards from the porch to the dirt road in front. The shells were large enough to cover the side of my head when I held them up to hear the ocean. But the amazing thing about the shells was that they hadn't been imported by any of my family from a visit to some far-off sea; instead, they had come up, over the course of eons, from the earth where they now lay.

For the story of 501 Holly to emerge, you have to begin with the ground itself.

A hundred or so years is far enough back—1890, to be specific. That was two years before Melissa Retan paid eighteen hundred dollars to the recently formed Pulaski Heights Land Company for this and several other parcels of land in a hilly, wooded area a mile west of Little Rock. Understand that when I say "parcels of land," I mean squares drawn on a map; this lawn I mow was nothing but rocks and trees, as was all the land around it. But two men from St. Johns, Michigan, Henry Franklin Auten and his law partner, Edgar Moss, had come here in 1890, willing to bet their livelihoods that someday people like me—and lots more before I ever got my turn—would want to live among the trees on the high ground outside the city.

Frank Auten was, by all accounts, an intense young man haunted by a search of his own. By 1889, he had decided that St. Johns wasn't big enough to hold his dreams. During a train trip, he picked up a brochure that told about Arkansas. He was impressed, and came to investigate. Little Rock—population nearly 26,000 as of the 1890 census—was a city on the move. Some of the streets were even paved, a large improvement over a mere decade before, when a state legislator had introduced a bill classifying two of the city's major streets as "navigable streams." Sewer pipes were in the ground. Telephone service had been available for a dozen years, electric service for half a decade. Electric streetcars operated throughout the business district of the city. Downtown was even lit up at night by four strategically placed 125-foot towers, atop each of which were five carbon arc lights known as "star lights." There was a med school and a horse track and even a baseball team—the formidable Little Rockers. Most of the town's power brokers lived in grand style in ornate houses a mere stroll from the business district.

But Auten knew that as long as there have been cities—even back to biblical times—there've been people, usually the wealthier ones, who've looked beyond the city limits for a lifestyle that included healthier air, less noise, more greenery, greater space  and, yes, sometimes, more homogeneity. Auten and Moss played to that historical precedent. They formed a syndicate and bought eight hundred acres of land just west of Little Rock, land they named Pulaski Heights— Pulaski being the name of the county Little Rock is in, and Heights being an apt description of the property itself, whose cooler and healthier three-hundred-foot elevation was going to be one of the big selling points. Another selling point was homogeneity: "It is and will be exclusively for white residents," Auten wrote in a slick brochure. "No property will be sold to colored people." On my first day of research for this book, I ran into a fellow journalist at Beach Abstract. "Oh, Pulaski Heights," he said. "Little Rock's first white-flight suburb."

Auten and Moss persuaded several Michiganders to invest in their syndicate, and a few of those investors moved to Arkansas, too. Auten's plan was for the founders of Pulaski Heights to set an example by building fine homes in this wilderness. The targeted Little Rock gentry was skeptical, of course. The problem with Pulaski Heights was that, while it lay little more than a mile from downtown, there were only two ways to get to it, and neither of them was pretty. You could take your horse and buggy and trot out along the River Road—but then you had to climb a steep and winding hill to the top of the ridge, where all the development was going to be. The other way involved taking the Seventh Street hill road, which ran out, becoming nothing more than a cow trail, just beyond the city limits, at what city folk considered the absolute end of the road—the insane asylum.

Truth is, Auten had been promised a streetcar line, and he was banking on that to make Pulaski Heights an accessible Eden instead of a local joke. He had no way of knowing that it would be ten long years—not until Thanksgiving Day of 1903—before a streetcar would connect Little Rock to the Heights.

But by the time he found out the streetcar was going to be delayed, it was too late to back out. The Autens and seven other founding families had already built and moved into their houses. They settled in two areas, generally: Some made their homes near Moss, who built on a ridge above a wooded ravine, beyond which flat bottomland stretched a half mile or so to the Arkansas River; others followed Auten, who, about a quarter mile to the southwest of Moss, actually found and refurbished an old two-story farmhouse with Italianate detailing.

One of the original Michiganders was Albert Retan, listed in Pulaski Heights Land Company literature as a "capitalist." He had retired from his general store in Michigan and joined this adventure with his wife, Melissa, and their two daughters, Zillah and Carrie.

The Retans, who built next door to the Autens, took seriously Frank Auten's mission of impressing the Little Rock elite: They built a showplace, a Queen Anne mansion just as big and just as fancy as the ones downtown. Behind the Retan house stood an imposing carriage house, and behind the carriage house was a rocky piece of ground that, thirty years later, would form a hilly corner lot where Holly Street ran into Lee.

Seventy years after that, you could drive by on any other summer Saturday and watch me pushing my old lawn mower up that very hill.

The first picture I ever saw of *any* of this house's past lives was sent to me by Ruth Chapin, who had grown up across the street. It was actually a photocopy of a snapshot, dated "1927 or '28," and it was gray and grainy, like memory itself.

In the foreground are two young women, identified as Ruth Ream—at that time—and Clara Young, who lived in the house next door to 501. It's a snowy day, and Ruth is holding what looks like a black-and-white dog. I can see Clara's house in the background and, next to it, the unmistakable shape of the one I've come to know. But there are disturbing differences. There's a nakedness to my house. Then I realize the massive elm tree by the driveway seems to be missing. No: Resorting to a magnifying glass, I can just make out a thin vertical line that looks, comparing it to the house, to be about ten or fifteen feet tall, and *skinny*.

Then I look up from my desk and out through the front French doors upstairs. Broad limbs, heavy with age, stretch up and out, their span not even contained within the double window frame. Three years ago, I even had to have that tree cabled together at the Y to keep it from splitting from its weight. I look back at the grainy picture. It's hard to reconcile the two images.

Photographs are tricky, and I've come to believe that most of us don't really see what's in them. More than once over the past year, I've studied faces and bodies in a picture snapped in this yard, and then I've stepped outside to look at the very spot where it was taken half a century, or more, before. No one is there, of course. I pore over the backgrounds to see if I can pick up an echo.

Over time, though, I've become able to summon up the figures and faces, and I realize now that this process is one of the great benefits of this quest of mine. One of the major characters in this saga is time. Most of us see the world only the way it is as we're looking at it. We take a snapshot of that moment and believe we've captured something. But time, that invisible trickster, is the real subject of every photograph. Every item in every snapshot is shaped, or colored—or faded—by time in one of its permutations. A brilliant writer named Robert Grudin has called time "the fourth dimension," and I've become increasingly able to see this house in that way: height, width, depth, time. When I first moved into 501 Holly, the rooms looked empty. Now I live with ghosts.

One of them drove the car parked in front of the house in that grainy snapshot Ruth sent me. That it's not a normal car is apparent even without the magnifying glass. It *looks* like an old wooden barrel on wheels, with a flimsy canvas top. I've since learned that it was an automobile built in the shape of a Nu Grape soda pop bottle, that it was painted purple, and that the radiator (which I can't see in this picture) was made to look like a bottle cap.

The man who created that car was named Charles Webster Leverton Armour, known to his wife, Jessica, as Charlie. Charlie and Jessie, as he called *her*, had met in the still-frontierish town of Fort Smith, Arkansas, sometime around 1908. Jessie Jackson, then age twenty-one, was a bright, outgoing, self-confident young woman from St. Paul, Minnesota. A graduate dietician, as successful home ec majors were known in those days, she had sent letters to schools all over the country announcing her qualifications and her willingness to relocate. She was a woman ahead of her time. One day, Jessie

*Jessie Armour with her children, Jane and Charles.*

heard from the principal of the high school in Fort Smith. He wondered if she would come establish a "domestic science" program at his school. It was just the kind of adventure Jessie was looking for. She packed up her best friend and took her along, too.

Jessie's best friend also happened to be her mother. Cynthia Jane Paxton Jackson had been widowed when Jessie was three, and the two of them had gone to live with Cynthia's brother, Ben Paxton, a bachelor doctor and world traveler. Jessie's father, William Malcolm Jackson, had also been a doctor. Back in those days, doctors made house calls—even out to the country in the middle of a Minnesota winter. After one such visit, Dr. Jackson caught pneumonia and died. Cynthia never remarried.

The above story was told to me one crisp blue day in the fall of 1992. I had driven out to the Scott community northeast of town to see Jane Armour McRae, then seventy-six, the only surviving child of Jessie and Charlie Armour. Jane is a tall woman, angular, and on the day of that first meeting I noted that she was wearing heavy blue eye shadow and a rinse on her hair the approximate color of Windex. She laughed heartily and often. On a later visit, the color was less vibrant, but her attitude was the same: When she looks at you, you get the feeling there's a party going on behind her eyes.

Her mother, Jane said, had two great loves: talking and dancing. In Fort Smith, she met a man who shared both of those passions.

A garrulous real estate salesman from Kansas, Charlie was seventeen years older than Jessie, and he had a past. For one thing, this was his second career. He had studied civil engineering at the University of Kansas and had spent several years surveying for a railroad down in Louisiana. He was brimming with tales about that exotic land, which was about as different from his own home state as any place could possibly be. He mesmerized Jessie with stories of wildcats and things up in trees that would howl in the night. He could still make the sound of a panther. He had loved Louisiana, had been taken with its food, its eccentricities, its attitude. He had adopted those Southern ways with the passion of one who happens upon a new part of the world and discovers himself in it. To Jessie Jackson, who had lived her entire life in the North, this smooth-talking fellow seemed the epitome of Southern charm, especially with his three first names. Up where Jessica came from, they're more frugal with their appellations.

He had also been married once, and had a young daughter, a toddler, Caroline, called Carolee, who lived with him. He was a widower, he said. He and his daughter lived in an imposing Queen

Anne mansion on a hill outside of town. It was the kind of estate that had a name—Lone Pine, which referred to a massive old tree that towered over the house and stood out in solitary splendor against the sky. There was a story about that house. Even if Charlie hadn't told Jessica about it, she would've heard. It was the sort of story that people would whisper behind their hands whenever Charlie walked into a room.

His first wife had killed herself at Lone Pine. One day Charlie and his daughter were walking out in the large yard when Charlie heard a shot. He swept Carolee into his arms and ran back to the house. When they got to the front steps, they saw her—his wife, and Carolee's mother—sprawled dead on the porch, a pistol in her hand. If Charlie had any idea why she did it, he never said. All his family ever knew was that his first wife was "nervously unbalanced" and took her own life.

Jessie and Charlie were both big people, tending toward heaviness, he standing five foot nine or ten, and Jessie five six or seven. They had big spirits, too. Each threatened to outtalk the other. Charlie teased Jessie *and* her mother, and both women were smitten by him. In 1912, when forty-two-year old Charlie asked Jessie to marry him, she responded with an unqualified yes. She and her mother moved into the big house on the hill, and for several years they lived there together, a blended family—rare in those days. Charlie pursued his real estate business and Jessie taught school. Cynthia Jane, now known as Grandma Jackson, spent her days taking care of Carolee, this instant grandchild who had washed into her life by fate. Carolee was six at the time of the marriage.

In 1914, Jessie gave birth to her first child, a son. All four of his father's names were bestowed upon him, and he went by Charles. Two years later, a daughter was born. She was named Jane, after Jessie's mother.

\* \* \*

*Charlie Armour as a young grid star in Kansas. His son, Charles, would always feel that he never quite measured up in his father's eyes.*

In time, through research, I would come to know things about her parents that even Jane didn't know. Still, I worried that they were eluding me. It's impossible to get inside another person's heart, even if you live together. But these were people I had never met, people who had lived in a completely different age. I stared at photographs and read stories into them.

Jessie displays a face straight from a Grecian urn—strong chin, prominent nose, high forehead, with a tousle of thick dark curls. Her eyes are intelligent, hawklike, *ready*. I imagine her dancing, whirling. I imagine her as a fiercely protective mother.

As for Charlie, I can't see much at all in his pictures. In every one, from his college days as a football player to his middle years as head of a household, the camera doesn't catch his spark. With some people, it does. He had a face like Kansas—wide, open, no sharp angles. With him, the rest of his family will be smiling, but he stands there expressionless. It's not anger, not pomposity, not shyness. It's just *nothing*: no hint of the salesman with the gift of gab; no glimpse of the music lover undaunted by a dance floor; no sign of the searching heart that would cause this man to reinvent himself time and time again.

Charlie scares me. He strikes me as a man who was forever chasing something but never quite held it securely in his hands.

Jessie and Charlie were married for eleven years before they built the house on Holly Street. In that time, they had lived in four other houses in three other towns. They left Fort Smith in 1918 because Charlie was offered the chance to manage a cotton plantation in Elaine, Arkansas. They left Elaine after a race riot erupted and many people were killed. They next moved to Memphis, where they lived in a big two-story rented house and Charlie went back into real estate. They moved from that house to a smaller one when, in 1921, Charlie's head was turned by the discovery of oil in south Arkansas. He just *had* to try his luck in the oil fields, but there's no evidence that he had any luck—not the kind that would've *changed* his luck. He was fifty-one and still struggling.

While he was gone, Jessie made sure the family was well clothed and well fed. She sewed their outfits, cooked their meals. Carolee was a teenager by this time, and the smaller children were both in school. Young Charles may've been glad to have some time away from his father. Charles was a worrier, and he wasn't particularly athletic. Many years later, he would confess that he never felt he measured up in his father's eyes.

In the spring of 1923, the Armours packed themselves into their Overland touring car and headed west from Memphis toward the site of Charlie's latest incarnation. It was to take place in Little Rock, Arkansas. The family was moving so Charlie could try his hand in the hot new industry of soda-pop bottling.

It looked like a sure bet for the times—especially now with Prohibition, when people couldn't openly slake their thirst with beer. More than that, though, bottled soft drinks seemed a perfect response to the whimsy, the mobility, and the pleasure seeking of the 1920s. I can imagine Charlie bursting with anticipation. This was totally different from anything he had ever done, and yet it was right up his alley. He was a people person, and this was a people business. He had lots of ideas that he wanted to try. Everybody knew that men all over the country had gotten filthy rich owning Coca-Cola bottling plants. This wasn't going to be that, exactly—Charlie was becoming a partner in something called Arkola, which had started in 1920 to take advantage of the cola craze. The company also bottled ginger ale and root beer. But the big reason Charlie was so excited was that the company had just landed the contract for Nu Grape, and this was going to be Charlie's baby.

It didn't take the Armours long to find out that the most desirable neighborhood in Little Rock was a western suburb called Pulaski Heights. By this time, the Heights had become annexed to Little Rock. Charlie and Jessie took the family on a spin through the hilly, winding streets. The old trees—oaks and elms and walnuts and pines—formed canopies over the paved roadways. By now, there were different neighborhoods within the Heights itself, and commercial areas had sprung up at different points along the streetcar line. The area where Auten and Moss had built their homes was now called Hillcrest, and its commercial district included a beautiful two-story Spanish Gothic building that encompassed the town hall, the civic center, and five storefronts facing Prospect Avenue. Across the street was a fire station. The Heights was home to Little Rock College, to a Catholic girls' school called Mount St. Mary's, and to several elementary and junior high schools.

Another big attraction to the Armours was an amusement park that some old-timers still called Forest Park but that had recently been refurbished and renamed White City. The ostensible reason for the name change was that all the structures had been painted a sparkling white, but the not-so-subtle message to Little Rock Negroes was no doubt considered a happy by-product. The park—which, the Armours learned, had originally been built to attract a streetcar line to the Heights—now featured an outdoor swimming pool that was a whole city block long and half a block wide. Parkgoers could even enjoy the recent invention called the "dodgem"—four padded cars with erratic steering and guaranteed collisions. The automobile culture had changed the park in other ways, too—White City now included a campground for tourists traveling by car.

Charlie and Jessie liked what they saw. When they drove along Woodlawn Street, they found it a kind of church row. There were a Methodist, an Episcopal, and a Presbyterian church all within three blocks of one another. On down Woodlawn, there was even a Baptist church just where Woodlawn ran into Prospect. In Hillcrest, no matter what denomination you were, you could get up on a Sunday morning and *walk* to church if you wanted.

It was time. Jessie knew it, and Charlie knew she knew it. It was time to dig in and make a stand, if ever they were going to do it. The stars hadn't been so auspiciously aligned at any time during their eleven years of marriage. Building a house, which they would have to do, was a major commitment—especially for Charlie. It's a frightening thing, especially for a man, to say, This is it. This is where I live and where I'm going to live—no matter what. You cross off all your options. You have to make it work *here*. At least Charlie could be comforted by the fact that nice houses in Hillcrest didn't sit empty—if, God forbid, something happened and they were forced to move again.

They began searching for exactly the right lot—one close to schools, churches, and the shopping district. Finally, they found a large parcel of land on the corner of Lee and Holly. It was on a hill, which was nice—the better to catch the breezes. The property was owned by a Melissa Retan, who, the Armours were told, had once owned the big Queen Anne house right behind this lot—so close, in fact, that shade from the imposing Retan carriage house fell on this property in the mornings. Melissa and her late husband, Albert, had been part of the original group who had developed the Heights. The house next to the Retan house was the Auten place, home of another Heights founder, who had died only recently, in 1918. Albert Retan had died way back in 1909, and Melissa had decided the big house was too much for her and her remaining single daughter, Zillah. So she had sold the property and moved to a smaller place.

Charlie and Jessie were impressed with the neighborhood. Holly Street was only one block long, and it was a very nice block. Across the street from the lot they were considering was a smallish but very neat bungalow with an interesting Oriental trellis on the gable. A substantial house stood next door to the north—a wooden two-story with a porch and decorative woodwork on the windows. Catty-cornered across the street was a big, comfortable-looking house with a porch and columns out in front. And next door to that, on the corner of Woodlawn and Holly, there was a *fabulous* house—huge, with upper and lower wraparound verandas and exotic mimosa trees in the yard. Combine that with the Retan and Auten houses just to the rear—you could even say the Retan house was *next door*—and, yes, this was a neighborhood anyone would be proud to drive home to every day.

On July 18, 1923, Charlie and Jessie paid Melissa Retan two thousand dollars for the land, which was officially known as "Pulaski Heights block 004, lot 007, the west one hundred feet of 007, and the south 40 feet of the west 100 feet of 008." A month later, they took out a loan of $5,800 to build the house. In the 1920s, the average annual income in the United States was one thousand dollars. What Charlie was to be making at Arkola, I have no idea. But while there were certainly many houses more expensive in Hillcrest, this was nevertheless a major expense.

They also had the added fee of their architect, a man named H. Ray Burks. The generally acknowledged "best" architect working in Hillcrest in 1923 was Charles Thompson, who designed very large and very showy homes. He had been working in Little Rock for many years, and in fact was said to have designed the Queen Anne house for the Retans in 1893. Another well-known Heights architect was K. E. N. Cole, who specialized in bungalows. Ray Burks would go on to create numerous houses and buildings in Hillcrest, but in 1923, at age thirty-three, he still had his best work ahead of him. He was a member of Kiwanis, as was Charlie Armour. I like to think of their meeting over rubber chicken and too-green English peas, two loyal clubmen happy to do business within the fold.

But what *kind* of business? In 1923, the trends in house design included a fair amount of harkening back to the romantic styles of the past, architecture that whispered—or sometimes shouted—its alignment with English, Spanish, or French designs. When Charlie and Jessie drove through the Heights, they saw quite a few houses that were English Revival, Colonial Revival, or American Foursquare. The style they saw the most, however, was the Craftsman bungalow, or some variation on it. During the period of Hillcrest's first major development—between 1910 and 1920—the Craftsman influence, an architectural offshoot of the English Arts and Crafts movement of the late 1800s, was at its peak in the United States.

Arts and Crafts celebrated individual craftsmanship as opposed to tasteless overmechanization.

I think I can understand why Charlie and Jessie were the Craftsman type. Jessie liked her nice clothes and her clubs, but essentially she was a practical woman. She was a Minnesotan, and I've lived in Minnesota. Minnesotans are unemotional, at least compared with the Southern women Jessie now lived her life around. She was sure of herself and her abilities. In a sense, she applied the Arts and Crafts ideals to the running of her home: She took joy in cooking, in making the children's clothes, in being a hands-on mother and wife. Charlie may've been less practical than his wife, but he wasn't a pretentious man. Besides, the Craftsman bungalow was the most house you could build for the money, and it was infinitely adaptable.

He and Jessie opted for a house larger than the smallest bungalow, but smaller than a high-style Craftsman. It wouldn't be as big as most of the other houses in the neighborhood, but it wouldn't be the smallest, either. Also, the extra property would carry some weight. When you approached from the west on Lee Street, you would see the house there on the high ground. The overall effect would be impressive. And the house would be very nice—one story with a big porch, plus a garage and servant's quarters. A good, sturdy middle-class house.

Charlie spent much time with Ray Burks trying to figure out the most advantageous layout for breezes and air flow. He wanted a house that *breathed.* The house would face west, and the porch would stretch two-thirds of the way across the front and wrap slightly on the south side—that way, it could catch the wind from all four directions. Wide eaves would keep out the rain and the hot southern and western sun. Casement windows, a traditional Craftsman touch, would allow the Armours to open the house, and interior French doors throughout much of the downstairs would let the air circulate from one side to the other. Those French doors also had another purpose.

As Charlie and the architect were planning, Jessie said to her husband, "Wouldn't it be wonderful if we could *dance* here!" "It would indeed," Charlie said. The French doors, which opened the house to a world of such possibilities, were immediately sketched in.

While their house was being built, the family rented a place nine blocks east, on a street called Midland. Every day before school started that fall, young Charles and Jane would trudge up Lee Street—Charles half a block ahead so as not to be seen walking with his seven-year-old sister—past the Pulaski Heights Elementary they would attend, toward the construction site. Charles monitored everything that happened. For a while, he even got himself hired on as a kind of water boy and nail fetcher, necessary credentials for mingling in that world of men. As for Jane, she stood by on the Holly Street side and watched the workers framing in the room that she had already moved into in her mind.

For the Armours, who had wandered so long, this house must've felt like a new beginning—the first step toward finally making a *home*. Jessie was beside herself. That Christmas, when they were finally in, she sent photographs of the house to friends and relatives. "The new house on Holly," she wrote on the back, "—complete at last!"

*Charlie and Jessie Armour in the side yard. This was in the late twenties, when all things still seemed possible.*

# Chapter Two

# Armour

*1923 🍂 1926*

All houses are fantasy, constructed as much of desires and dreams as wood and brick. They're receptacles to hold not just us but also everything we want to be. Sometimes we don't even know what that is. Sometimes we move into houses empty and expect them to fill *us* up.

Houses have such power because they live in us as much as we live in them. I know a woman, a psychologist, who tells me that Carl Jung's theory of a collective unconscious came to him after he had dreamed about a house. He described the dream this way:

*I was in a house I didn't know. It was my house. In the upper house there was a kind of salon furnished in Rococo style. I did not know what the lower floor looked like. There everything was much older. This part of the house must date from the fifteenth or sixteenth century. The floors are of a red brick, the furnishings are medieval. I went from one room to another thinking, "Now I really must explore the whole house." I came upon a heavy door and opened it. A stone stairway led me to a cellar. Descending again, I found myself in a beautiful vaulted room which looked exceedingly ancient. The walls dated from Roman times. The floor was of stone slabs, and in one of these I discovered a ring.*

*The slab lifted. I saw a staircase of narrow stone steps leading down. I descended and entered a low cave. In dust were scattered bones and broken pottery, like remains of a primitive culture. I discovered two human skulls, obviously very old and half disintegrated.*

*Then I awoke. It was plain to me that the house represented an image of the psyche.*

No *wonder* we have such strong feelings toward our houses: They are us; we are them. Dream analysts will tell you that when you dream about a house, many times you're actually dreaming about yourself. Jung used his house dream to develop a theory about certain universal symbols—the house among them—and the reason people all over the world respond so emotionally to them. He believed that dreams are the way our unconscious self communicates with our conscious self. What excited him about the house dream was that he had spoken to himself from a deeper level, and with a structure that illustrated what was happening. To Jung, the salon represented consciousness, and the ground floor stood for the first, or personal, level of the unconscious. Many dreams come from there. As he went deeper, though, the scene became darker and more alien. He interpreted the Roman cellar and the prehistoric cave as signifying past times and past stages of consciousness—times and consciousness beyond the personal self. From this dream, he began research that resulted in his notion of *archetypes,* primordial images shaped by the repeated experience of our ancestors and expressed in myths, dreams, religion, literature. These images are prelogical. They're imprinted on the deepest levels of our being. So when you see a house with a cozy front porch, all sorts of feelings and urges—many of them entirely irrational—may wash over you. It's happened to many people right here at 501 Holly.

Jessie and Charlie were the first.

\* \* \*

I like to think that the house was the way they saw themselves. Outside, the dark red brick spoke of strength and practicality and endurance. The great square porch columns seemed solidly rooted in Arkansas rock. The white concrete capping on the arch and half columns evoked images of new snow on rich old ground—or maybe white hair on a couple who had lived long and watched life pass from that very porch.

Inside, the house was warmed by cream-colored walls. There was a fireplace, too, and on either side of that was a built-in bookshelf so the family could sit in the living room on winter nights and read good books by the fire. The mantel was more classical than Craftsman in design. On either end, squares of molding sat above rectangles, evoking columns. Larger squares of the same decorative molding refined the walls. Over the casement windows in front, Jessie shut out the world with heavy drapes hanging on thick rods from large wooden rings. The floor in the living room was strewn with several six-by-nine-foot Oriental rugs. After supper, the children would lie on the rugs and read or draw. Jessie placed a pair of morris chairs—something I imagine to be like early recliners—on either side of the fireplace so Charlie could smoke his pipe and read and she could tend to her sewing. Grandma Jackson sat on the sofa, listening to music from the Victrola or the player piano.

The house was basically built along two parallel lines. You entered from the front porch into the living room, and straight beyond that were the dining room, the breakfast room, the kitchen, and a back porch or utility room. Left of the front entrance, French doors opened to a small front bedroom, shared by Carolee and Jane. Beyond that was a middle bedroom—Jessie and Charlie's. Then came a hall—where Carolee would sit for what seemed hours talking on the heavy black telephone—with a bath to the left, and a large back bedroom, which was shared by Grandma Jackson and Charles.

I can imagine Jessie loving the French doors. She was a woman who appreciated elegance—in clothes, in furniture—and there's something undeniably elegant about French doors. There's also an inherent sociability to them. If you're shy and private, you can't hide behind double glass doors. French doors, you *fling* open with both arms, and, in so doing, you open your arms wide to the world. That strikes me as Jessie. She even had pongee-covered French doors separating her and Charlie's bedroom from the dining room.

Passing from the living room through the double French doors into the dining room, you would've come upon a large Oriental rug that formed the perfect base for Jessie's pedestal table. It could easily seat twelve and often did. A china cabinet stood just inside the room, to the right. There, Jessie displayed her beloved Haviland china. But her favorite piece was placed against the east wall, straight ahead, so that even people in the living room could see it. It was an Empire sideboard with a rounded glass front that opened. She kept her fine glassware in there. On either side were a couple of drawers in which she stored candles and silverware and place cards and such. Below that were four drawers for linens—Jessie liked big, elegant, twenty-four-inch napkins, and tablecloths that draped to the floor. The sideboard also had two little pull-down doors. In one of those was where, after Prohibition, liquor was kept.

The breakfast room represented a triumph of Jessie's domestic science. It was a small space, but very efficient. In the wall between the breakfast room and the kitchen was a cut-out panel with sliding doors that opened to a counter on the breakfast-room side. Jessie could keep meals hot in the kitchen, and then, at the last minute, could open the sliding doors and set the platters of food on the counter. The family would serve themselves buffet-style. She had a small gateleg table that she folded out when the family took meals in the breakfast room. In the mornings, they would sit at that table in elegant bentwood chairs—there were eight of them throughout the house—with the sun streaming in through the French doors that led out to the side steps and yard. It was a serene way to begin the day.

There were no built-ins in the kitchen. The sink was under the south windows. To the left of that was a tall freestanding cupboard with two doors on one side for storing bowls and pans and plates. On the other side was a single door, which, when opened, revealed Jessie's flour sifter. She would pour her flour into the large container for storage. Then when she wanted to use some, she would fiddle with a lever that allowed flour to sift down into her bowl. Jane was mesmerized by this process. It was so ingenious, so *modern.*

But that was nothing compared to the stove. Standing against the big wall across from the sink, it was a gas stove of state-of-the-art design. It was cream-colored, the approximate hue of eggnog or boiled custard, and it was trimmed in pistachio green. It had legs, instead of being set squarely on the floor. In Jessie's home, the stove was always the cornerstone. She and Charlie had bought this stove brand-new for this house.

The back bedroom was given to Grandma Jackson because she had developed asthma, and that room was the most private. Charles slept in her bed at first. As he got older, he used a roll-away bed, but he still stayed with her. Jane recalls thinking Charles was their grandmother's pet.

The hall must've been Charlie's tribute to Grand Central Station. It's not a hall in the long and narrow sense of the word; it's simply a small room in the center of the house, a room whose only purpose is connecting the other rooms with one another. The hall has no fewer than seven doors—back bedroom, attic, coat closet, breakfast room, dining room, middle bedroom, bathroom. It's hell to wallpaper, but a good place to wait out a tornado warning.

In Charlie and Jessie's time, the bathroom was clean and entirely white, like a medical room. It had a pedestal sink and a floor comprised of hundreds of tiny octagonal tiles that played tricks on your eyes if you stared at them too long. There was a built-in wall heater to keep you warm when you stepped out of the big tub.

In the middle bedroom, Charlie and Jessie slept in a huge sleigh bed whose head was placed in the center of a bay window on the north side of the house, next to the driveway. Mostly, the curtains on those windows were kept drawn because the Armour house was lower on the hill than the house next door. If you weren't careful, the neighbors could look right in and catch you in your underwear—or worse. Jessie had a dresser on the east wall, and she kept her clothes in the closet opposite. For all their attention to detail in this house, Charlie and Ray Burks hadn't drawn in many closets—just one small one per bedroom, and the one in the hall. Charlie's suits, hats, shirts, shoes, and accessories were stored in a massive armoire on the wall between the French doors and the door leading to the girls' room. The armoire was made of a heavy mahogany. To young Charles, it must've been a magical piece—dark, brooding, filled with the rites and rituals of manhood.

Before they moved to 501 Holly, Jessie already had a set of beautiful white wicker furniture. As it became obvious that Carolee and Jane would share a room until Carolee—now seventeen—left for college, Jessie went out and found another piece of wicker—a long couch that opened into a bed. In the daytime and evenings, the front bedroom could be a charming sitting room, one where Carolee could have privacy with her beaux and still be in sight of the living room, thanks to the French doors. At bedtime, Carolee and Jane could fold out the couch.

And when they did, Charlie and Jessie would sometimes go out on the porch alone, if the weather wasn't too cold. Jane says they sat on the porch a lot, especially in the beginning. I can see them watching the stars sparkling in the western sky. You could do that then, when there weren't so many man-made lights west of Holly to dim the view. Other times, they would go out at day's end to wait for the glorious red sunsets. They'd hung a swing on the porch's south end, so they could see the front and side of their house at the same time. They'd planted evergreens around the porch, and several trees in the yard—that spindly elm in front of the house, near the driveway, and a tulip poplar on the edge of the hill overlooking Lee. On the side of the house, near a mature walnut tree, they'd planted a young maple. Charlie and Jessie had, quite literally, put down roots.

It was—it is—a good feeling. There's something especially warming about certain accomplishments around a house—a new purchase, a big project crossed off the list, even a simple thing like a day of yard work completed. It's as though all is right with the universe. It's the feeling of *home* distilled—a feeling that you're keeping up, not losing ground. Many's the evening Beth and I have sat on that very porch, and we've marveled at our industriousness and our good fortune, as Charlie and Jessie surely must have at theirs. I wonder if, during dusks like that, they felt as I have—that the silhouetted rafters in the porch overhang looked like the swags of a theater curtain.

These are moments in a house you have to cherish, like the sunsets. One minute the sky is a blaze of color. The next minute everything is gone.

*Soul* is a hard word to pin down. It's the word we use to name something ephemeral, but just giving that something a name doesn't capture it. Soul isn't captured. It's *revealed*.

In Jessie and Charlie's house, it manifested itself in optimism, gregariousness, efficiency, pride. It floated through every room on the scents from Jessie's kitchen—from her incomparable sweet-potato croquettes, or Grandma Jackson's famously sinful doughnuts, or the apple pies Grandma said she baked "especially for Charlie—though others can have a taste if they wish." In the mornings, the aroma of coffee announced that Charlie was up and ready to go to work. In her back bedroom, Grandma Jackson would prop herself up in bed, because Charlie never failed to take his mother-in-law the first cup poured.

Music was another revelation of this family's soul. It makes me happy to know that this house was filled with music—was *conceived* with music in mind. My parents seldom played music in our houses when I was growing up. They liked music, but it just wasn't a priority. I think a house without music robs you of something, both at the time and later, too. My forty-seven-year-old brother, Phil, recently went back to see the house on Churchill Drive in Jackson, Mississippi, where we had lived for a while in the early fifties. He says that just *looking* at it after forty years didn't take him back. Where memory is concerned, the senses of sight and touch aren't as evocative as smell and taste and hearing. Hearing music is the best transporter of all.

Music works on memory like the emulsion on film—it freezes time into keepable slices: *Standing in the backyard in Jackson talking with my mother through the window, asking if I can keep the stray dog I'm holding, while somewhere a radio plays "Young at Heart." Waking up in Miami at 3:00 A.M. to the sound of sultry Keely Smith singing "Love for Sale" on my brown-and-orange bedside radio. In a star-crossed bedroom in Minnesota, hearing my five-year-old son singing a line from his favorite song: "I'm on the top of the world looking down on creation. . . . "* None of it is especially important— except that, after it's over, that's what you've got.

Almost three-quarters of a century after the fact, Jane Armour McRae remembers her grandma Jackson sitting by the radio and listening to "Tiptoe Through the Tulips." Radio took off in the early 1920s, and Grandma Jackson was one of the first people in the neighborhood to have one. She had been fascinated by the idea that you could sit there in your house and listen to someone sing "Barney Google (with the goo goo googledy eyes)" from a box on the table. You could also hear news. Grandma Jackson *had* to have a radio.

It was a big one, a console, and she placed it in the dining room, near the windows. That was as far away from the bedrooms as she could get it—she didn't want to disturb anyone while she sat up till all hours twisting the dial. Jessie and Charlie put her chair next to the radio, and that became her throne. She sat there from morning till night, listening. Not only did she know all the latest songs but she became the family's ear to a world that was getting larger by the minute. Every night at dinner, she would tell them all the amazing things she had heard that day.

As planned, Jessie and Charlie did dance in this house. They belonged to a dance club, a group of eight or ten couples who organized dances at one another's houses. Jessie would open all the French doors, and Charlie would move back the furniture and roll up the rugs. Jane's job was always to wind the Victrola and change the records—or, if they were using the player piano, she had to change the rolls and pump the piano. Her parents and their friends mostly fox-trotted or two-stepped, so Jane would play current favorites like "Always" or "Rhapsody in Blue." If somebody was feeling frisky, they might request "Sweet Georgia Brown." Carolee and her group were also dancing by the time she moved to this house. Carolee's coming of age had coincided with that of a new dance called the Charleston. On nights when Jane deejayed for her sister's crowd, she played songs that rocked the entire neighborhood— "Five Foot Two, Eyes of Blue" and "If You Knew Susie Like I Know Susie." Jane learned to dance early, because some of the older boys and men would ask her to take a turn around the room with them. If she could prevail on someone else to take over her duties— Charles would do it, but then she *owed* him—she would get to enjoy the party even more. Jessie was happy for Jane to dance. Dancing was a celebration of the soul.

\* \* \*

So is humor. Jane Armour McRae remembers her father as charming, outgoing, the kind of man who would walk guests out to their cars and never stop talking. People could hardly *escape* his hospitality. His dour photographs aside, the man obviously had a sense of humor. How else could he have created the Nu Grape car?

Nu Grape was going well. Over at the White City pool, you could hear young girls say, "If you can swim all the way across, I'll buy you a Nu Grape." The distinctively cinch-waisted bottle certainly helped. "She has a shape like a Nu Grape bottle" was another popular saying—usually from the young men watching those girls swim in the pool. But though business was good, Charlie decided he needed a gimmick. Selling had gotten sophisticated. With radio, the public had lots of new demands on their attention. You had to reach out and *grab them*. The idea Charlie came up with was to build a car in the shape of a Nu Grape bottle.

He began with a Chevrolet chassis, but by the time Charlie got through with it, you wouldn't have recognized it as a Detroit product. Actually, the car became a kind of work in progress. At first, it didn't have the roof I saw in that first grainy photograph—just two seats up front and a back end shaped like the Nu Grape bottle. The radiator looked like a bottle cap from the start. Naturally, the car *had* to be painted purple. The back opened so Charlie could carry cases of soda, or proposals, or whatever a Nu Grape bottler needed to have on hand. Immediately, the car achieved Charlie's purpose—people all over Little Rock knew about "the Nu Grape car." It was good for business. As for Charlie's image, he had finally acquired a degree of that Southern eccentricity he had admired so in Louisiana.

He took to driving the Nu Grape car back and forth to work every day. At night, he would park it out in front of the house so people couldn't miss it. In the mornings, before he went to the office, he would drop Charles and Jane off at school. Poured them out with everyone watching. They weren't the least bit embarrassed. They

*To help sell soda pop, Charlie Armour created this car shaped like a Nu Grape bottle. Jane and young Charles—here outside his dad's bottling plant—loved it.*

loved the car, found it enormously funny. Their classmates considered Charles and Jane celebrities because of it. The car also advertised the fact that Charles and Jane had a never-ending supply of soft drinks cooling in their icebox at home. After school, 501 Holly was a very popular hangout.

Eventually, Charlie decided that having no top on the car was impractical. He commissioned a canvas top, with curtains that could be locked into the windows on cold or rainy days. He even installed a primitive heater. All this "winterizing" belied an ulterior motive. There was to be a bottlers' convention in Buffalo, New York, and

Charlie wanted to drive his purple pop bottle the two thousand-plus miles to Buffalo. Not only that, he wanted Jessie to go with him.

She thought it was the most ridiculous thing she'd ever heard. This was a *gimmick*, not an automobile. And highways were unpredictable, not to mention unpaved. Jessie's world didn't allow for such tomfoolery. She lived a swirl of meals and sewing and grocery shopping and child rearing and club work. She belonged to the Culture Club, one of the finest women's organizations in the Heights. She also taught a young women's Sunday school class at Pulaski Heights Presbyterian Church. Yes, she had a maid, a Negro woman named Mabel, but Mabel wasn't always dependable. She lived out in back over the garage, and though she was good when she was working, sometimes she would just leave. She once went to Brownsville, Texas, for a year. Then, one day, she showed up again, asking for her job back. Jessie gave it to her.

So Charlie had to woo Jessie about the Buffalo trip. He was persistent, and he could be charming. He would take everybody for drives on Sunday afternoons, making sure Grandma had a blanket to cover her legs. Sometimes he would surprise the family by buying tickets to the Majestic Theater downtown. It was a movie theater with vaudeville shows between the films, which were still silent. Jessie and Grandma Jackson loved the Majestic, losing themselves in the flickering pictures while the piano player matched the mood. The kids loved the vaudeville acts, because if you went on your birthday, you got to sit in a special box and the entertainer would come over and talk to you. Charlie would usually get tickets for Friday or Saturday nights, the best nights, when it was reserved seating only.

When time for the convention finally arrived, Jessie went. It took *days* each way. She was exhausted when she got home, but Charlie was beaming. His Nu Grape car had been the talk of the show.

\* \* \*

In the spring of 1926, Charlie received a letter saying that his mother was coming to live with them. This was not considered good news.

A severe, humorless woman, Elizabeth Leverton Armor spelled her surname like warfare—minus her son's softening *u*. Charles and Jane didn't remember her, so Jessie told them stories of when Grandfather and Grandmother Armor had visited in Fort Smith when Charles and Jane were little, or even before they were born. Grandfather Armor's name was Charles Webster Armor. He had fought in the Civil War on the Union side, and he loved to tell stories about his exploits. Whenever the Armors had visited Fort Smith, Mr. Armor was the center of attention for the duration of the trip. He was a character, a raconteur. As a young man, he had ridden for the Pony Express. That was a very dangerous job, Jessie told Charles and Jane—both of whom were spellbound by this rambunctious relative they had never really known. They wished he were coming instead of his widow.

Jessie told them they were to address Mrs. Armor as Grandmother Armor—*never* Grandma. What she didn't tell them was that Charlie's mother was a strict, straitlaced, ill tempered old biddy and that Grandfather Armor's most perilous exploit had been living with her.

Charlie, meanwhile, had more practical concerns—such as where to put everybody. This house just wasn't large enough for another person. And yet they loved it here and didn't want to move. One night at supper, Charlie announced a bold plan. "What we'll do," he said, "is add on."

In August, he and Jessie borrowed money from the Prudential Insurance Company, and the work began immediately. Architect Ray Burks recommended adding a second level at the back of the house. Charlie wanted to add three bedrooms and a bath—and, by now, some good-size closets. As before, they didn't stint on details. The upper floor would be reached by the stairs that previously had gone to the attic. At the top of the stairs, you took a right and there was a small bedroom with casement windows on the east and south sides. That room was connected by French doors to a larger room with windows all across the south wall and two more on the west side. This room also had a huge walk-in cedar closet. The plan was for Charlie and Jessie to move up here, and Jane would take the small room adjoining. Across the hall was a nice-size bedroom for Charles. It had windows on the east and north walls, so that when you woke up in the morning, you felt as though you'd slept in a tree house. A door in Charles's room led to a bath with a pedestal sink and a beautiful black-and-white tile shower. Charlie, Jessie, and Jane could also get to that bathroom by a door that opened to the hall. It was a well-thought-out floor plan. Carolee would need a place when she came home to visit, so she and Grandma Jackson would keep their rooms, and Grandmother Armor could have the middle one that Charlie and Jessie had been using. Until the new addition was finished, everybody would just have to make do.

Elizabeth Armor arrived, as best can be determined, with the chill of autumn. It was a difficult fall, with all the dust and noise and the workmen tramping in and out. Then, too, there was this stranger in their midst. Jessie did her best to soothe frayed nerves. There was little entertaining because of the work, but she cooked up great steaming platters of comforting foods for the family. Grandmother Armor, with her mouth set hard and her hair bound in a bun, was not comforted. At suppertime, if Jessie served her something she didn't like, instead of eating it graciously, she would take her index finger and slowly push the plate away. The children found her impossibly strict and unapproachable—as opposed to their Grandma Jackson, who fried them doughnuts and read to them and occasionally talked Jessie into letting them go to the picture show. Grandmother Armor had little use for anybody, much less children.

*Elizabeth Armor, Charlie's mother.*

The addition was finished by Christmas. That year, 1926, Uncle Ben, Grandma Jackson's brother, came to spend the holidays in Little Rock. He was on his way to the Hawaiian Islands, just another in a long list of his exotic jaunts. The man traveled almost as much as he practiced medicine. Charles and Jane loved it when Uncle Ben would come. He was so funny when he talked about the places he'd been. The truth was, he was kind of a snob about travel. Once he had come to see them after a trip to Venice. All he could talk about was how bad the place had smelled.

Grandma Jackson was overjoyed to see him. She wanted to show off her new radio, not to mention their new house. She was seventy-

*Christmas Day 1926. Despite Uncle Ben's visit and the house renovations being completed, nobody in this picture seems to be having a happy holiday.*

four that year, and her health wasn't all that she wished. The asthma was getting worse—even though Jessie sent notes with the Christmas cards saying Grandma was "spry as a cricket." Cynthia and Ben sat by the radio for hours that year, listening and talking, reminiscing. It was a wonderful Christmas. The new addition, made of stucco and painted white, sat atop the old structure like a big white cake from Jessie's kitchen. On Christmas Day, the family posed outside in the yard—everyone but Carolee, who wasn't there, and Charlie, who took the picture, and Grandmother Armor.

Looking at that photograph, you'd never know it was a happy occasion. A frown creases every face. It's as though a vague communal uneasiness had now permeated this house, filling each member of the family with an unnamed dread.

Only Jessie, indomitable Jessie, seems to be trying to summon up something resembling a smile.

*Here's the house with the second story Charlie added when his mother came to live with them. It was the fall of 1926, the beginning of the troubles.*

*Chapter Three*

# Armour

## 1926 ❦ 1937

For much of my life, even my adult life, I thought that you worked hard, you achieved and acquired things, and that those things would forevermore be yours. It's an embarrassingly naïve view of the world.

The thing that opened my eyes was a simple pair of socks. It was in that bedroom in Minnesota. In my sock drawer, I discovered a pair of socks that wasn't mine. I asked my wife about them, but she said I must be mistaken. I knew I wasn't. Not coincidentally, her boss soon left his wife and moved away, taking a job in New England. And my wife asked for a divorce and took our two sons home to her mother's house in Florida. Shortly after our divorce was final, she moved to New England and married her ex-boss. Though I certainly wouldn't have been able to script out that specific scenario, I knew, from the moment I found those socks, that my life would never again be quite the same.

That's part of what fascinates me about houses—how major life changes are precipitated, or at least revealed, in the most mundane ways. To my mind, Elizabeth Armor was a harbinger. Nobody alive today remembers why she came, and maybe there never was a plausible answer. But it's as though she were the embodiment of some larger, darker disturbance loose in the land. It's as though this pinched soul from the heart of America interrupted the Armours' happiness as a warning: that life, and fortune, can shift with the suddenness of a letter being plucked from the mailbox. Whatever her reason for coming, the truth of the matter is this: She lived with them for more than two years. And even after she was gone, their life at Holly Street was never as good again.

Maybe you can trace a portion of that to Charlie's decision to build a second story onto the house. That was a gesture born of hopefulness, of optimism, of confidence. And why *wouldn't* Charlie have been confident? He was successful—didn't his fine house with all its elegant appointments prove that? He had built this house from nothing. I've never commissioned the building of a house, but I can imagine that, once the work is completed and you realize that indeed you *have* afforded it, a heady feeling of power might ensue. You've put something on this earth that wasn't here before, something that will stand a hundred years. It's natural to believe you can keep doing it.

Besides, the Nu Grape business had been going well—so well that Charlie had invested more and more of his money in it. By 1928 he had two plants, the main one in Little Rock and a smaller one in Pine Bluff, forty-three miles south. Charlie believed in making his money work for him. Pem McRae, Jane's husband, remembers Charlie saying, "Money tied up in a house is wasted. That's expensive living. That money could be making money for you somewhere else." All over the country, businessmen were doing exactly as Charlie Armour was doing—investing in American business.

Even young Charles wasn't immune to the lure of big money. Much to his mother's horror, he decided to drop out of Little Rock High School to go into business with his dad. Charlie gave Charles a job loading cases of Nu Grape on and off one of the big trucks. Later, Charles graduated to driver, with a truck of his own. He was making more money than he'd ever seen in his life. Meanwhile, Jessie remained distressed at his dropping out of school. One day, one of her friends came over to have coffee, and as Jessie poured the cups, she also poured out her fears. The friend told Jessie not to worry. "Charles will be all right," she said. "Just wait'll he gets over fool's hill."

Before the decade was finished, many an American businessman older than young Charles Armour had gotten over fool's hill the hard way—by tumbling down the steep side. On October 29, 1929, when the dizzying rise of stock prices finally imploded in the famous crash, people went broke overnight. Businesses began closing. Over the next two months, $15 billion in paper value would simply vanish.

And, though it wasn't obvious at that moment, so would the market for soft drinks.

Most of us, when we're growing up, have no idea how hard it is to hold the center. If we're lucky, we never have to think about there being such a thing as a center to hold. Economic and emotional gravity keep us tethered, keep us believing that we're part of something solid, something warm, comfortable, and secure.

For a long time, Charles and Jane weren't aware of how precarious their world had become. There was food to eat; there were clothes on their backs. Charles and his father still had a bottling business to go to. Even after the Depression had begun in earnest and Charlie was forced to close the Little Rock plant, his children had no idea how bad things were.

At first, Charlie tried to scale down. In 1930, he gave up the big plant at Second and Rector and moved his operation to a smaller building on Broadway. He worked out of that office for a couple of years, but he could see that things were getting worse instead of better. Orders were dropping off at a steady pace. It couldn't have made him feel any better to read in the trade news that even gigantic

Coca-Cola, which owned some two-thirds of the market, was feeling the pinch. Coke's sales declined more than 20 percent between 1930 and 1932. Nobody had even a nickel to spend on soda pop.

In the house at 501 Holly, there was, added to this external gloom, a sadness of a more personal nature. Grandma Jackson died in January 1932. She had been getting weaker, and for the past year Jessie had moved her into the middle bedroom, where she could remain in bed and still be part of the goings-on. Everyone who came to the house wanted to see her; it had always been that way. Now Jessie would just open the French doors, and the bedroom became a kind of salon, where Jessie and her guests could drink coffee and chat while Grandma lay propped up in the big sleigh bed. Some days were better than others. Some days, she just wanted to doze, with the radio tuned low at her side. She died in the evening, with her family around her.

Jessie's feeling of emptiness must've been overwhelming. She was forty-five years old and had never, other than during college, lived apart from her mother. She turned her attention to her garden, planting two huge Cape jasmine bushes just outside the kitchen door. She had always planned to wallpaper those wall panels in the living and dining rooms, but the window had closed on that—wallpaper cost too much money. She stepped up her church work. Even during the weekdays, she spent many hours "going calling," as she termed it, visiting young women to try to persuade them to attend Sunday school.

Charlie's mother soon prompted a different kind of mourning. On July 18, 1932, probably at work, Pulaski County Sheriff Blake Williams came to see Charlie. The sheriff reached into his coat pocket and placed a summons in Charlie's hand. "In the Circuit Court of Pulaski County," it began. Then the words became almost unbelievable: *"Elizabeth Armor, Plaintiff, vs. C. W. L. Armor (also known as C. W. L. Armour), Defendant."*

It's possible that Charlie knew this was coming—though the idea that your own mother would sue you, especially when you were already on the ropes financially, is hard to comprehend. The suit claimed that Charlie owed her $2,154.28, that she had demanded payment, and that Charlie had refused. An affadavit, signed in a shaky hand by Elizabeth, charged that she had lent Charlie one thousand dollars on May 1, 1926 (which was just before she came to live with him). That loan was to be repaid in full, plus 6 percent interest. Then in late 1929 and 1930, Charlie had received four thousand dollars, three thousand dollars, and five hundred dollars, which was to be his share of Elizabeth's estate after her death. The stipulation, however, was that he would pay interest on that money during her lifetime. Finally, he had drawn $112.71 from an account she maintained in Little Rock. Between January and September 1930—about the time Charlie was scaling back his business—he had made six payments, totaling $215; after that, nothing. Now she wanted her money.

I can imagine Charlie and Jessie sitting on the front porch late on that July night in 1932. We give up in stages. We draw invisible lines, across which we won't allow the world to encroach. Then when that line is violated, we draw another—tighter, closer in. It's a helpless feeling, waiting for the end to come. Charlie must've felt that way about the business. It was a losing battle. The Depression was bigger than he was. The summons, like Elizabeth herself, was only symbolic—what's another couple thousand dollars in the face of total ruin? For Charlie and Jessie, the tighter line now had to encircle the family, the house: the home. Others were losing that battle, too, but *they*, the Armours, had to find a way to hold the center.

At the end of August, Charlie settled with his mother for the sum of $1,994.82, plus 6 percent interest from June 10. That fall, he set about dismantling the Little Rock Nu Grape plant. He still had the one in Pine Bluff, but that wasn't enough to keep the family going.

The spring of 1933 brought the worst of the Depression to Little Rock. On March 4, to avoid a run on the banks, the Arkansas banking commissioner ordered all banks closed. They didn't reopen until March 13, after they had been pronounced sound and new procedures had been adopted. But that was a long week in Arkansas. That was a week in which many people were paid in produce, or in anything else that still had value.

By that time, the frivolous little Nu Grape car seemed as alien as the memories of the decade just past. Charlie replaced it with a two-door Chevy in sober black.

Seemingly overnight, 501 Holly was transformed from a place of gaiety and well-being into a retreat. No more would there be elaborate dinners or festive dances with the rugs rolled back. Instead of a place into which the world was invited, this house had become a refuge from it.

Charlie's presence at home on weekdays was unsettling for the rest of the family. Charles, back in high school, was now in the same grade as Jane. In the mornings, they would catch the streetcar a couple of blocks away on Prospect, then ride it back home again after school. Upon their return, they would often find their father sitting in the living room by the radio, wearing casual clothes instead of his customary suits, his pipe cradled in his mouth as he listened to the state of the world. His sitting there told Charles and Jane all they needed to know about the state of the world.

Not that Charles and Jane spent a lot of time worrying about their father's situation. They were, after all, teenagers. Both would be seniors during the 1933-1934 year, and both had their own friends, their own schedules, and their own concerns. Even though he made better grades than Jane, Charles fretted that he wasn't going to do well. And he was compulsive—he wanted things done *just right*. Jane seemed to be more comfortable in her skin than Charles was in his.

She was dating a nice young man named John Pemberton McRae, called Pem. Like people all over the country, Jane and Pem escaped to the movies as often as they could afford it during the 1930s. On hot summer evenings, there was nothing better than a cool, dark theater to take you away from your troubles. There was a new Disney cartoon that seemed—if your mind worked in such a way—to be a commentary on the times. It was about a trio of pigs, and after the show you could hear people singing or whistling the catchy theme song, "Who's Afraid of the Big Bad Wolf?" as they left the comfort of the theater and walked off in pairs into the night.

Meanwhile, Charlie and Jessie worked at keeping his spirits high. Behind that noncommittal exterior, Charlie Armour had a temper, though he usually managed to contain it. Jane remembers witnessing his anger through the window one day when she was a child. Charlie was in the front yard with a Negro man, who was there doing some work. Suddenly, Charlie grabbed the man by his shirt and practically lifted him off his feet. Charlie was saying something, but Jane couldn't hear what. The man was obviously petrified. Then Charlie put him down and the Negro went back to his work, cowering like a dog that had been disciplined. From Jane's point of view, the entire vignette was acted out in silence, which gave it a power—the power of imagination—beyond what it might've had otherwise.

Jessie kept busy, of course, and Charlie really did, too—as much as possible. He worked on the grape arbor he'd built in the backyard, and he tended his tomato plants, as he had every year. He had a knack for growing tomatoes, and at harvest time he made the rounds of the neighborhood, sharing the bounty with the folks on Holly and Lee. He phoned friends, visited with people he'd known in business, church, and civic affairs. Sooner or later, some job prospect would turn up. At least he and Jessie weren't having to go out and humiliate themselves by dancing for dollars in dance marathons, the way so many other couples were.

In mid-October, there was an item in the *Arkansas Gazette* about one of President Roosevelt's new programs, the Civilian Conservation Corps, generally referred to as the CCC. Hundreds of boys would soon be shipped to Arkansas from places like California and Oregon. These young men were going to be put to work building all sorts of public facilities, bridges, and dams. The plan, according to Guy Amsler, head of the State Parks Commission, was to house some of the boys in barracks to be built at Fair Park, just a few blocks from Holly Street.

Charlie Armour had a degree in civil engineering. Maybe, he thought, these untrained crews needed just such a person to supervise their work. It seemed to be a sign—especially since Guy Amsler, the Parks Commissioner, happened to be Charlie Armour's neighbor to the side, right across Lee Street.

He and Amsler talked, and yes, there were definite possibilities. One of the CCC projects was to be the construction of Boyle Park, a 231-acre parcel of land southwest of the city. The Parks Commission was going to need a superintendent for Boyle. Charlie Armour, Amsler said, had just the right qualifications.

So at age sixty-three, Charlie became a civil engineer again. His self reinventions had come full circle.

If there's peace in your heart, your house will reflect it. If there's rage, your house will reveal it. If there's indecision or indolence, your house will bear the brunt of it. In Jessie's case, her new concern about her home showed itself in a feverish rearrangement of the downstairs rooms. She moved the player piano from the living room to the front bedroom, which she was now calling "the music room." The middle bedroom was now "the sitting room." Jessie had furnished it with a couple of easy chairs, good lamps, and a lighted fish tank designed to provide a much-needed touch of serenity.

Of course, she probably attributed these moves to practical concerns. Radio had taken over the living room—by late 1933, Charles and his father could sit by the fireplace and listen to "The Lone Ranger," or Jessie and Jane could fill the wicker popper and listen to "The Romance of Helen Trent." Now, suddenly, you needed a different place for reading and playing music. The other factor was that the house was just so much larger with three fewer people in it. Grandma Jackson was dead, Grandmother Armor had moved in with her other son in California, and Carolee had gotten married and was living in Boston. It seemed a shame to let all that space go to waste.

Jessie's brilliant idea no doubt resulted from just this sort of antsy preoccupation with the house. Not content to sit and wait for events to overtake her family, she began to take stock of their strengths, their abilities, their holdings. The only thing they had in excess, she decided, was space—the house itself. With so many people losing homes—or not able to afford them in the first place—she suggested to Charlie that they start taking in boarders.

It was perfect: Jessie was, after all, schooled in the efficient running of a household. The going rate for room and board was thirty dollars a month. Besides using the center to *hold* the center, they would be helping others who needed a place in these tough times. And one other thing in their favor: Arkansas had passed a lenient divorce law, and people from all over the country were coming to the state to live during the three-month residency requirement. This house, a family house, would be ideal for a young woman all alone and miles from home.

Jessie began advertising, and before long she had plenty of business. There was a lot of coming and going, but word of mouth kept the house full most of the time. She and Charlie moved back downstairs, back to the middle bedroom. Charles moved to the back bedroom, the one he had once shared with Grandma Jackson.

Jane insisted on keeping her small bedroom at the top of the stairs, but that still gave Jessie three rooms to rent. Mabel was back living in the room above the garage, so she could help Jessie. And if she left again, they could rent out *her* room.

The first boarder was an old-maid schoolteacher named Miss Hairston. She taught first grade at Pulaski Heights Elementary, just down the street, so she was delighted to find a homey place so close. She took the big upstairs room with the cedar closet, the room separated from Jane's by the pongee-covered French doors. Every night when Miss Hairston saw Jane's light go out, she would say the very same thing, never a variation. It drove Jane crazy.

"Good night, Janie dear," she called out in her chirpy, school-teachery voice.

"Good night, Miss Hairston," Jane dutifully replied.

"Sleep tight, Janie dear." With that, Jane pulled the covers over her head and burrowed in as deeply as she could.

It must've been strange at first, having other people in the house. I can't imagine it myself—I feel a vague unease even when our cleaning lady is here, no matter if she's downstairs and I'm up in my office. But Jessie liked having new people to talk with. She told them all about the neighbors, how they lived and what they did and who their people were. She talked about her Sunday school class and tried to line up new members. She provided her boarders two meals a day, breakfast and supper. At night, the boarders were welcome to come downstairs and sit by the fire or out on the porch. Charlie would tell them stories about growing up on the farm in Kansas, or about the panthers in Louisiana.

Having boarders was almost like having parties again. A young lady from New York named Olive Hoeffleic came for a divorce, bringing her mother with her. They waited out the three months eating Jessie's good cooking, which had become more quintessentially Southern than that of her Southern-born neighbors. Jessie didn't cook Cajun-style, though, and one of the boarders was a young woman from Louisiana, Jeanne Breaux, who missed her own mother's cooking. Jeanne's husband was a salesman whose territory was Arkansas, and he wanted her in a family-type boarding-house. The Armours could see why. Jeanne was as coquettish as they come, and she immediately took over the social life of the house. In her Cajun accent, she led giggling conversations at the dinner table. Her people were both French *and* Italian, and she would write to her mother, asking her to send recipes—red beans and rice, and all her other favorites—which Jessie would then try. Jeanne would stand in the kitchen, translating while Jessie cooked, and everybody would be laughing the whole time.

In 1935, Annabelle Ritter came. A Mississippian, she had moved to Little Rock in the late twenties to work in a branch office of the General Motors Acceptance Corporation. She would become one of the Armours' longest-running boarders, staying eight years—longer than some of the future owners of this house.

It was as though the Armours and their boarders were an extended family. People came to Jessie looking for a home, and she took them in. If they stayed long enough, they all got to know one another's moods, quirks, nuances. Most of the boarders could tell the Armours were having financial trouble, though the words were never actually spoken. Maybe it was just an occasional look in Jessie's or Charlie's eye that gave it away. But it was no surprise, really, nor was it a stigma—*everybody* was having financial trouble to some degree.

One day in what must've been the fall of 1936, the Armours' situation took a noticeable turn. Jessie announced to the boarders that she was taking a job outside the house—she was going to be a dietician at the state mental hospital a few blocks away. It was understandable. Charles and Jane were now in college, and two children in college at the same time would be hard for any family. Of course, the boarders wondered what this meant for them. No, Jessie said, she wasn't closing the boardinghouse; she was just taking on additional work.

She still cooked breakfast for everyone in the morning before going off to her other job. In the afternoons, she would come home with jars of food left over from the meals she had prepared for the patients. These leftovers would often be the evening meal for the residents of 501 Holly.

Then, in early 1937, Jessie called Annabelle Ritter aside and told her she had some bad news. The Armours were going to have to move. The present arrangement just wasn't working. They were keeping the house, however, and Jessie had arranged for a family called the Kemps to rent it and to allow the boarders to stay. Unfortunately, they would no longer be boarders; they would just be renters—but they would be welcome to keep their own food in the refrigerator and prepare it themselves.

Annabelle was astounded, but Jessie waved aside any show of pity. They would be fine. They had taken an apartment farther into the Heights, she said, over on North Tyler Street. It was a nice apartment—a duplex, actually. Charles and Jane were going to drop out of college and get jobs until the family got back on its feet.

What Jessie didn't tell Annabelle that day was that Charlie had already declared bankruptcy. They had held on for a long time, but the odds were stacked too high against them. Charlie had gone to court the previous summer, in August of 1936. He had been sixty-six years old at the time. The paperwork on the bankruptcy was surprisingly brief. "In the matter of C. W. L. Armour, Bkcy. No. 4499," it began. "At Little Rock, on the 31st day of August, A.D. 1936, before the Honorable John E. Martineau . . ." Though it was written in legalese, certain phrases stood out as brutally to the point: ". . . having been heard and duly considered, the said C. W. L. Armour is hereby declared and adjudged a bankrupt. . . ."

When moving day came, Jessie had packed their clothes and a few pieces of furniture. After checking the house one last time, she closed the door and got into the car, where Charlie was waiting. In my mind's eye, I see them driving off, bravely, without looking back.

The writer Mark Twain lived for many years in a flamboyant Stick Style house in Hartford, Connecticut. It was there that he wrote some of his most famous books—*The Adventures of Tom Sawyer, The Prince and the Pauper, The Adventures of Huckleberry Finn, A Connecticut Yankee in King Arthur's Court.* For Twain and his wife, Livy, the years in that house were the best of their lives. "To us," Twain wrote, "our house was not unsentient matter—it had a heart, and a soul, and eyes to see us with; and approvals and solicitudes and deep sympathies; it was of us, and we were in its confidence, and lived in its grace and in the peace of its benediction. We never came home from an absence that its face did not light up and speak out its eloquent welcome—and we could not enter it unmoved."

Those lines inevitably come to me when I think of the Armours driving away from their house on Holly Street. They had lost its approvals, its confidence, the peace of its benediction. Without those things, they were unsheltered in a way that's ultimately more damaging than simply not having that roof over their heads. Especially Charlie. His heart and soul were now open to the elements.

*The Armours tried to hold the center, but finally they had to leave 501 Holly.*

# Chapter Four

# Armour

## 1937 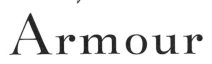 1947

Every weekday morning, I drive my stepdaughter Bret to school. Though Bret would tell you there are some days when I'm the grumpiest of chauffeurs, I nevertheless enjoy these moments—they're a comforting ritual, and no doubt part of the reason I feel at home at 501 Holly. My own two sons have lived in a different state from me since David was seven—they moved on his seventh birthday, actually—and Matthew was seven months. Herding eleven-year-old Bret and our miniature schnauzer, Snapp, into the car every morning, I feel, when I think about it, that I've managed to double back and recapture a piece of something I had lost.

The subject of loss often crosses my mind on the way to school. That's because, following Kavanaugh Street (called Prospect until the mid-thirties) farther into the Heights, I pass right by North Tyler Street, where Charlie and Jessie and Charles and Jane moved when they had to leave the house on Holly. The duplex they lived in is the second one from the corner, and I give it a respectful glance every day as I drive by.

But it's not the duplex that rivets me. It's a utility pole on the north side of Kavanaugh, just west of Tyler. I look at it both going and coming, but it's after I've dropped Bret off and am on my way home that I begin to really focus on it. I start eyeing it several blocks away, passing Fillmore Street, then Taylor Street, then Polk. Then, in the block between Polk and Tyler, I grip the steering wheel tighter and begin to imagine that I'm Charlie Armour on that August day in 1937.

The whole family had gotten jobs, but Charlie was looking for a better one. Toward the end of that summer, he got a lead about a position in Hot Springs. It's not clear today what the job was, but he was interested enough to go investigate. On Monday, August 16, he and Jessie and Jane drove the fifty miles to Hot Springs to get a sense of the town. August of 1937 was terribly hot in Arkansas. In fact, it was scorching all through the midsection of the country. The day the Armours made that drive to Hot Springs, the temperature in central Arkansas hit 96 degrees—with Arkansas's usual stifling humidity. They took the black Chevy, which absorbed the heat. When they got back to Little Rock, they were all glad *that* trip was over. Even at almost 5:00 P.M., the thermometer still stood at 93 degrees.

Jessie wanted Charlie to let her and Jane out at the duplex so they could start fixing supper, but they needed a twenty-five-pound block of ice. The icehouse was only a short distance away on Kavanaugh, close to where White City had been. Charlie dropped them off and went to get the ice. A few minutes later, he was on his way back home, driving east on Kavanaugh past Fillmore Street, Taylor Street, Polk. Then, on this very block that I'm driving down on my way back from taking Bret to school, Charlie ran into an unseen force that smashed his chest and squeezed his heart with a grip that made him blind with pain. He lost control of the car, which swerved across the oncoming lane and smashed into the utility pole—probably not this very piece of wood, but a pole that once stood where this one now stands.

Half a block away, in the kitchen of the duplex, Jessie and Jane were starting supper when they heard fast footsteps on the front porch and a rapping at the door. Jane opened it, and a little neighbor boy was standing there. The color had drained from his face. "Come quick. Come quick!" he blurted. "Mr. Armour's had a wreck and run into the telephone pole!"

Jessie heard him from the kitchen and came running, banging the screen door against the wall as she hit the porch and tore down the steps. Jane lingered just long enough to call Pem at work and tell him something terrible had happened. Then she went out after her mother. As soon as they got to the front of the yard, they could see that a crowd had gathered on Kavanaugh. The black Chevy was smashed against a utility pole on the opposite side of the street from the direction Charlie was traveling. He was slumped over the steering wheel. As Jessie and Jane reached the crowd, they saw that a doctor they knew, a man named Thompson, had pulled over and was lifting Charlie from the wreck. The doctor placed Charlie on the ground. Jessie ran to her husband, but Thompson stopped her in her tracks. "He's dead," the doctor said.

By the time I get to that part, I've passed the spot and am on my way back home to the house Charlie Armour never saw again.

In 1938, Jessie moved back to 501 Holly. I like to imagine that, like Mark Twain's Stick Style sanctuary, Jessie's bungalow brightened and welcomed her with a moving eloquence. That can happen if you really love a house. You can step through the front door after an absence, even a brief one, and the room will light up as though it were a theater set. At that moment, you're able to see your house in dual dimensions—one, through the eyes of a stranger coming into a warm and comfortable room for the first time; and, two, through the eyes of one lucky enough to call this place home.

Though much had changed in Jessie's life in the few long months since she had been away, this house rewarded her return with a comforting familiarity: the front porch with the creaky swing, the fireplace where so much popcorn had been popped, the elegant

French doors, the well-worn rugs, the cozy breakfast room, the way the sun crossed the kitchen at certain times of day. If it had been summer, Jessie could've flung open the side doors and inhaled the sweet scent of Cape jasmine.

Of the Armours, there were just Jessie and Charles here now. Jane and Pem had married during the time in exile and had rented an apartment downtown. But there were boarders, such as Annabelle, who were glad to have Jessie back. And Jessie was glad to have the boarders, a family she could mother. She served them meals again, and she did some sewing for Annabelle. During the weekdays, she continued working at the state hospital, overseeing preparation of the food for her less fortunate family there.

At night, after supper, Jessie often retired to her bedroom to read, while Charles, now a restless twenty-four, disappeared with some of the boarders into the darkness, bound for any number of places where a young person could pass an enjoyable evening. But on many nights in 1938 and 1939, Jessie would *not* retire to her room, nor would Charles and assorted boarders go out in search of fun. There were many nights during those years when the radio pulled all of them into the living room to share the experience of impending catastrophe in Europe. Grim-voiced radio announcers told of Hitler's Nazis in Czechoslovakia and of a Japanese pledge to support Germany. They outlined the jockeying of nations, the form-ing of pacts. On September 1, 1939, they reported Hitler's military invasion of Poland. Two days later, they relayed the news that England and France had declared war against Germany.

It was a war that would change the lives of many of the people listening in that quiet, comfortable living room at 501 Holly. But of that group, it would change no one's life as much as it would that of young Charles Armour.

Annabelle Ritter remembers that after England entered the war, Charles started talking about joining the Royal Navy. This war, he seemed to feel, went deeper than mere nationality, and he wanted to have his part in it. By 1940, when the United States was gearing up for the inevitable, Charles signed with the U.S. Navy. Jessie received the news stoically, the way she had taken so many other blows.

Charles left Little Rock for the Great Lakes Naval Training Center in Chicago, where he was to be molded into an officer. He and his commissioned cohorts in all the services in those days were often referred to as "ninety-day wonders," a jab at the speed with which this country was turning out military leaders. But there was no choice—war was raging in Europe by now. Italy was in on the side of the Nazis, and France had fallen to Hitler's troops. The British vowed to fight on alone.

Sporting his new ensign's bars, Charles came home for a few days before shipping out for good. He was a hero in the neighborhood. Of course, he was especially fawned over at 501 Holly, where his mother cooked his favorite meals and all the boarders listened to his tales of sea life—such as he now knew it. As the time came for him to go, he took a last good look at the house he had grown to manhood in. Then he boarded a train west, transferring to a troop ship bound for his duty station, a base in the Pacific called Pearl Harbor.

For the longest time, no one was able to tell Jessie whether or not Charles and his ship, the cruiser *Louisville,* had even been in port the morning the Japanese attacked. After war was declared, Jane and Pem moved to Massachussetts so Pem could work on radios for the Raytheon Corporation. Jessie was alone now, except for her boarders. She pored over the newspapers, looking for any scrap, any hint, any information at all that she could cling to. She called the navy, and she wrote letters, but so did thousands of other mothers and wives and girlfriends. You had to send your letter to the fleet post office in San Francisco, which sometimes felt like putting a note in a bottle and dropping it into the sea. You had no idea whether your letter would get to anyone who even knew Charles Armour.

The dates are fuzzy from this period, but finally, one day in what I believe was the spring of 1942, Jessie came home from work and found an official-looking envelope in her mailbox. It was from the chaplain on the *Louisville*. The ship had been at sea when the base was bombed. Charles had become sick aboard ship and they had put him ashore at a hospital in Manila, in the Philippines. The Japanese had captured Manila a few weeks after Pearl Harbor. As far as the chaplain knew, Charles had been in the hospital at the time Manila fell. That was the last anyone had heard of him. And that would be the last Jessie would hear for more than a year.

It was a terrible way to live, not knowing whether her son was dead or alive. But if she had to go through this, it was good that she was back in her own house. Our houses are where we go to find order and certainty against the disorder and uncertainty of the world at large. In our houses, we're surrounded by familiar things, familiar people. We have our comforting routines. Jessie had her boarders and her job to keep her occupied. But she also did something interesting involving how she lived in her own house.

One day, she announced that she was moving her quarters to the small, narrow pantry/porch behind the kitchen. This is where Beth and I keep the washer and dryer, and where the girls pretend to try to hang their coats. This is where Snapp eats, where we put our wine rack and keep canned goods. This is where the closet for the hot-water heater is, tucked beneath the stairs to the second floor. This is a room five feet wide and fifteen feet long, with the door to the backyard right in the middle, so any sleeping arrangements would have to be in half that space. Jessie placed a cot on that porch and moved in.

In my family, the word *cubbyhole* was part of the lexicon, and I absorbed a concept of that word very early on. I say "a" concept because the dictionary defines *cubbyhole* somewhat differently from the way I think of it: "A snug or cramped space or room; a small compartment." To me, those definitions sound vaguely negative compared to the cubbyholes I've known and loved. One old house I lived in as a child had a secret room behind the fireplace, and another tiny room beyond that; another had a trick closet, so you could enter in one room and come out in the closet of another; still another house had a space *above* one closet, with sliding door panels. To a young boy growing up in the Roy Rogers era, the dominant impression of these spaces wasn't that they were cramped. It was, instead, that they were wonderful hideouts. Even as an adult, I've been charmed by such secret hideaways in houses I've considered buying.

I'm sure Jessie would say that her little cubbyhole of a bedroom was a practical move, that it was more convenient to the kitchen. But I believe she was drawing the line around herself closer and tighter. In times of uncertainty, it's helpful to keep life simple. You want just a few true things you can count on without thinking.

A look at the newspaper each morning told her there were a lot of families with the same uncertainty she felt—or worse. Reading the *Arkansas Gazette* had become a different experience from the one it had been even as recently as the late 1930s. Back then, there were the usual stories about gangsters on the loose, but there was also a sense of fun, even with hard times just past and war in Europe on the horizon. There were splashy automobile ads every few pages. There were big store ads showing slinky evening wear, the hemlines hovering teasingly at midcalf. There were movie ads and announcements of big-band performances.

Now the tone had changed. You still saw movie ads and lists of radio shows. There were still weddings and club announcements and funny papers. Downtown stores all had big ads showing what the well-dressed man and woman would be wearing at various seasons. Despite all that, the paper was grim. There were no automobile ads—Detroit couldn't get rubber for tires. Even the clothes that were advertised featured practicality over glamour—hemlines were shorter to save on material. The war dominated the news. Even the gossip columns dealt with the war: "Aimée Semple McPherson has a message for her followers: 'Drive slowly and use less rubber.' "

No doubt a lot of people in Jessie's situation turned to the second page of the paper first. At the top, inevitably, were photographs of young men in uniform under the headline MISSING IN ACTION, or, all too often, KILLED IN ACTION. These were local or state boys, some of whom may even have known Charles. The obituaries were on that page, too—long lists of the dead. At the end was a separate section headlined DEATHS OF NEGROES. It was a page you had to pore over while holding your breath.

On December 7, 1942, a year after Pearl Harbor, the paper reported that a total of 42,635 U.S. fighting men were now missing in action. "Most," the article said, "are presumed to be prisoners."

By this time, the effects of wartime deficits were really beginning to be felt in Little Rock. Because of gasoline rationing, streetcars were overcrowded. Sometimes they even had to pass up people waving to them from the curb. One large department store reported that it had sold out of walking shoes and had no idea when it would have new stock. Food stores were hanging SOLD OUT signs on coffee, lard, patented brands of shortening, butter, tuna fish, imported olive and salad oils, meat products, and dozens of other items. At restaurants, diners had become used to asking what was available rather than telling the waiter what they wanted. Beauty shops had begun requiring customers to bring their own hairpins. The variety of cosmetics was shrinking rapidly. Imported castile soap was no longer available. Lipstick now came in plastic containers.

This was a time when Jessie's home economics training came in handy. She knew how to stretch a dish. Efficiency and organization were also at a premium. You had to watch the food stamps and make sure you were using the right stamp from the right ration book. Every so often, the newspaper would publish a list: "Sugar—last day for No. 12 stamp in Ration Book 1; Coffee—first day for No. 23 stamp in Ration Book 1." You wanted to use every stamp you had, and that took planning, organization. To let a stamp lapse was simply wasteful.

Even though it was wartime, there were light moments. Late one night, Annabelle was sound asleep when her door suddenly swung open and the overhead light glared in her face. "Get up, Annabelle!" a voice said. "Someone's murdered Gene Driver and thrown him in the front door!" Annabelle rubbed her eyes and began to realize that it was Jessie standing there. The Gene Driver she was talking about was a neighbor. From her little cubbyhole behind the kitchen, Jessie had been startled awake by a thud at the front of the house. Grabbing her robe and going to the door, she flipped on the porch light and there, in a clump by the doormat, was Gene Driver. He sure *looked* dead.

Annabelle went and took a peek. While that was happening, Jessie called Miss Alice Ream across the street. Her brother was staying there, and he soon came over and inspected the body— which turned out to be an inebriated Gene Driver. Some of his drinking buddies had dumped him on Jessie's porch by mistake.

At some point during the war, Jessie decided she could no longer serve meals to the people who stayed there. She told Annabelle that she was welcome to keep food for herself in the refrigerator. Annabelle appreciated it, but—well, she had something to talk with Jessie about. Her company, GMAC, had had to close down the Little Rock office because nobody was selling cars. The company had left one contact man there to keep in touch with the dealers, and Annabelle had stayed to work for the contact man. But there was nothing to do. Her days were empty, boring, depressing. After eight years at the Armours', she had come to the hard conclusion that it was time to go back home to Mississippi.

Jessie hugged her tightly. With Annabelle's departure, Jessie was losing much more than a boarder.

It was the spring of 1943 when word came from the navy that Charles was a prisoner in the Philippines. About that time, she also received the first of five cards that she would get from him over the next year. The cards, on a deep manila stock, bore as heading the imprint of the Imperial Japanese Army. They were form postcards. Using a typewriter with a spotty ribbon, Charles had been allowed to fill in the blanks or underline certain multiple-choice answers:

1. I am interned at <u>Philippine Military Prison Camp No. 2</u>
2. My health is—<u>excellent;</u> good; fair; poor.
3. I am—injured; sick in hospital; under treatment; <u>not under treatment.</u>
4. I am—improving; not improving; better; <u>well.</u>
5. Please see that <u>Caroline and Art are notified. Take care of all my things.</u>      is taken care of.
6. {Re: Family}: <u>Hope you and Jane well. Please write to me and let me know how you are % Red Cross.</u>Love to all. Dont worry.
7. Please give my best regards to <u>all of my friends.</u>

After all this time, even this strained missive seemed like a long, chatty letter. At least Charles was alive! All the neighbors came to see the card. This little rectangle of paper was a real connection: Charles had actually held it in his hands. Now Jessie held it. She read and reread it a thousand times, always looking for some previously hidden clue to his condition. He was worrying, as usual—of *course* she would take care of his things.

She received one other card from him that spring, then two more in the late fall and winter. The final card was slightly discomforting.

In the form sentence reporting on his health, this time he had underlined *fair*. His worrying was also evident: "Wish I could have been with you for Xmas. Am looking forward to receiving a letter from you. Do not dispose of any of your property. Hope that you, Jane, Caroline are all well and that I will be with you again soon. Love to all." On the signature line, he had signed "Charles W. Armour."

Toward the end of January 1944, the Office of War Information released the shocking story of Japanese brutality during the Bataan Death March nearly two years before. The country was enraged. A few days after the revelations, Jessie picked up a new magazine and began to shriek: There was a photograph of the Death March, and she thought she saw Charles in the picture. Hysterical, she called Jane and Pem, who calmed her down. Later, the family decided it hadn't been Charles, after all.

Jessie scoured the news stories for names of people she could write to who might know something about Charles. Comdr. M. H. McCoy, stationed at Fort Blakely, Washington, answered in mid-April 1944. "I knew your son quite well and his health was good at the time I escaped," McCoy wrote. They had met in Camp Number 1 and had then gone on to Camp Number 2 together. His recollection was that Charles had been on the "vegetable-gathering detail."

That appears to have been her last word about Charles for more than a year.

In February 1945, the Associated Press circulated stories of two different Japanese prison ships that had been torpedoed or bombed by American planes, with heavy losses among the American POWs. The ships had been en route from the Philippines to Japan. Obviously, the Japanese were beginning to feel the heat and were attempting to get their prisoners back to Japan. A few months after those reports, she heard from a man whose name had been mentioned in one of the stories.

*22 June 1945*

*My dear Mrs. Armour:*

*You probably, this week, received the good news that your son, Charles, is alive and now in Japan. While I did not know him intimately, I was in prison camps in the Philippines until last December 1944, and the Casualty Section of the Navy Department, where I am now on temporary duty, has suggested that I write you about your son.*

*Most of the time Charles was at the prison camp in Davao, Mindanao; he then came to camp # 1, where I had been the previous 2 years, and I met him here for the first time.*

*We met through a mutual friend, Lt. James Lynch of the Army Engineers. . . . Charles, Lt. Lynch and I were among the 1600 prisoners who were on the prison ship which sailed from Manila on 13 December 1944. It was sunk on 15 December 1944, at which time I escaped. Charles and Lt. Lynch were recaptured and later shipped to Japan, as we learned just a few days ago.*

*We all hope with you that the end of the war is not long distant and that your son will again be with you.*

In my mind's eye, I always see Charles's homecoming in slow motion, as though it were a movie.

*Pem, back from Massachussetts, is mowing the lawn at 501 Holly, struggling with the steep Lee Street hill, when he sees the taxi coming toward him on Lee. For some reason, he stops his mowing and, instead, watches the cab as it gets closer and closer. When it reaches Pem, it slowly makes the turn onto Holly, then pulls up at the curb in front of the house. The door opens and a gaunt man in a naval officer's uniform slowly unfolds himself from the backseat. By this time, Pem sees that Jane has already seen Charles arrive and is running out to meet him. Her arms are outstretched, and tears are streaming down her face.*

*I picture Charles, arm in arm with Jane, walking up that sidewalk toward the red-brick house with the comforting front porch, the house of his mother and father and sisters and grandmother, the house that had been secured with nails he had carried for the workmen so many years before. They had held. No matter what he had seen or done or been through over the past forty-four months, the house still stood. It was what he had gone to war for.*

In real life, even if Charles was thinking such lofty thoughts, they weren't the only thing on his mind. He was sick and worried, and there's evidence that he was also angry: He would tell a friend, "For thirty years I've been the fuckee. Now I'm going to be the fuck*er*." After the atomic bombs and the Japanese surrender, Jessie had received word that Charles was coming back to the States, to Memphis, 127 miles away. Jane and Pem and their two children—Janesy and Anne—were back in Little Rock by then. But the navy made no suggestion that the family visit Charles during the two months he had to spend in the navy hospital. Charles needed time to recuperate.

Then one day, he showed up in a taxi in front of 501 Holly. On the surface, he was home.

But when Jane ran out to the cab and threw her arms around him, she had the feeling that she seemed like a stranger to him. "He looked at me so strangely," she says. Jessie was still at work when Charles got there. While Jane took her brother inside, Pem ran all over the neighborhood shouting, "Charles is at home! Charles is at home!" Before long, the house was filled with neighbors. They didn't speak of the war, at least not in detail. Charles told them he'd been treated for beriberi and scurvy. They could see, by the scars on his face, that he'd had skin cancers removed. When he first came back to the hospital, he'd also had hives on his legs and terrible intestinal problems from dysentery. For the time being, he was only going to be home on weekends; later, he would be mostly in Little Rock and would go back to the hospital for short checkup visits.

When Jessie got home and the family was alone together, Charles told them something else: There was a woman in his life. Her name was Mildred Ahrens—or Millie, as he called her. She was a navy nurse whom he had met in the hospital. They'd been going out since shortly after he got there. She was—well, she was a Yankee, from New York. Jessie had been in the South so long—nearly forty years—that she thought of herself as Southern. It was obvious that Charles was smitten, though, and Jessie told him he should bring Millie home with him some weekend. He thought that was a splendid idea—one he'd already had himself.

To the family, Charles seemed distant. He would sit in the house by himself, sometimes just staring off into space. Most afternoons, he would put on his uniform and catch the streetcar to the movie theater. There were lots of movies about the war, and Jane thought he was trying to find out what he had missed. Sometimes he would sit through the same movie two or three times, coming home in the early dark of winter to a house warmed by lights.

It wasn't long before he took Jessie up on her invitation to Millie. They rode over together on the train and were met by Jessie at the station. Millie still remembers how intimidated she was by Jessie. She seemed so *tall,* so self-assured. She was a handsome woman dressed to the nines, and she talked nonstop. As Jessie drove them to Holly Street, Millie took in the neighborhood. Kavanaugh was curvy and tree-lined, with old Craftsman houses and stone-fronted apartment houses. It all looked quaint to a girl from New York.

Millie was embarrassed to talk—she felt awkward about her Yankee accent—but with Jessie around, that was no problem. Jessie filled the rooms with words. Millie had never encountered anyone who knew so much about the neighbors. Jessie even took out Charles's christening dress, telling her about Charles as a baby and holding the dress up for Millie's inspection.

There were no longer any boarders. Charles slept downstairs in the bedroom he had once shared with Grandma Jackson. Millie slept upstairs in Annabelle's old room. Jane and Pem and their babies were across the hall in the room that opened to the upstairs bath. Millie would share that bath, entering from the hall, and Jessie had given explicit instructions on how to lock both doors. Still, Millie was uncomfortable knowing those strangers, with unpredictable little children, were just on the other side of the bathroom door.

In the morning, Millie woke to find Charles in her room, giving her a good-morning kiss.

That June, the summer of 1946, Jessie's Cape jasmine bush bloomed thick and sweet outside the kitchen door. She cut armloads of flowers for the wedding, which was held in a Presbyterian chapel in Memphis. Afterward, the new bride and groom, his family, and five or six of the couple's friends had an elegant dinner at the Peabody Hotel, where Millie and Charles had done much of their courting. There was a ballroom on top of the hotel, and a restaurant that Charles especially liked. Even if he and Millie had been going to a movie, Charles had insisted on dinner first. He couldn't get enough to eat. In prison camp, he and his fellow POWs had passed the time trading recipes, sustaining themselves on the sheer memory of the scents and tastes of home.

Jessie also decorated the dining table with Cape jasmine. There was an abundance of champagne, and many, many toasts. Jessie insisted that Charles use some of his considerable back pay to buy Millie a fur coat. Millie, who wasn't used to alcohol, drank too much and passed out at the table. The next morning, her husband had breakfast brought in. When she felt better, they made up for the night before.

After a few days in Memphis, the newlyweds came home to 501 Holly. They moved into the back bedroom downstairs. It was only temporary, until Charles figured things out. He was trying to get a retirement so that if anything happened to him, Millie would be taken care of. He would go to Washington for up to two weeks at a time, partly to be treated for his skin cancer and partly to work on getting the retirement. His worry was palpable. Beriberi caused heart damage, and he seemed to have an acute sense of his mortality. Many—too many—of his sentences began with "If anything happens to me . . ."

With Charles in Washington and Jessie and Pem at work, Millie and Jane were thrown together all day long. They would do chores like washing the clothes and hanging them out to dry in the backyard. Jessie would come home from the state hospital with jars of food, which she would pour into pans and heat up for supper. One night about a month after the wedding, Millie said, "I can't eat; I'm sick." Jessie took one look at her and said, "You're pregnant." Jessie was right. That complicated Charles and Millie's plans a little, but they were ecstatic.

Charles had decided to go back to the University of Arkansas at Fayetteville to finish up and get his law degree. Millie was thinking of getting a graduate degree in nursing. They had their sights set on the spring semester of 1947. Jane and Pem had big plans, too. They were planning to buy a house, but they weren't going to put *all* their money down, because Pem wanted to start his own radio-repair business.

During that fall of 1946, Jessie worked with Millie to get ready for the baby. They embroidered sixteen little receiving blankets, and they had a whole layette fixed. They enjoyed doing that together. It was a good time in the house, the first truly hopeful time in almost twenty years. On the other hand, in a matter of months all the children would be gone and Jessie would be left there by herself. She was almost sixty years old. It was too much house for one person, and boarders weren't an answer anymore. It was postwar—people were going to college, having children, buying houses of their own.

Besides, Jessie didn't need the money now. Uncle Ben had died and left everything to her. Why stay here? Why not take an apartment at the state hospital and sell this place? She might even travel a bit— might finally get to visit some of those exotic spots in the world that Charlie, with his kindred adventurous spirit, had hoped to see but never had.

One night at dinner, Jessie brought up the subject: Despite the pain that these walls had known, this house had been good to her, to *all* of them. They had made many memories here—the music and the dancing and the slow, cradling arc of the porch swing on summer nights—but those memories were theirs forever, no matter where they might live. Maybe, after nearly twenty-four years, more than a generation, it was time to move on.

I have a photograph, probably taken their last fall at 501 Holly. Jessie and Charles and some of their neighbors are gathered around the front steps just feet from where the Nu Grape car and the spindly elm were in that photo from two decades past. Charles is telling a story, and everyone is laughing.

But I see another snapshot within that one: Charles is frail and balding, and Jessie is an old woman with white hair and the stiff stance of age. In the upper right-hand corner, mature tree leaves rustle near the house, casting shadows.

*Ruth Taylor and Billie Lee Murphree courting in the 1930s.*

# Chapter Five

# Murphree

*1947 ❧ 1948*

These words are being written in mid-March, which means spring in Arkansas. The French doors to my upstairs office are open. The baby leaves on the elm tree are backlit by the sun, rendering them a translucent yellow-green. Golden jonquils sway in the yard.

The older I get, the more I appreciate spring. The other day I sat on the steps outside the kitchen, eating a bowl of cereal. I watched a cardinal hopping in the hedge. I noticed the shoots of new lariope pushing through the ground. I saw a squirrel sail from the upper branches of the walnut tree, which already has buds popping, to the maple, which doesn't. Used to be, spring meant I could play golf or run on real ground instead of a treadmill. Now I welcome spring from a deeper part of me.

To a homeowner, though, spring is like the aftermath of an accident: You've apparently *survived,* but you have to check yourself all over to see if your parts are still in working order. I took my coffee out into the yard and inspected the house. A board has bowed away from an upstairs window. A little more paint seems to have flaked off from the eaves. The part of the porch roof that was rebuilt two years ago already looks a tad warped, and more nails are pushing up through the tar paper on top. The required physical therapy includes serious splints and skin grafts, most of which I won't find the time or the money to do right away. Instead, I'll worry about it while attending to the relatively simple acts of regrooming, like a man who needs a heart bypass but gets a haircut instead.

Inside, Beth prunes the girls' closets, while I tend to the bushes that clothe the house. We buy herbs, and in time we'll plant a host of impatiens, the only flower that blooms with any consistency in the shady back garden. I carry plants from their inside winter quarters back out to the open-air porch. I round up dead leaves from the driveway and patio. Sometimes, when I want to stretch the job and dream, I use the big new push broom Beth bought me. Other times, I go to the trouble of hauling out the orange electric cords and cranking up my noisy leaf blower—the one half-covered in dried tar from when my stack of paint cans and roof tar caved in and spilled last summer in the darkness of the shed when I was away on vacation. There's something disconcerting about a tar-encrusted electric yard tool. I remind myself more and more of my father.

Ivy patrol is one of my spring rituals. Ivy and houses, both con artists, have joined forces in a fascinating collusion. Ivy on a house speaks to us in soothing terms of permanence, stability, stateliness, even money. The truth is, ivy is nothing but death in a green suit. When growing on a brick or stucco wall, ivy will leech out the mortar and fester the skin. Last year, I spent a day ripping the ivy away from the north side of the house. No matter how hard I tried, I couldn't remove some of the pieces of the vine itself, short sections marked with tiny cross-hatchings from which leaves used to grow. They're still there, looking like sutured slashes. The people who painted this house last time simply coated over old ivy scars, incorporating marks of past mortal encounters into the building's newest face.

Spring always surprises me by revealing a kind of amnesia on my part. I guess it's a self-protective forgetting, a way to forge ahead blindly instead of being debilitated by focusing on all the things that are wrong with this life—or, more specifically, this house. For example, during the winter I inevitably forget how absurdly slanted the back patio is. It's true that the ground itself slopes from north to south, but you'd think that whoever built this brick patio would've considered the genial rite of balancing a gin and tonic on a table rather than simply going with nature's flow. Actually, I now know who constructed this patio, a story I'll tell in due time. Knowing who built it only amazes me more.

In spring, I inevitably think how nice it would be to open all the windows and catch some of that cross ventilation old Charlie Armour so cunningly cultivated. Then I recall that the windows are painted shut. Downstairs, the windows are still sealed. Upstairs, we've spent thousands of dollars refurbishing the casement windows and screens so we can open the house to the breezes of spring. Casement windows require a cranking tool, however, and all of the original window-opening tools were lost. We had one of the workmen make a couple of ersatz tools, and now we know why we couldn't find the originals—half the time, we can't even find the new ones. "Have you seen the thing?" is a question that will forever mean spring to me.

Spring is also the season when I curse poor old Charlie Armour just a little bit. Surprisingly, it's because of the front porch, that charmer that has seduced so many starry-eyed buyers, including me. The porch makes an L, the short end jutting a few feet along the side of the house, the long part stretching across the front. And yet the porch roof only goes three-fourths of the way across the front of the house. This means that I pull my car into the driveway and, if it's raining, I step out and walk ten feet or so uncovered. What was the sense in that? Why on earth, if you were going to have a porch at all, wouldn't you cover it all the way over to where you park your car?

I usually ponder this as I scrub that unprotected portion of the porch in spring. All winter long, that section has been exposed to the elements, which, in one cracked spot particularly, have built up layer by layer into a nasty deposit of sediment. But here's where my annual amnesia comes in. It's while I'm scrubbing the porch that I'm reminded of the seasons *within* the season. Beginning in spring, the elm tree that hovers above the open part of the porch is always dropping something. First, there's the joyous bud season, followed closely by an intense week of what can only be called spring bird-shit season, followed by the delicate baby-leaf season, followed by some kind of translucent-spore season, which coincides with pollen season, whose hallmark is a coat of green dust over cars, rocking chairs, and, certainly, the unexposed part of the porch. Then comes summer, with the elm's glorious leafy shade. I'm convinced that that elm tree saves us hundreds of dollars every year in air-conditioning costs. In summer, the branches are full of chirping, singing birds, which are wonderful to listen to on the front porch. They don't announce their presence as insistently as before, but it's still inadvisable for me to own a convertible. Then fall comes, producing some kind of seed that results in *fall* bird-shit season. Then the leaves dry up. Finally, they die and float gently to the ground.

I guess it's just life. Maybe Charlie Armour left part of the porch uncovered to remind himself that a house can't protect you all the time.

Spring is an appropriate season to be thinking about the Murphrees moving to Holly Street. There's a rhythm to life itself, an ebb, a flow. After a quarter century, the Armours' time here was spent. But as Jessie, old and tired, was coming to that decision, seven blocks away a woman half her age named Ruth Murphree was complaining to her husband, Billie, that they had to have more space. Their conversation wasn't warm or wistful. Ruth was angry and had been for years. Billie had been away in the navy since 1942. When the war was over, his discharge had been frozen for reasons Ruth couldn't fathom. They didn't release him until February 1946. By then, everybody was home, the good jobs taken. But the main complaint was that while Billie had been stuck in the South Pacific on a mail ship, Ruth had been cooped up in a tiny house on Pine Street with two preschool daughters *plus* Billie's recently widowed mother and *her* nine-year-old son, whom Ruth referred to as a "menopause baby," *plus* having to work as secretary to U.S. congressman Brooks Hays. No, Ruth hadn't been charmed by this arrangement. "The next war we have," she told her husband, "I'll go and you'll stay home."

Once Billie got a taste of what Ruth had been putting up with, it didn't take him long to say to her, "Go find us a bigger house." They preferred to stay in Hillcrest. One morning, she saw an advertisement for a house at 501 Holly. It had five or six bedrooms, depending on your needs. Ruth thought that sounded heavenly. She called the Realtor and arranged a viewing. It was love at first sight. She was enchanted by the front porch, the beautiful hardwood floors, the music room, the overwhelming *spaciousness* of the place.

She took Billie back that very afternoon. He was impressed, too. Besides, if it pleased Ruth, that was saying a lot. In the decade they had been married, he had found that she wasn't easy to satisfy. They bought it without quibbling, paying Jessica J. Armour $13,500 in cash for the right to play out their own dreams of home.

The Murphrees lived in this house during a seasonal change in the country, too. It began as a kind of springtime, a postwar blush of budding promise, though it didn't end that way. I remember the beginning of that time as a brief moment when it was possible to believe in goodness and mercy and safety and peace—to *assume* those things. That was in the period from the late 1940s until the mid-1950s. I was a child then, age five to about eleven, and I'm sure that was a good part of it, the illusions of childhood. But the times seemed to foster illusions—maybe even to depend on them. I know now that my parents dealt in those years with the timeless trials of adulthood, but even they appeared to cling to the idea of something approaching innocence.

For me, those were days of roaming loose through my neighborhood, of playing army and cowboys and, occasionally, doctor under the house with neighbor girls. They were days of comic books and baseball cards and bike riding with no hands. There were heroes like Mickey Mantle and Eddie Mathews and Roy Rogers and Lash La Rue. There were fears of the requisite neighborhood bully, in my case a strange bird called "Booger Red," who leapt out of trees onto people. There was a first bite of a new dish called "pizza pie," and a sip of my dad's Schlitz, a taste that lives in my memory and still defines beer for me. There were after-church dinners of fried chicken with rice and gravy. There were lightning bugs, and games of kick the can until dark, when you heard your mother calling you for supper and you reluctantly parted from your friends for the night and trudged in the blue dusk toward the lights of home.

Most of all, those were days when your home and your neighborhood were the nucleus of your life. You went to church in the neighborhood, you shopped in the neighborhood, from merchants you knew, and you played with friends in the neighborhood. Nobody's mother hauled children all over town to take gymnastics or tennis lessons. You learned the games you needed to know from the kids you lived near. Life seemed as easy as a shortcut through the neighbors' yard. I lived in Mississippi during that magical time. Five hours away, in a big corner house in Little Rock, the Murphree family lived their own version of the same illusion.

I met Ruth Murphree in the fall of 1992. I simply called the number in the phone book, and she answered. It had been twenty-six years since she'd lived in this house. She listened warily while I made my spiel. Then, to my slight surprise, she agreed to see me.

A widow since 1989, Ruth lives today in a retirement complex in west Little Rock. Her apartment is relatively new, and the scale of the rooms doesn't suit her preference in furniture, which is Victorian— large, dark, imposing. But these pieces are here because they're not just objects; they're memories, many of them from her days on Holly Street.

Ruth is a small woman, and her reactions are often obscured by the glare of her glasses. Nor does she betray much through expressions or mannerisms. Occasionally, she'll chuckle. During that first meeting, I got the feeling that she's very careful about what she says, and to whom. Once, after I had told her daughter Joyce that I wanted to talk with some of her parents' friends, Ruth complained to her, "Why does he need to talk to *them*?" And yet she seemed pleased enough to talk with me about her husband, who died shortly after their fiftieth wedding anniversary, about her three daughters— Martha, Pat, and Joyce—and about 501 Holly, where the Murphree family lived for nineteen long years, from the big-band era to that of the Beatles. Between that initial meeting in 1992 and the beginning of 1995, I would have several conversations with Ruth and with all three of her daughters. I would visit Martha in Florida and Pat in Atlanta. Joyce, here in Little Rock, would help me read the animosities and the alliances and would tell me what I was seeing in family snapshots and on Murphree home movies.

Through it all, I would come to absorb the story of one family struggling to hold together through the wrenching changes of mid-century America—changes that were reflected, always, within the walls of 501 Holly.

The postwar world seemed specially scripted for Billie Lee Murphree. It was a time when a smart, energetic, and morally upright young man could make a real mark for himself. Billie was all of that, and more. A country boy with city polish, he was movie-star handsome, and he exuded self-confidence. He liked people, and they liked him. His gift of gab would eventually take him into teaching for a while, even though he'd dropped out of college following the 1929 crash. That's what he was doing when he met Ruth Taylor. Later, he would go into county politics, serving as comptroller for Pulaski County before the war.

He wasn't a man to sit back and live on a salary, though. His sideline business was real estate. He would buy houses and fix them up to rent out, remortgaging them and using the new money to buy still more rental houses. Billie's daughters love retelling the family legend of how their daddy established credit. He went to the bank and borrowed one hundred dollars, which he put in a drawer and didn't touch. When the note was due, he paid the money back with a small amount of interest. Then he asked for a larger amount— three hundred dollars, say—and did the same thing. Finally, when he was known at the bank as a good credit risk, he hit them for enough to buy a small house. He was off and running.

Shortly after his return, Billie pulled strings to land a job with the Veterans Administration. Congressman Hays, Ruth's boss and Billie's former Sunday school teacher, simply phoned the head man at the VA. "My friend Bill Murphree needs a job," the congressman said. The GI bill offered all the returning veterans favorable terms on money to go to college, to start a business, to buy a house or a farm. Billie began work in the mortgage department of the Little Rock VA. He took to the work naturally. With his interest in people, his war experience, and his knowledge of real estate, it was an almost fateful fit. Before long, he would rise to the position of supervisor, in charge of GI mortgage loans throughout Arkansas and a portion of Texas. A lot of soldiers had been dreaming of home for a very long time. Now, in his part of the country, Billie Lee Murphree would become no less than gatekeeper to the American dream.

But for all his charm and ambition and entrepreneurial skill, the thing that made Billie Murphree so perfect a reflection of his times was his moral certainty. A strict Baptist, he lived the way he thought: Never lie, never drink, never smoke, never break the law, go to church regularly, live by the Ten Commandments, and your life will turn out wonderfully. He took great pride in telling the story of how, when his daughter Martha was born, he picked Ruth and the baby up at the hospital, dropped Ruth off at home, and took Martha with him straight to church. He did this, Martha now realizes, not just to show her off but also to indoctrinate her into the life he wanted her to lead. He felt the same way about the other girls when they came along.

Most people who knew the Murphrees then probably thought Ruth shared her husband's sense of certainty. She surely wasn't timid about expressing her opinions. But now, approaching her eightieth year, Ruth can admit to a weakness of the soul: She was inclined toward envy and had to fight to avoid letting it get the best of her. She says the worst time was when she envied a friend whose banker husband hadn't had to go to war, and Billie had—banking was an "essential" job and being a county comptroller wasn't. It made Ruth bitter. Later, Ruth's daughters thought she envied people who drove bigger cars, lived in better houses, had newer things.

She was a petite thing from the same general area of northeast Arkansas that Billie came from, but even in early photographs you can tell her tastes were far from country. As a wife, she was a hard worker, helping Billie with the paperwork on his rental-house business, but she enjoyed playing bridge, being a member of women's clubs, and going downtown to shop. Downtown was nice then. The Gus Blass department store had a mezzanine restaurant where ladies in hats would meet over salmon croquettes and iced tea. Blass's also had a new escalator, the first in Arkansas. The ladies laughed about a matron who, seeing it for the first time, said,

"It's nice, but shouldn't they have somebody here to show us how to use it?"

It was a perfect world, at least on the surface, and Ruth's daughters say that she worked hard to maintain that appearance. Whenever one of the girls breached their mother's idea of the norm, Ruth would say, "What will the neighbors think?" She wanted to keep anything potentially embarrassing within their own walls. The things that were embarrassing were whatever belied the happy image of *family*—devoted mother, successful, good-natured father, obedient children.

This image extended even beyond Billie and Ruth's immediate family. At age thirty-eight, Billie was the patriarch of his own sprawling clan. His youngest brother, Tom, refers to him as the family's "Godfather." Billie helped them financially, and when he bought 501 Holly, it became the de facto family home. Even if Ruth hadn't wanted to spend so much time with her in-laws, she would've been outvoted by Billie. To him, family equaled home. At Christmas, Easter, and on the Fourth of July, this house throbbed with the energy of brothers and sisters, aunts and uncles, cousins and nieces and nephews.

I can't help feeling that Ruth was the one member of the clan not quite in the loop. Ruth's daughters say they had more of a bond with their father than with their mother. Sometimes this manifested itself in the form of pets. The Murphree house was a veritable menagerie— at various points they had dogs, cats, turtles, birds, chickens, ducks, a goat, and an alligator. Billie loved animals, loved seeing the children playing with them. Never did he come home from a trip that he didn't bring the girls a turtle or two. "Go look in the car," he would say, and they would race to the driveway, to find an old terrapin hunched down in the backseat. They would keep him a few days, maybe painting the date on his shell with fingernail polish, and then finally they would let him go back to the wild.

Ruth loved the dogs; some of the other pets were underfoot because she was simply outnumbered. To this very day, Martha seems to be only half-joking when she claims her mother pushed her pet goat off the garage stairs and broke its neck.

They moved in on a March day in 1947, but the weather wasn't springlike, the way it is this year. Instead, the wind howled and the rain beat down. Little Pat, three years old, stood weeping in the drafty living room. "I want to go home!" she told her mother. "I want to go home!"

Ruth hugged her baby tight. "But this *is* home," she said. Pat wailed all the more.

It's one thing to build the house you've already constructed in your head, the one you've calculated will be right for you; it's another to move into what was once someone else's dream and try to reshape it to match a vague template in your heart. Those of us who've done it know what Ruth was feeling. You're standing in the living room of a house you've walked through no more than a few times, maybe only once. You know—in your head—where the various rooms are, but still the whole place looks alien. It almost seems to float. If you've moved a few times, you know that eventually you'll come to see these very rooms differently, and that later it'll be fun to try to remember the way you saw them on this very first day. Later, the space will take on a different measure; rooms will seem to have been viewed from a completely different angle. By then, the alien place will have become centered around your own things.

*Things:* I'm talking about our personal possessions—mementos, heirlooms, cherished pieces of furniture or art, totemic objects that ground us, that connect our present with our past. Surely, only things allow us to move as often as we do. Whenever I think of things and their importance in making a home, I think of the way my mother moved to Florida. The year was 1957, and we were leaving

Hazlehurst, Mississippi, bound for Miami. This was at the end of a strange interlude in my father's working life. After he had gotten out of the service he, like Billie Murphree, had gone to work for the Veterans Administration. He did that in Tupelo and later in Jackson. Then there were cutbacks. My father was told he could stay on, but at a lower grade. He refused. For a time during our Jackson years, he worked for a company that sold toys. He traded the car for a panel truck. My brother and I, blissfully ignorant, were excited about the toys, though I remember being embarrassed going to church in the truck. Then my father took a job running a grocery store in Hazlehurst for a nephew of my uncle Alex, Aunt May's husband. My uncle's family owned a lumber business, and this store sold to people who worked at the mill. My father was promised a share of the profits, but then he found out this store wasn't supposed to turn a profit. It was a disaster for my parents, but, like Charles and Jane Armour during Charlie's crisis, I was unaware.

Finally, my father was offered a job with Vocational Rehabilitation in Florida. He would go on to great success there, eventually becoming director for all of South Florida. In the fall of 1957, though, he couldn't wait to get out of Hazlehurst, where he had run through his savings and his pride. He couldn't, or didn't, hire a moving van; instead, he hooked up a U-Haul trailer to our blue 1955 Ford. He told my mother they could take only what they could fit into the U-Haul. She left many things, including the bedroom suite of her mother's, in Hazlehurst with her sister. There was an understanding that Mother was going to get them later, but of course life seldom works out that way.

Ruth Murphree understands the importance of things. Today, her red velvet mahogany settee still comforts her the way it did on that March day almost half a century ago. When she moved her family into Holly Street, she placed the settee—then covered in green velvet—on the left side of the living room, with her leather-inlaid coffee table in front and her two green velvet Victorian side chairs flanking the fireplace. Her gold brocade wing-back chair sat in the corner between the dining room and what Ruth had decided was the music room. Across from that, between the front door and the music room, her red brocade chair echoed the gold in regal symmetry.

A visitor walking into the Murphrees' house back then could glance straight ahead through the French doors and catch sight of an impressive oak dining table in the center. Against the far wall, where Jessie Armour had placed her Empire sideboard, stood Ruth's antique buffet. The music room provided a more modern vista. Under the windows to the front porch was a sleek beige couch that evoked the stylishness of the 1930s. Ruth placed their record player/radio console under the north windows. On the east wall was the spinet piano. Both Ruth and Billie loved music—classical, jazz, gospel—and they encouraged their girls to love music, too. Billie's mother had taught piano, and Ruth believed every girl should be able to play. The Murphree girls would grow to love this room, but not in the way their parents hoped. For the girls, the music room would become a conduit to a wider, less certain world.

Beyond the music room, for the time being, was Ruth and Billie's bedroom. A mahogany four-poster and dresser anchored this space. Martha and Pat started out sharing the downstairs back bedroom, the one young Charles Armour and his Grandma Jackson had slept in so many years before. As it happened, just as Billie and Ruth bought this house, Billie found another rental house for his mother and Tommy. All during the war years, Ruth had yearned for a day when she would no longer be constricted by circumstance. Now she found herself living in a house with *three* empty bedrooms.

Not all was perfect, however. Ruth saw problems and felt an uneasiness that couldn't be solved by the simple positioning of cherished possessions. She had some painting done before they moved in, and she noticed that the downstairs bathroom tile was loose. When the tile man began poking around, he found that all the joists beneath that floor had rotted. Water had been seeping in from somewhere. Ruth and Billie had to put in a whole new subfloor, but that wasn't the worst of it. From then on, Billie would worry about water and whether more of it was coming in—and, if so, from where. A house is man's attempt to stave off the anarchy of nature. Ripping up that floor had allowed a disturbing glimpse into the house's secret life. It's more comfortable not to know about such things.

Ruth remodeled the whole bathroom in pink-and-black tile, a color combination then still considered avant-garde but one that all the trendy magazines would be touting before long. She also replaced the single pedestal sink with two chrome-legged lavatories. As for the rest of the problems, they would have to wait. The kitchen still had one of those old four-legged ceramic sinks with the built-in drain board; Ruth surely wanted to replace that. Also, the house was a freezer. There was no heating system, just a few small stoves here and there. In the living room fireplace, a gas heater had been stuck into the space where the logs used to go. At some point, Jessie Armour had plugged up the fireplace and inserted the heater to try to ward off the cold. The Murphrees knew nothing of Jessie Armour's life, of course. All they saw was an old heater that should've been vented but wasn't, and that didn't put out much heat anyway. Fortunately, warmer weather was coming. Ruth made a note to have floor furnaces installed as soon as possible.

Beyond that, Ruth had problems with Jessie's French doors. All that glass between the dining room and the bedroom bothered her, made the bedroom feel too public for Ruth's taste. Besides, French doors were too formal for the postwar style. The modern house was loose, open, more free-form. If you sat in the living room of this Craftsman bungalow, browsing through *The Saturday Evening Post* and *McCall's,* when you looked up at your own surroundings, this house suddenly felt old and tight. The flow that Charlie Armour had worked so hard to achieve with French doors seemed, to the Murphrees, to make the house feel "all chopped up." That indictment extended to the doors separating the living and dining rooms, and even to the narrow breakfast room with its clever built-in serving counter that Jessie had loved.

New times require new thinking. So do new owners.

One year after they moved into this house, Ruth and Billie took part in a ritual that was symbolic of the new postwar optimism: They conceived another child. The baby, their third daughter, was born three days after Christmas. They named her Joyce. She was the very first child born to this house.

As if in celebration of the postwar ideal of family, Billie surprised his girls with a special gift that Christmas of 1948. It was one of the new 16-mm Kodak movie cameras that were all the rage. Using it was quite a production, but Billie didn't care—not, at least, on birthdays and holidays, when the clan was over and the table was set and everyone was all smiles. And on nights when he would show the home movies, they would gather in the living room, Martha and Pat fighting for the best spot on the floor. As their grainy figures tottered across the screen, the Murphrees would laugh and clap, basking in the flickering image of family that danced from the projector on a smoky beam of light.

*The Murphree girls—Pat, Joyce, and Martha—in the side yard in 1949.*

# Chapter Six

# Murphree

## *1949* 🍀 *1956*

I'm riveted by a photograph of the three Murphree daughters taken in the early summer of 1949, posed in the side yard in approximately the same spot where Jessie, Jane, and Charles Armour and Grandma Jackson were pictured with Uncle Ben on that long-ago Christmas after Charlie's mother had descended upon the house. The photo of the Murphree girls is every bit as revealing about its era as that other frozen moment of time was about its own.

Pat, just-turned six, and Martha, almost nine, are sitting on opposite edges of the table surrounding Joyce's built-in baby seat. Pat, her hair in little-girl bangs, is wearing a lace-shouldered little-girl sundress and white socks and Mary Janes, with a little-girl skinned shin and a little-girl absence of front teeth in her open mouth. She's facing the camera straight on, imploring it to—what?—not overlook her? Meanwhile, Martha all but languishes on the table, her eyes coyly downturned, her hair pulled to the side. All that's missing is a flower over her ear. She wears a ruffled bare-midriff top and skirt and shows an astonishingly long, bare leg, tapering to a sockless foot in an open sandal. Wide-eyed, six-and-a-half-month-old Joyce, oblivious to the drama going on around her, studies the camera not as something to be responded to emotionally—something to be needed or seduced—but as merely a fascinating gadget with moving parts she'd like to get her hands on.

I find this photo compelling because the Murphree household was one dominated by females—much like the one I now live in— and the rivalries are palpable. The great unseen presence, of course, is Ruth, with whom all of the girls in this picture—even baby Joyce, later—were in some degree of competition. As was Billie, I guess, husbands and wives being the way they are.

Despite her precocious glamour in this snapshot, Martha was the tomboy, the adventurous one—the one Ruth found irrepressible. She and two other girls in the neighborhood had a group they proudly called the Lee Street Terrors. When a new house was built at Woodlawn and Holly, Martha and her friends were so incensed over the homeowner's taking *their* vacant lot that they poured a concoction of black ink, Kool-Aid, and mud through the mail slot, and it landed on the people's new carpet. Another time, just after Ruth had bought some fashionable new pull-cord draperies, she came home and found that Martha and her friend across Lee had rigged up a tin-can phone using the drapery cord.

Martha was almost six and Pat nearly four when they moved to Holly Street, and, even then, the two spent much of their time at each other's throats. Martha thought Pat was a crybaby. "She whined and complained about everything," Martha says, "and she was prissy. I just didn't have much patience with that type of individual." Martha loved dogs; Pat loved cats. Not only that, but every year each daughter got to choose the meal that would be served on her birthday. Pat always asked for liver and onions.

Their shared bedroom was a war zone. "We played the games all sisters play," Pat remembers: "'You're on my side of the bed. Here's the line—don't get your foot on my side!'" When Joyce came along, Ruth and Billie separated the older girls. Martha, being the older and more aggressive, claimed the big room with the cedar closet. Pat and her dolls shared the smaller bedroom across the hall.

In the fall of 1992, Martha and Joyce returned to 501 Holly Street. Joyce had been in the house once a few years before, when it was for sale, but for Martha this was the first visit in twenty-six years. The sisters were now mothers and wives, but as they walked through the rooms of their childhood home, I watched them become girls again. They reminded me of Jung's story of probing deeper into himself the further he ventured into the house of his dream. At first, they spoke of halcyon days with no worries; then as they talked, their memories grew darker and more complex.

Martha remembered straddling the floor furnaces Billie and Ruth installed in the music room and the hall. Joyce remembered riding her tricycle down the stairs, knocking out her front teeth on the oak dining table. Martha remembered living in a secret world in which her bedroom floor represented vague and unnamed dangers, and the only way to avoid them was never to touch the floor. She mastered the art of walking the entire circumference of the room on doorknobs, swinging over to dressers, and so on all the way around. Joyce remembered the day the hot-water tank caught fire and destroyed part of the kitchen (giving Ruth an opportunity to redecorate). She recalled the neighborhood as a wonderful place to roam—with the exception of the creepy old Retan house on the next corner, which she was scared to walk by because everybody said it was haunted.

Then Joyce asked, "Is my dog's name still in the sidewalk by the house?" I told her I had never seen it. She took me outside. In the spot where the fieldstone walk curves away from the house toward Lee, she pulled back the grass that had grown over the edge of the walk. There it was—AUSTA, along with Joyce's initials. How many other secrets, I wondered, have time and this house tried to conceal?

\* \* \*

For the Murphree girls, life at 501 Holly breaks into two parts—before the mid-1950s, and after. Before was magical; after was torment.

I imagine the early Murphrees as very much like one of those sitcom families on TV. Billie was among the first in town to buy his family a television set. It was a big dark mahogany console model, with an octagonal screen and rabbit ears on top. They put it in the living room, but then Ruth decided the children would ruin the good furniture. That gave her a good excuse to do something about those French doors to the bedroom: She had them ripped out and replaced by a solid wall, with a floor-to-ceiling bookcase on the bedroom side.

Except that this was no longer the bedroom—it was now the den. It was a quiet and cozy spot for Ruth to thumb through her *Saturday Evening Post* and for Billie to concentrate on his Saturday-evening Bible study for Sunday morning's lesson. Ruth had her bedroom furniture moved to the back room, where Martha and Pat had slept before Ruth separated them. In the den, Ruth arranged a couple of easy chairs and a long sofa. The TV set was also brought in, positioned near the door to the music room. Billie didn't allow much TV watching on school nights, but on Fridays the family gathered to watch *The Adventures of Ozzie and Harriet.* The nearest TV station being Memphis, Martha and Pat had to squint through clouds of snow to catch a glimpse of their heartthrob, Ricky Nelson.

As long as she was adding the bedroom wall, Ruth went ahead and removed the one between the kitchen and the breakfast room. That gave her live-in maid, Mattie (who resided in the garage's "servant's quarters," one room with a chain-pull toilet tucked into a tiny space beneath wooden outside steps), more space to prepare sumptuous desserts for Ruth's afternoon bridge parties.

Those parties had become more frequent in 1950, when Ruth quit her job with Brooks Hays to become a full-time bridge-playing, house-remodeling mother and housewife. She wore hats and went shopping downtown. She lunched. She sent her sheets out to be pressed. Life was good. There was a picnic table in the side yard, and on those pre-air conditioning summer evenings, Ruth and Billie would frequently invite their friends or family over for cookouts. Later, the webbed lawn chairs would be arranged in a circle in the dark, and the talk would be as soft as the air itself, a comfortable mur- mur of prosperity punctuated occasionally by sparkling laughter.

Ruth and Billie's competition was relatively low-key in those days. The girls say Ruth resented Billie's interminable hand shaking and socializing after church, but, then, Billie was a deacon and superintendent of the Sunday school. Sometimes, especially later, the girls saw Ruth try to pick fights with Billie, but he would never engage her. Ruth called Billie by his given name, but he called her "Mama." At times when he needed a little extra leverage—such as when he got Martha the goat—he would call her "Mommy." For all his Baptist piety, Billie Murphree was a bit of a flirt with women. "Now, Mommy," he would say, "you're not going to be mad at your old daddy, are you?" Everybody said Billie had the patience of Job. He never got angry at Ruth—or, if he did, he didn't show it.

In the Murphree household, the females referred to Billie as "the king of duct tape." For most jobs, that wide gray tape was Billie's answer to the problem. In later years when he began driv- ing the Cadillac Ruth wanted, he even taped on a broken taillight. That embarrassed Ruth, though maybe not as much as when he patched his Bible with great swaths of the tape and carried it to church that way.

He insisted on doing most of the repairs at his rental houses— "If you hire everything out, you can't make any money," Billie would say—as well as at home. If he couldn't use duct tape, he resorted to what was known among the Murphrees as "nigger rigging"—a tor- tured, make-do solution, such as the wires he and Tommy ran all over the house to hook up extra, unreported telephones. When the Murphrees moved into 501 Holly, the old heater in the fireplace had a couple of ceramic burners that had slipped. Billie rigged up a pair of coat hangers to hold the sagging burners in place.

The subterranean water problem baffled him, though. He had worried about it after the bathroom floor repair, but his concerns grew after he'd had floor furnaces installed in the hall and the music room. The girls began to notice that the grate to the music room's floor furnace would rise whenever there was a hard rain. The grate appeared to be *floating*. If that was so, it meant that the water under the music room was so high that it was washing up against the bottom of the furnace.

Martha says you could always tell when Billie was wrestling with a problem. He would put the tips of his fingers together and press them into a point—into the shape of a steeple, or a temple. His index fingers, especially, would be pressed against each other so tightly that the knuckles would pop. He would stare at the temple he'd made with his fingers and continue to pop his knuckles. When the popping stopped, his decision was made. Years later, Martha read in a psychology magazine that people who hold their fingers together that way think of themselves as superior to everyone else.

Billie tried a sump pump to remove the standing water, but the pool kept building up. Then he decided water was seeping down from the house next door, which stood higher than his. To fix that, he gathered a pile of brick and fieldstone—whatever he could find— and mixed them with concrete, fashioning a retaining wall along the driveway on the line between the two houses. He and Tom also paved the old strip-concrete driveway, toddler Joyce adding her initials in the wet cement for good measure. The idea was that maybe now the water running off the roof would trickle away and not steal into the darkness of the foundation, where the very structure of the house would be at risk.

I find myself thinking of Billie and the water in symbolic terms, as though the water were the physical incarnation of all the undercurrents of society that he tried desperately to keep from seeping into his family's life. In the 1950s, Billie was appointed to the Little Rock Censor Board, a group formed decades before when the local PTA had become alarmed by movie scenes it considered unfit for youngsters. The ordinance creating the censor board stated that its purpose was "to protect the public peace, sense of decency, and safety," and it went on to name those things that would from then on be illegal:

*Scenes and acts in which the names of God and Jesus Christ were used without veneration; scenes and acts exhibiting nakedness; scenes and acts in which dialogue and jokes, gestures, and songs had a double meaning, suggesting obscenity or sex relations; scenes and acts in which proper home life was ridiculed and immorality or underworld life or unfaithfulness in marriage was made to seem attractive; and scenes and acts where marriage or love scenes between different races were portrayed.*

The board had been lax during the war, but by 1947 it was clear to those concerned that something had to be done about the increase in lurid magazines and books and pictures. A new ordinance was written, one less didactic than the original. The new one left definitions of lewdness to the discretion of the censor board.

Billie took his board duties very seriously—after all, he had two daughters about to come of age, and he owed an all-out effort to them. That meant his house, *this* house, had to be an ark capable of withstanding the flood.

Sunday was a day of rest at 501 Holly. Billie's rule was: no television, no card playing, no music, no wearing of shorts on that day. Sunday was a time to be quiet and praise the Lord—and besides, the preacher often came for after-church dinner.

Pat remembers that the day inevitably started with her father singing hymns as he dressed for Sunday school. Billie wasn't an accomplished singer, but he loved the old Baptist standards. As he shaved in the new pink-and-black bathroom, he would hum or sing "The Old Rugged Cross," one of his mother's favorites. From behind the shower curtain came his lilting melody of "Just as I Am." Putting on his white shirt, blue suit, and red tie, he launched into "How Great Thou Art."

Ruth and the girls could hear him throughout the house as they ate breakfast and got themselves ready. Then, at the appointed time, the family would walk out the door to the car, Bibles in hand. There's a scene in one of the home movies, probably at Easter, when the Murphree females come swishing out of the house in hats and gloves and full-skirted dresses like a gaggle of Loretta Youngs on the way to a party. During the ten-minute ride to Second Baptist downtown, Billie drove and the whole family sang along:

> On a hill far away
> Stood an old rugged cross. . . .

Every one of the Murphrees went to Sunday school and then to church. On Sunday afternoons, the girls were required to attend Baptist Training Union—BTU—and then evening church service. On Wednesday nights, there was prayer meeting. The Murphrees were typical of the times. In 1954, *McCall's* reported that church membership "has rocketed from 50 million in 1929 to more than 95 million—a gain of 90 percent, while the population was increasing only 31.4 percent." Even outside church, the trend was reflected in the public's choice of reading. Norman Vincent Peale's *The Power of Positive Thinking,* Catherine Marshall's *A Man Called Peter,* Thomas Chastain's *The Silver Chalice,* and the new Revised Standard Version of the Bible all hit the best-seller lists in 1952 and stayed there into 1953. In 1954, President Eisenhower changed the

Pledge of Allegiance to reflect the mood of the country: He added the words *under God.*

I think I understand how deeply the Murphrees' religion affected the life inside this house. I grew up Baptist, too, attended BTU and prayer meeting, and I remember that church felt mighty *aggressive* in those days. Maybe it was the Russians—the Cold War against "Godless communism" was heating up—or maybe it was simply an expression of postwar superiority. Preachers had a lot of power, and they weren't shy about telling their flock how to live their lives. For most of my childhood, we had a Sunday-morning ritual much like the Murphrees', though with more grumbling and less singing. Then one morning—I guess I was in high school—it became noticeable to everyone that my father wasn't getting dressed. We couldn't see him, but we knew he was still sitting in the living room reading the paper. My brother and I exchanged meaningful glances. Finally, my mother had to break the ice. "Honey!" she said. "It's time to get ready!"

Phil and I held our collective breath. Dead silence for a long moment. Then we heard our father's voice from the other room. "I'm not going," he said. "I'm not going ever again." As he later explained it, he was fed up with the hypocrisy of the Baptist Church. He shopped around for a while, and eventually he and Mother began going to the Presbyterian.

But the Murphrees lived a mid-century Baptist life. Joyce remembers that Catholics and Jews weren't spoken of highly in their household (never mind Negroes). Pat recalls that her mother wouldn't let her play with one little girl whose mother had been divorced. When Billie took the family out to eat, if they walked into a restaurant and Billie noticed alcohol being served, he would quietly say, "Let's don't eat here." In general, says Joyce, if you didn't come from a family in which the father went to work, the mother stayed home, and everyone attended your kind of church, then "the Murphrees didn't need to be friends with you."

* * *

Home is a fragile ecosystem. One person's dark mood can suck the very sunlight out of a room. An icy stare can steal a house's heat. It's part of what makes the concept of family—a group of angst-ridden individuals living together under one roof—almost laughably difficult. In the midst of that hothouse jungle, most of us think and act as individuals, rather than putting the family above ourselves so it can have what it needs to flourish. Once the precarious balance is out of whack, then blooms fade. Roots wither.

In the mid-1950s, the mood in the Murphree house changed dramatically. Martha was a willful teenager by then, and Pat was right behind her. At the same time, Ruth started becoming ill a lot. She complained about horrible headaches. She was hospitalized several times for what were diagnosed as bladder infections. She was irritable, and everyone in the house had to walk on eggshells to avoid setting her off. This spell lasted four or five years.

Today her daughters suspect the onset of menopause, but at the time her family thought her ailments were psychosomatic. "She never suffered alone," Martha says. Joyce remembers her father telling the girls, "I'm going to put your mother in the hospital. It's the only thing that'll make her happy." Whatever the causes of Ruth's pain, the effect in the household was profound. Ruth would hole up in the downstairs back bedroom and not come out for hours. She would try to pick fights with Billie, which he would quietly deflect. She began talking about moving to a different house—one newer and finer. There was one farther into the Heights that she particularly wanted, and the whole family went to look at it. Eventually, Billie put his foot down. He liked 501 Holly, and that's where the Murphrees were going to stay.

For a time, he moved upstairs to a corner of the attic, which he had finished off—in his way—so Pat could have bunking parties. The floor was still nothing but splintery attic planks, but Pat liked the room so much that she moved there, too. She slept in the corner nearest Lee and Holly, and Billie had his bed at the opposite corner, toward Woodlawn and Elm. Pat pasted silver stars all over the slanting plasterboard ceiling so she could pretend she was sleeping under a peaceful sky. The attic was a make-believe place. It was a hideout.

Martha was the one most at odds with her mother. That was due partly to Martha's being the oldest, but also to Martha's rebellious, even belligerent nature. Her mother made her crazy. Whenever Ruth said, "What will the neighbors think?" Martha could barely contain herself. "Who *cares* what the neighbors think!" she would scream. And, with that, she would stomp up the stairs and slam her bedroom door. She says she soon decided it was just better to avoid her mother whenever possible. Coming home from school was like approaching a minefield: Would she trip the explosion, or would she make it through safely? "If mother was in the kitchen, I went in the den," Martha says. "If mother was in the den, I went up to my bedroom."

Even when the rest of the family thought Martha was up in her room, she sometimes wasn't. She had matured early, and she liked boys. With the same resourcefulness and agility that had allowed her to circumnavigate her floor on doorknobs, she'd now calculated a way to sneak out of her bedroom at night without anyone knowing. She would crawl through her window onto the flat landing on the roof just outside, and from there her long legs could reach the trellis that held up Jessie Armour's sultry Cape jasmine bush. Ruth and Billie would be downstairs in the den reading—poring over the *National Geographic* or one of their numerous books on history or religion—and Martha would be outside in the dark meeting her boyfriend. Hours later, she would simply use her key and walk in through the front door, knowing everyone else was fast asleep.

Martha also began having conflicts with her father. As a member of the censor board, Billie once wrote a stern note to Martha's literature teacher protesting a play the class was reading, and he kept his ears open to the music she was listening to. None of the girls would ever take to piano the way Ruth and Billie had hoped. By the mid-1950s, popular music was becoming too hot for Mozart to match. The week Martha turned fifteen, the number one song in the country was "Rock Around the Clock" by Bill Haley and the Comets. It was an exciting sound, and new, at least to white kids. Only later was it obvious that that song had marked the absolute end of one era and the beginning of another.

Martha spent a small fortune on 45-rpm records, which Billie monitored the best he could. He had a troubling suspicion that something insidious was seeping into his home through the lyrics to some of the new music. One of Martha's favorites was a raucous song by Etta James called "Roll with Me Henry."

Just what in the world did *that* mean? Billie was taking no chances—he confiscated that record, as well as others he deemed equally offensive, from Martha's collection.

Billie's daughters and widow all hasten to make the point that Billie Murphree wasn't seen in the world as a sanctimonious man. He certainly had his standards, but he was nevertheless a regular guy— a backslapper, a political insider, a man who never met a stranger. He was kind and fair, and he could bend his moral judgments when a higher moral was involved. Once, he got word that one of his mortgagees had been killed. The man had been a kind of shade-tree mechanic, and a car had fallen on him and crushed his chest. Billie drove down to the Delta town where the man had lived to see what kind of benefits he could arrange for the man's family. He talked to the wife, who in the course of the conversation told him that, in fact, she and the late father of her three children hadn't technically been married. That meant she wouldn't be eligible for a widow's pension, which in turn meant that Billie would have to foreclose. But he didn't. Even though he disapproved of the concept, he managed to have her declared a common-law wife, and she was able to keep the house. When Billie told Ruth about it, she was stunned: Never before in her life had she heard the term *common-law wife.*

I've come to suspect that there was even a part of Billie that identified with the dangerous secular world he was fighting on the censor board. He certainly understood sex appeal. When young girls would come over to the house, he would tease them. "How's your love life?" he would say. He was vain about his own good looks. In photographs, he was never shot candidly—he *posed,* the way people who know they're attractive learn to do, making sure he showed himself off to best advantage. Martha once even caught him in the bathroom applying a little makeup to a blemish on his face.

Maybe that side of him explains the car. The year was 1956, a busy year for Billie, both at the censor board and at home. First, a writer named Grace Metalious published a scandalous book called *Peyton Place.* Second, a singer named Elvis Presley was inciting ever-more-unseemly riots among young women. Third, Pat became a teenager, which meant Billie now had two teenage girls, and an angry wife, at home. But as if to add fuel to the fire, when Martha turned sixteen, Billie honored that milestone by giving his oldest daughter a 1955 baby blue Ford Fairlane convertible. Forty years later, Martha remembers it as "the sexiest, greatest car."

On the censor board, Billie was a member of the motion picture committee. That meant he focused on movies, but of course he was privy to discussions of all the printed materials, and those discussions had a deep effect on him. I found a grainy news photo of the censor board in action, sitting around a raised table at the front of what appears to be a vast but empty auditorium, somewhat like a court-room. The women are in hats, the men in coats and ties, reflecting the importance of their mission. Billie sits at the extreme left in the picture, listening intently, his fingers pressed into the shape of a temple.

Martha's new car and Billie's censor board duties clashed in as perfect a portrait of the conflicting strains of the times as you're likely to find. A car is freedom, and a car like *that* approaches anarchy. That car had a radical effect on life in the Murphree home. Now, whenever Martha wanted to get away from her mother, she would simply jump into her baby blue convertible and take off. She carried her Kent cigarettes in a metal Band-Aid box in her purse, and as soon as she was out of sight of 501 Holly, she would fire up a cigarette and turn up the radio. Elvis's "I Want You, I Need You, I Love You" was playing everywhere in mid-summer of 1956, and Billie had little use for Elvis. But so what? Gripping the steering wheel of her very own car, Martha felt, for the first time, that she had control of her own life. Today she realizes that some of Ruth's outbursts were caused by frustration over losing control of her daughter.

Martha sometimes even threw that loss up into her parents' faces. Once, when the family had a maid who didn't live in the garage apartment, Ruth asked Martha to drive the Negro woman home. The "Negro problem" had become a hot topic ever since 1954 and the Supreme Court's ruling against school segregation. Ruth was opposed to integration, and she was very vocal on the subject. That gave Martha just the ammunition she needed.

Knowing her traditional place, the maid started to climb into the backseat. "No, no, no," Martha said. "You sit up front with me." As she backed out of the driveway, Martha could see her mother standing at the front door scowling. When Martha got home, Ruth was waiting. "Don't you *ever* do that again," she said. "The maid is not to sit in the front seat of the car with you."

"She'll sit in the front seat if *I'm* driving," Martha said. It wasn't that Martha was so liberal; it was just that her mother was so demanding.

Pat wouldn't get a car when she turned sixteen, and neither would Joyce. But it was too late to backpedal on that score with Martha. So

*Billie and Ruth (here with Joyce) made the rules and expected them to be followed.*

Billie and Ruth became even stricter. Martha says they wouldn't let her go on a real "car date" until she was almost seventeen. Even when she was eighteen, Billie laid down the law regarding the movies she could and couldn't see. One he was particularly adamant about was *The Long Hot Summer,* starring Joanne Woodward and Paul Newman. Martha lied and said she was going to see something else, then went to see it anyway. When she came home, she told her father that not only had she gone to see it against his wishes but also that there wasn't one thing worth censoring in the entire movie.

"Well," Billie said, "don't you remember that she walked around the bedroom in her slip?"

Despite the freedom the Ford convertible gave Martha, it also became a powerful tool of punishment for Billie. Once, Martha had picked up several friends, and one of the boys wanted to drive her car. She let him. When she got home, Billie was waiting. "Martha, you let somebody else drive the car," he said. She tried to lie, but he knew too much. He knew the street she'd been driving on, knew that the boy had been smoking, knew that he'd had his arm around Martha. "I won't tolerate that," Billie said. She was grounded for a week. Later, he told her that one of his and Ruth's bridge-playing friends had driven past Martha's entirely too recognizable car and had promptly called in a report.

That baby blue 1955 Ford convertible had a spirit of its own. I know that because I remember the year of that car so vividly. It was the year of *Blackboard Jungle* and *Rebel Without a Cause*. It was a seesaw year, the year that finally tipped the balance away from Billie and Ruth's (and my parents') big-band postwar innocence toward something younger and freer and not nearly as certain. Martha drove that car across that seesaw as though it were a bridge. And even when she parked the convertible outside, its spirit came into the house with her.

Martha's parents didn't allow her to have boy-and-girl parties at home, so she had them only when they were away and her grandmother was staying over. On such nights, Martha and her girlfriends and their boyfriends would spend most of the evening in the music room with the lights low and the music high. There was a good deal of what was then called "smooching" going on. Martha would also inevitably perform her specialty, the "dirty bop," a slow bump-and-grind shown off to best advantage when done to a libidinal chant like Gene Vincent's "Be-Bop-a-Lula."

Of course, Martha had to take special care on nights after the weather had been rainy. That water under the music room would make the floor furnace float, and a girl could trip in the dark if she didn't watch out.

*Pat Murphree (foreground) at age fifteen, July 1958.*

*Chapter Seven*

# Murphree

## 1957 ❧ 1959

I n a house, you never can tell where the next trouble will erupt. A doorknob will suddenly come off in your hand. A heating duct in the belly of the house will lose a screw and pop out of its fitting. Even if you think you know the trouble spots, you'll still be taken by surprise. A piece of upstairs trim will swell up and warp, and the next thing you know, the rain will be leaking in downstairs and two walls away.

That's the way it was both literally and figuratively at 501 Holly during the second half of the 1950s. For all Billie and Ruth's efforts to control their world, or at the very least to *appear* to control it, the world now seemed bent on showing how powerless they were.

When Joyce was in the fifth grade, she came down with mononucleosis. She had to stay home from school for a month. On the day she was supposed to go back, she pleaded with her mother for just one more day of lying on the sofa watching TV. Her older sisters would later say that Joyce was "the perfect child." She was enough younger than Martha and Pat so that she wasn't involved in their fights. Plus, she wasn't spoiled like Martha, and she wasn't angry like Pat. Ruth said okay.

In the early afternoon, Ruth left to go play bridge, and Joyce was savoring every minute of her final day in the darkened den. Suddenly, she thought she smelled smoke. She got up and walked into the back bedroom, where the large window fan was. Nothing was burning there. Then she went into the kitchen. What she saw stunned her: Flames were climbing the wall to the left of the back-porch door. It was amazing that the fire could've become so intense so silently.

Joyce ran back into the den and called the first person she could think of—the neighbor across the street. The neighbor called the fire department, and they came immediately, men in hats and coats hauling heavy equipment into the house and across the polished hardwood floor of Ruth's living and dining rooms. They found that the hot-water heater in the back-porch closet had gone bad and burst into flames. The men attacked the kitchen wall with axes. They flooded the room with the power of their hoses.

By the time of the fire, the Murphrees had already been assailed from directions they never would've imagined in the good old clear-cut days after the war. First they found themselves in a battle at school. Next they were broadsided by the church.

In the fall of 1957, Martha began her final year at Little Rock Central High School. Her mother and father were on a much-needed vacation in England when school started, and Billie's mother was staying with the girls. But nobody had to prod Martha to get up and go to class. She was eager: This was an important day—she was now officially a *senior*. There had been a lot of talk lately about integration, but Martha hadn't been paying attention to that kind of stuff. "It wasn't a factor in my life," she says. What *was* a factor was making good grades. Martha had partied a lot in the tenth and eleventh grades, and her grades had slipped. Over the summer, she had come to the conclusion that she had to make a strong showing her senior year, or otherwise she wasn't going to get into a decent college. Part of the partying had had to do with becoming romantically involved with her boyfriend, Jerry Leazure. Now she was secure in that relationship, so she could focus her attention on other things.

That first morning, September 2, Martha picked up her carpool and drove to school in her baby blue Ford. When she got within a couple blocks of the school grounds, a police car was parked, blocking the street. Martha rolled down the window and asked what was going on. "We've closed the parking lots," the officer said. "You'll have to park on the street and walk to school today." When Martha had found a spot and she and her friends had hiked back to the front of the school, they saw that it was cordoned off. There were people everywhere, and many of them didn't look like students.

The teachers kept the students in the classrooms with the shades drawn that entire day. They had no idea what was happening outside. That night at home, Martha and her grandmother watched Governor Orval Faubus on television. Nine Negro children were attempting to go to school at Central, and Faubus swore he wasn't going to permit it. He said he was activating the Arkansas National Guard to keep it from happening. Martha called one of her uncles and asked him what she should do. He told her that as long as the school was open, she had to go.

The students were in the dark for seventeen days. A few blocks away in the governor's office, Faubus wrangled with a federal judge, with the Department of Justice, and even with President Eisenhower. Finally, on September 20, Faubus withdrew the Guard. Three days later, the nine Negro students were admitted to Little Rock Central High School. An angry crowd appeared out front, and school administrators ordered the removal of the black students through a side exit. The next day, the mob was even more unruly. President Eisenhower responded by federalizing the Arkansas Guard and ordering in one thousand troops from the U.S. Army's 101st Airborne. For the next month, the nine Negro children were escorted to school—and from classroom to classroom—by armed soldiers.

Martha had several classes with the Negro students. "The classroom activities were very stressed," she recalls. "In those classes with the blacks in them, the soldiers, four or five of them, would have duty standing around the walls in the classroom. Then, five minutes before the bell would ring to indicate that class was over, the soldiers would circle the black students and carry them down the hall, like they were little peas in a pod."

Martha and her friends found the entire process terribly disruptive. "My French class had two black girls in it," she says. "This was second-year French. These girls had had first-year French, but they might as well have had only three weeks of French. They didn't have the slightest notion of what was going on. It was sad, because they were obviously going to fail. And they were slowing down the progress of the classroom, which I and the rest of us resented."

A lot of people felt that way—Billie and Ruth among them.

While Martha was trying to concentrate on her senior year, Pat was a ninth grader at Pulaski Heights Junior High. It was nice, for a change, not being in the shadow of her sister. Pat had developed a full social life of her own, and in junior high she had talked with her parents about even going to sock hops. Ruth and Billie responded in an amazing way: They volunteered as chaperones.

This was probably Ruth's influence, combined with the coming of age of a second child. Over time, parents learn to choose their battles. Still, for a Baptist deacon and member of the censor board and his wife, this was a revolutionary leap. Second Baptist, the church they attended, was very strict: no mixed bathing, no movies on Sunday, and, certainly, no dancing.

One day when Ruth was at home, the phone rang. It was the Baptist preacher, and he wasn't pleased one bit. He'd heard that the Murphrees allowed their daughter to go to *sock hops*, and he was calling Ruth on the carpet about it. Unfortunately for him, word about Ruth's moods hadn't made it to the parsonage.

At the beginning, Ruth tried to be reasonable. She told him yes, she *did* let her daughter go to sock hops—that she'd rather Pat be at the school dancing, where Ruth knew what she was doing, than in the backseat of a car parked in the dark. The preacher didn't see it that way. "I'm going to church you," he told Ruth, meaning he intended to run her out of the congregation. "Do you hear me? I'm going to *church* you."

And that's when, as Ruth remembers it, she "told him how the cow ate the cabbage." That's an old Arkansas expression meaning she verbally crucified him. One thing she said was, "Well, if you're going to call the rules, I'll just join the Catholic church, where I can have someone to pray *for* me."

The next phone call rang in Billie's office at the VA. It was the preacher telling Billie that his wife had committed the unpardonable sin of disagreeing with the head of their church. The call made Billie angry, though he maintained his composure. But before he hung up, Billie gave the preacher a word of advice. "When you tangle with her," he said, "you're tangling with someone who can really hand it back at you."

The preacher didn't take the hint. Instead, he began preaching about the abomination of allowing children to go to sock hops. Ruth never heard a word of it, though. She quit Second Baptist immediately, and took her three daughters with her. Billie, because of his position in the church, felt he had to stay. Ruth and Billie never had another conversation about it.

For a while, Sunday at the Murphrees' was a day of unrest. On those mornings, as Billie hummed his hymns and clutched his duct-taped Bible for the drive downtown, Ruth and the girls would walk the three blocks to Pulaski Heights Baptist Church. The rift lasted a year, at which time Billie left downtown and "moved his letter," as the Baptists say, to the Heights—closer, in so many ways, to home.

My mother used to sing me a sad song about two brothers, Tobias and Cachunky. Tobias won their sibling competition at every turn. When the brothers grew up, they went off to war. I used to feel a terrible ache in my heart whenever she sang this verse, to the tune of "Auld Lang Syne":

> *These two boys to the army went,*
> *And both high places filled—*
> *Tobias was a brigadier,*
> *Cachunky, he got killed.*

Martha got through high school, dashing across the finish line in her baby blue Ford convertible just before the red flag fell. She was accepted into a good out-of-state school, Mississippi State College for Women, where girls from prominent Southern families had gone for generations. In the fall of 1958, she packed up her stylish clothes and her new records, and her Band-Aid box full of Kents, and she drove off to a bright future—deliriously happy, too, to be out of her mother's house at last.

Standing in the driveway waving, little sister Pat must've felt that life wasn't very fair.

When the first year of integration was over, Governor Faubus called a special session of the Arkansas legislature. The legislators granted him the power to close public schools being integrated by force. Faubus wanted a delay in the order to integrate, but when the U.S. Supreme Court refused to allow that, the governor played his stunning new trump card: He announced that he was shutting down the city's high schools for the 1958–1959 school year.

Suddenly, Pat had nowhere to go. Staying home was out of the question. That was the year of the fire, and there were workmen around constantly, laboring under Ruth's watchful eye. The kitchen and back porch had to be redone again. Also, Ruth had finally decided to remove the wall and French doors between the living and dining rooms and to replace the casement windows with picture windows in each of those rooms. Picture windows were the style now. They were what the *new* houses had. The carpenters put up a massive support beam where the wall and French doors had been. On the casement windows, after they had puttied in the giant panes of glass, the real trick was patching the sills and window frames so that the transformation wouldn't be so obvious. If you wanted to make a house look modern, you couldn't leave a lot of reminders around that it really wasn't.

There's a photograph of Pat taken at the War Memorial Park swimming pool in July 1958, the summer before the lost year at school. She's fifteen. She and a friend are sitting in their one-piece bathing suits at a picnic table on the hot concrete, eating Dreamsicles. On the table in front of them are their impossibly thick billfolds, the kind teenage girls have carried since time immemorial. In the background, showing through the cyclone fence, are the cars of teens lucky enough to have real wheels. For the others, there are bicycles parked in a row. Pat no longer looks like a child in this photograph. She's at that awkward age: too young for cars, too old for bikes—an age when the tensions build up tighter than your wallet.

One of the things that doesn't show in this photograph is that Pat now had a steady boyfriend. His name was Larry Sparks, and he was in the same school situation she was in. Maybe his was even worse— Larry was two years older, so he was losing his senior year. All around them, their friends were trying to figure out what to do. A segregationist group had arranged for the opening of a private school, for white students only. Some kids went there. Others were tutored in the basement of one boy's grandmother's house. One girl's parents were so eager for her to get a good education that they

*Billie and Ruth at the height of hostilities in their household.*

allowed her to be legally adopted by relatives in Texas so she could qualify for the resident requirements and go to school there.

For the entire month of September, Pat was at loose ends. There was a lot of anger in the house—Ruth and Billie were upset because of the Negro problem that had started this whole series of events, and Pat was bored, frustrated, and cut off from her friends, who had been scattered to the winds. One day, Pat and a couple of girls were in the music room listening to records. Suddenly, Ruth burst in and snatched the record off the turntable and broke it into pieces, right in front of Pat and the other girls. "You *know* your father doesn't approve of that music," Ruth said. Nearly four decades later, Pat remembers that the song said something about "I want you, I need you, I love you"—it was Elvis, of course, that other dark force in the modern world. Ruth doesn't recall the incident at all.

In October, Pat began attending a school out in rural Pulaski County. One of Pat's aunts, Billie's sister, taught there and had finagled spots for Pat and one of her cousins. For a city girl such as Pat—a girl from Pulaski *Heights*—this was an awful comedown. The county school was a wood-frame building, with individual stoves in each classroom. Compared with what Pat had been used to at Pulaski Heights, this was like going to a pioneer schoolhouse.

Her boyfriend, Larry, was taking courses at another county school. Meanwhile, Pat was so bored that she couldn't even make herself go to class. She made straight *A*'s anyway. The only activity was girl's basketball, but her parents wouldn't let her play: In Little Rock, *nice* girls didn't play basketball. So she spent most of her time in the study hall, trying to figure out what to do to keep from going crazy. She asked if she could take advanced courses, and the administrators said fine. Between October and April, she took and passed several eleventh-grade classes while making straight *A*'s in the classes she was supposed to be attending. At that school, if you made straight *A*'s, you could get out in April, six weeks early. It had been an awful school year, but she had survived.

Martha, meanwhile, had stolen the spotlight again. In the middle of the year, she'd announced that she and Jerry, now a medical school student, were getting married in June. At 501 Holly, this news had brightened Ruth's days. Not only was it going to be nice to have a doctor in the family but it had given her something to plan for, to buy for, to get the house in shape for. She was a ball of energy. There was a flurry of letters and phone calls between Ruth in Little Rock and Martha at school in Mississippi. There were details to work out about invitations. There were showers to go to, teas to attend.

On May Day, Pat turned sixteen. It was a far different experience from that on her sister's big birthday three years before. Pat had access to a car—an old Oldsmobile that all the girls had learned to drive on—but no car of her own. At least summer was almost here. Even though Billie would insist on summer school, she could go out with Larry at night and spend lazy afternoons at the swimming pool.

In June, Martha and Jerry married at Pulaski Baptist, followed by a reception in the basement of the church. Almost everyone involved was a nervous wreck. Billie woke up the day of the wedding with a fever blister on his lip. Martha had her eyebrows dyed, and they turned out way too dark. Ruth, wanting *her* side of the family to look as nice as the Murphrees', had sent money to her mother to help her get a nice dress, and it had hurt Mrs. Taylor's feelings. Pat, the maid of honor, and the bridesmaids—looking striking in bouffant hairdos and pink knit full-skirt dresses that they would never wear again—had to stand in spike heels until their feet cramped. It occurred to Pat that she didn't want to ever go through anything like this again. At one point, Billie joked to Pat that when the time came for *her* to get married, he'd pay her five hundred dollars to elope.

That summer, Pat dutifully went to school in North Little Rock, trying her best to pay attention to the teacher, who kept droning on about long-dead poets and dull-as-dust novels. It was the summer of "Lonely Boy" by Paul Anka, of "Lipstick on Your Collar" by Connie Francis, of "There Goes My Baby" by the Drifters. The name Drifters must've seemed ironic to Pat every time she heard it on the radio, and it was on the radio a lot that summer. She felt that *she* was drifting. She started adding up all the extra courses she'd taken, and she figured out something alarming: Even if the schools opened in the fall, she was now so far ahead of her friends that she wouldn't even be in the same class with them. What was the point?

On the morning of August 17, Pat told Ruth that she needed to go to the shopping center after summer school that day. There was nothing unusual about Pat's story. This was a new shopping center that had just opened a mile or so west of Holly Street. The downtown merchants were already feeling the pinch as the city moved steadily westward—a trend that had begun with the development of Pulaski Heights—and shoppers responded to the novelty of the new centers. Pat would be home late, she said, but not to worry.

Late that afternoon, Billie happened to be upstairs in the attic playroom when the phone rang. Joyce was there with him. Billie answered, and it was Pat. He talked with her for a few minutes, his voice sounding strained.

When he hung up, his face was pale. He went downstairs to find Ruth.

Many nights, I lie awake studying the shadows in my bedroom. Beth and I sleep in the middle room downstairs. On those nights when I can't doze off, I drift back to all that's happened inside *these* very walls, the walls within the walls of the house itself. Once I get started, it's not hard to summon up the characters and then to lie there watching them unobserved, like Scrooge in those heartbreaking visits to his Christmases past:

*Charlie Armour opens the doors to his wardrobe and carefully hangs up his suit. Jessie, still talking, crawls under the covers of the sleigh bed across the room. Suddenly, the person in bed becomes Grandma Jackson, who died with her head in that very spot. Charlie stands holding a coffee cup. Then the bed is replaced by easy chairs. A new air conditioner hums in the middle window as Ruth reads by lamplight. Billie comes in and says something to her. She begins to weep. This room is the precise spot where Ruth Murphree's heart was broken.*

She was sitting in the den, reading. I can imagine Billie taking a deep breath and telling himself he had to approach her very calmly, and then going in with that forced calmness that immediately unnerves anyone who encounters it. "That was Pat on the phone," Billie said. "She and Larry got married today." Thirty-five years later, Ruth marks August 17, 1959, as the day that "broke our hearts."

Billie didn't show it as much as Ruth did. Ruth shrieked and sobbed and paced the floor of the den while Billie sat in his black recliner in front of the air conditioner, trying to calm her: "Now, Mommy . . ." Pat had called from Texarkana, Texas. Pat and Larry had driven there to get married by a justice of the peace. Billie had told them to come on home, that they would all make the best of it.

On the three-hour drive from Texarkana, Pat and Larry were nervous over what they'd done. "I wished it was twenty years later," Pat says, remembering that trip back to Little Rock. She knew she had hurt her parents, but she felt that things would work out all right—*if* she could just avoid this homecoming at 501 Holly.

Ruth was on the phone, calling Larry's parents, calling Martha. Martha recalls that Ruth was in tears. Through the sobbing, she managed to get out what Pat had done. Martha and Jerry had only one car, and Ruth urged her and Jerry to come over the *minute* Jerry got home from medical school. Martha says when she and Jerry got to Holly Street, "Mother was hysterical. Daddy was very, very stressed and hurt." Billie was sitting in his chair, and Ruth was pacing and screaming: "We've got to get an annulment; that's all we can do! We've *got* to get this thing an*nulled*! What'll the neighbors think!"

For the Murphrees, it was the culminating moment of the post-war years, years in which old ideals had steadily given way to new realities. This situation, a middle-class sixteen-year-old girl running away from a life that had gone off track, running off to marry an eighteen-year-old boy—well, it was the pushiness of the Negroes and the rebelliousness of Elvis all wrapped up in one. It was *sex*—was Pat pregnant? Pat denied it then and does today, but everybody assumed she was. Those assumptions finally put the kibosh on Ruth's talk about annulment. The only thing more humiliating than a married sixteen-year-old daughter was a pregnant, *unmarried* sixteen-year-old daughter. Besides, Billie felt strongly that if you'd had sex, you needed to be married. And if you were married, you should *stay* married.

They were all on the cusp of a new era, the 1960s, and this was just a little taste of it. In two years, the censor board would be gone. In four years, U.S. Presidents would no longer be safe on the nation's streets. In six years, women's skirts would be scandalously short and men's hair outrageously long. There would be a divisive war. There would be rebellious young people living together in communes, smoking more than cigarettes. God forbid, but there would soon come a time when Elvis Presley would look tame.

They knew none of that, of course, that night as Ruth wailed her heartsick cry and Billie suffered in silence, in that middle room of the home they'd worked so hard to keep airtight against all manner of rising tides. The home as sanctuary—what a laugh. In the end, the ultimate flood came from the inside—from their own tears.

Jerry had sedatives with him. He gave some to Ruth and put her to bed.

# PART TWO

# Quarrel and Pilgrimage

*Mark, Scott, and Lori Grimes. Their family ushered in a new era, one in which change became a more frequent visitor.*

*By the late sixties, 501 Holly was feeling its age. And so was Billie Murphree, who told Ruth the Lee Street hill had become too steep to mow.*

*Chapter Eight*

# White Walls

*1960 ❧ 1966*

I'm happy to report that, for the Murphrees, there was life beyond that terrible August night in the den. The following spring, they welcomed two grandchildren—Martha's son and Pat's daughter— into the rowdy mix of the Murphree clan. They bought a place on Lake Hamilton in Hot Springs, where they and their sprawling extended family began spending vacations and parts of weekends, commuting the hour to the lake after Sunday-morning church, and then, after an afternoon of swimming and boating and water skiing, driving back to Little Rock in time for BTU and the evening sermon. They watched Joyce, their own baby, grow into a responsible teenag- er (though not without her *own* conflicts with her mother), and they watched Martha and Pat settle into marriage and motherhood (though not without Billie's occasional reprimands because their skirts were too short). They, especially Ruth, continued to work on the house. She had the front casement windows in the music room replaced by a picture window like those in the living and dining rooms. She also decided, after contending with years of dust and noise, to install wall-to-wall carpeting downstairs. She chose a beige wool with the very latest sculpted design.

Ruth says the reason they moved was that Billie finally got sick of mowing that terrace, that Lee Street hill. He'd taken to tying a rope around his lawn mower and tethering it to a tree, so that if he slipped, the mower wouldn't careen into the path of a car. It was, of course, ridiculous. After two decades, the hill had become just too steep. "I want a flat lot," Billie told Ruth one day. It was music to her ears. They decided to build a house farther west, in a newer, more fashionable part of town.

By the time they did, those of us in their children's generation had already launched our own pilgrimages. Our restless journeys would take many forms and would branch in wild new directions, but the destination would always be the same.

Some of us would think we'd reached it at a house on Holly Street.

Surely there's meaning in the fact that the first two families in this house lived here a total of forty-three years, while the rest of us, *six* families in all, have come and mostly gone over a period of only twenty-nine.

I don't pretend to know precisely why that is. All I know is that Billie Murphree's generation seems to have been the last to regard change as something not to be *sought*. Billie came home from World War II and stayed at one job for three decades. He was married to one woman for more than half a century. He and Ruth moved just three times during all those years. They bought cemetery plots and picked out their coffins when they were in middle age. And Billie, because of his sideline real estate business, turned out to be a millionaire.

Those days seem gone forever. To me, though, it sometimes feels like something epic has been lost—some sweep, some heroic, poetic willingness to stand against outside forces—only to be replaced by something that's festered up from deep inside us and caused us to *run*, and to keep on running, shifting directions whenever the wind blows. It feels as though the search has become indistinguishable from whatever it is we're searching for.

In house terms, I know from experience that this restlessness has its own palette. It's pale, neutral, not nearly as passionate as you might think.

My oldest friend has had the same telephone number and post office box since we graduated from college almost thirty years ago. Since he married in 1969, he and his wife—the same wife—have lived in one apartment and two houses, the latter for the past fifteen years. My friend claims he's had to fill out an entire Rolodex just to keep track of me. I hate when he says that, because it's so close to true. And yet I think I'm more nearly typical of American life—certainly of our generation—than he is. "In the United States," Alexis de Tocqueville wrote in 1835, "a man builds a house in which to spend his old age, and he sells it before the roof is on." I've read that the average American lives in some thirteen residences during his life-time. This is about twice the rate in England and France, four times the rate in Ireland, and half the rate for me—*so far.* People who ana-lyze such things attribute American rootlessness to several factors—a greater likelihood of divorce, for one; a wider geographic dispersal of economic opportunity, for another. Those strike me as mere mile-stones on a circle. Tocqueville suspected a deeper cause—that our classless society gives the average American more opportunity, which produces in him "anxiety, fear, and regret." As a result, he's always searching, always looking over his shoulder, always changing his plans "and his abode."

And when he changes his abode, he paints it beige or white so it'll sell or rent more easily the next time.

I've always loved color, loved its power to express the soul. And yet it took me years to sense what the expectation of moving was doing to the quality of my life. In 1968, after I finished graduate school, my wife and I moved to Kansas City, where I went to work for Hallmark. We rented an apartment, had a son, rented another apartment, then a house, then yet another apartment. All of them had white walls. I changed jobs, discovered the magazine business. The moment I got into it, I started angling for the next magazine, the next position. We bought a house, my first—an almost-new house. The only color in it was the gold shag carpeting and our icy blue drapes.

Then I got a better job and we moved to Minneapolis, where everything was white so much of the year. It was December 1973. We were lucky: We found an affordable *old* house in the best old area of town—it had big trees in the yard and a creek not too far away. I felt that I was home. We painted the living room a deep blue and had white carpet cut and bound. The inside of our house looked like a Minnesota winter day. I papered my son's room in bright red, white, and blue. I even painted my study a rich brown, that being the decorator color of the 1970s. Then we had another son, and I papered over my study for him. I remember the dominant color was a fresh green. Soon after that, I found the alien socks in my drawer. We lived in that house two and a half years.

I moved to an apartment—white walls again. I began dating—too seriously, too soon—for the first time in a dozen years. I bought my own town house, painted the walls a sunny yellow. Then I got a call from a headhunter. It was the job I had been angling for in Chicago. I sold the town house less than a year after I bought it. Some boxes I had never unpacked. In the fall of 1978, I got rid of my car and prepared for the urban life. The woman I was with told me she had always wanted to live in Chicago.

We moved into an old apartment building in Lincoln Park. The rooms were large, numerous, and as white as apathy. I threw myself into my work. I explored Chicago, that most Southern of northern cities. In the very first week, I met a black man, a janitor, who had come from Hazlehurst, Mississippi, and knew my uncle. I felt at home in Chicago and began looking for a place to buy. It turned out to be a condominium, an old and cozy one near the lake. The woman and I, still unmarried, though talking about it, moved in together. The walls were more of a cream than stark white.

In Chicago, I began consciously wrestling with this business of always angling for the next thing. It was time to stop, I told myself. Besides, I now had the very job I had wanted since college. It was time to dig in and make a home. It was during my time in Chicago that I realized my aunt May's house had such meaning to me. I traveled to Hazlehurst frequently during those years. I noticed that May's rooms were painted a soothing green.

I married again in 1980. Three years later, we bought the old house on Chicago's North Shore, the one whose sunroom renovations I later dreamed of while mowing the lawn. This time, I had my small study papered in a rich Chinesey red, almost the color of brick. I tried painting the downstairs sunroom terra-cotta, but it turned out all wrong—a horrible shade of pumpkin. We had someone come in and repaint it. I can't remember what color it finally was. We weren't there long enough.

When my disillusionment with my dream job reached the critical point, I began angling again. I wanted to start my own magazine, which, on the face of it, should've qualified me for permanent residence in a home for the hopelessly insane. My idea was to start a magazine about the South. Some people in Little Rock had the same notion, and I agreed to go in with them. My wife was stunned—she loved Chicago *and* her job—but said she would try it. I thanked her. The color of azaleas exploded in my head.

We made a lot of money on the Chicago house, and in 1986, we bought a big, relatively new place in west Little Rock. Starting a magazine, I was hardly ever there. Most of our many walls were beige, and some were light gray. In less than a year, my wife, a Minnesotan, decided she hated Arkansas, that it could never be

*No more white walls: Beth and the girls in our colorful living room, Mother's Day, 1992.*

home to her. She wanted to go back to Chicago, and eventually she did. We divorced after eight years of marriage, and finally sold the house—for a loss—after three. She lived in it a year and a half.

Now Beth and the girls and Snapp and I are together on Holly Street. Beth loves color, too. Her late brother Brent, a New York decorator who died too young, left her with these words of wisdom: "Matisse colors, Vuillard patterns." We painted the living and dining rooms an earthy terra-cotta, and next time we'll do it brighter. Our bedroom is periwinkle, a purplish blue that evokes hydrangeas. Bret's room is a bold Mediterranean blue, with curtains the color and pattern of Moroccan tiles. My office-studio, in the Murphrees' day known as the attic, is a warm yellow that could stand to be even warmer.

Most of us are afraid of color, no matter how much we yearn for it. I suspect it has to do with the way we've been conditioned. When Beth and I were trying to choose a color to paint the room where we watch TV—it's the former downstairs back bedroom—we wanted it bright, in a reddish hue. And yet we were timid, forever watering it down in the direction of a comforting white. The first run-through, we ended up with walls the color of Pepto-Bismol. Beth phoned her brother, who urged us to be brave—to make a *commitment.*

Now we call that room the Geranium Room, describing the color. It's bold, brilliant, and more soothing than I could've ever imagined. Every time I walk into it, I think about all those years I existed within white, easily transferable walls. I don't regret my running and my risks, but now the Geranium Room makes me dearly want to hold on to what I've got. Sometimes there's only a shade of difference between being ambitious and being lost.

*Roy Grimes and his mother in the fall of 1966. Roy wasn't an old-house person, and at 501 Holly even the trees needed work.*

*Chapter Nine*

# Grimes

---

*1966* 🍂 *1973*

J ust as I was getting started on this book, a writer friend of mine from New York drove through Little Rock on his way out west. As I was telling him about the history of the house, we walked out into the front yard, down by the Lee Street hill. It was early evening and the lights were on upstairs and down. We stood out there in the dusk for a very long time; I was pointing to this and that, and my friend was just listening. Finally, he said, "Do you want to know my impression of this house?"

I told him I did.

"I find it ominous," he said.

That was a shock to me. Never once had I perceived this house—the *appearance* of this house—as anything but warm and appealing. But I took another look at it, this time through my friend's eyes. I began to see what he was talking about.

It shows up often in photographs, especially at dusk, and especially in the late springtime. At that time of year, the trees are bushy and dark-leafed, and they loom over the house like giants stepped from a child's dream. At the end of the day, but before nightfall, there are still shadows—vast, unseeable places in that high yard on a hill, where the trees have blocked out light. The house takes on an air of mystery then. The porch that I find such a passive source of joy and contentment seems to jut out almost aggressively. The eaves that I find so architecturally interesting become, recast in long shadows, a row of daggers protruding from just beneath the roof over my family's heads.

My writer friend has long since gone home to New York, but I've never seen this house in quite the same way since his visit. It's probably just as well. Even the sunniest of us has a dark side, and to think anything else is folly. But for quite a while I wondered if what my friend had seen was the *true* personality of this house. Looking back over its history, you could make a case for portentousness and foreboding.

It started hopefully enough, as all houses—as all *lives*—do. Then in 1926, Elizabeth Armor brought her insidious message of evil and despair, which was soon followed by the stock market crash and the Great Depression and the unraveling of Charlie and Jessie's dreams. In some ways, poor Charlie didn't even see the worst of it—his son held prisoner of war for the duration of World War II.

The Murphrees' case is more subtle, but no less ironclad, it seems to me. I believe Billie invested this house with his own sense of moral superiority at a time when morals and manners were changing radically. The Murphrees had a good life here—some of the Murphrees more than others—but the house couldn't possibly protect Billie and his family from the erosion that was taking place all around them.

I said earlier that I feel as though something epic, and maybe heroic, has been lost since the time of the Armours and the Murphrees—since the end of the 1950s, I suppose. Partly, that's me romanticizing the carefree days of my childhood. But the times did change, beginning in the 1960s, and this house not only reflected those mostly unhappy changes; you could say it also presaged them.

Like the country itself, the house at 501 Holly had begun to feel the weight of age and the effects of decay at its core. By the time the Murphrees left in 1966, there was an ominous bulge in the wall above the window in the downstairs back bedroom. In the den, the floor felt suspiciously soft when you walked across it. Outside that infamous bay window, a row of bricks originally angled to lead water *away* from the house had now kicked upward, inviting runoff rain from the pane to trickle into the dark space between the brick exterior and the wooden dermis of the house itself. In the backyard, the garage, crammed with the detritus of decades, was tilting precariously. The Murphrees had even discovered termites eating at the floor beneath the music room. All Billie's brooding about the water had been justified: It *had* given birth to corruption, to compromise. Can a floor once damaged ever be trusted as before?

And could there be a more perfect symbol for the restlessness of the past thirty years than an uncertain floor? It seems to me that while the sweeping themes of the first half of the century were external, the themes of the second half have been internal—a crash of identity, a world war deep within, a great depression of the spirit.

At the house on Holly Street, those themes intertwined in an episode I call the Great Termite War. It was more than an episode, really—it was an era, twenty years in all. Sometimes it was a hot war, sometimes a cold war. Sometimes it took the form of active termites, and sometimes it showed up as dry rot. But no matter how the conflict manifested itself, the cause was water. Its dark, damp beginnings aren't precisely known, but its destruction is. The destruction affected more than the house itself, of course—it touched six families, eroding friendships, bank accounts, even marriages.

That being the case, *is* this house "ominous," as my friend suggested? Does it bring bad luck to those who live in it?

The other night, I fixed a drink and went out into the side yard and studied my house. I stood, hidden by darkness, under the long, graceful limbs of the maple tree. It seemed that every light in the house was on, which didn't surprise me. Like my father when I was young, I now spend much of my life walking around flicking off lights after other members of the family have departed a room. This time, though, I was glad we were burning so much electricity—it allowed me to see more. Windows are a house's eyes. Just like with a person, you can never tell exactly what's going on behind those panes, but if you peer deeply enough and concentrate, you can form an impression of the life inside.

Upstairs, Bret's bedside lamp was on, though she was supposed to be asleep already. I'd like to think she was reading, but she was probably playing with her Game Boy. Blair's overhead light and ceiling fan were both going—she's a teenager and hardly ever comes out of her room, except to snarl that her mother is ruining her life. She was probably writing notes to one of her friends. Downstairs, the tall lamps between the living and dining rooms cast a warm glow on the terra-cotta walls. I could tell, too, from the color of the reflection on the wall near the hall that the light in the Geranium Room was on. Beth was probably in there watching an old movie.

And I, of course, was lurking in the shadows looking for signs that my house was evil. I didn't see it. Oh, I saw odd things—for the first time ever, I noticed that the second story Charlie Armour added at the back of the house gives the structure the vague shape of one of those fanciful old sailing vessels, like the *Niña* or the *Pinta* or the galleon of Captain Hook. The second story is the bridge, the jutting front porch the bow.

But I don't believe that it's a pirate ship. It's just a ship of fools—always has been, always will be. The house is old now, and it's been through a lot in its days. I think that's what my friend was seeing—not the house's personality, but its damaged heart, a wise old soul reflecting what it knows about the ominousness of life itself.

\* \* \*

It's hard to say exactly when a house becomes old. Despite Ruth's efforts to update it, 501 Holly wasn't really old when the Murphrees bought it—it had been standing for only twenty-four years. Today, that would be a house built in 1972. That's not an old house, not in the way the word is used by people for whom *old* is a desirable quality. For those people, a house has to have patina, the sheen of another era. But beyond that, the era evoked has to be attractive in some emotional way. A 1972 house conjures images of bell-bottoms and platform shoes. Even if I live to be a hundred, that won't be *my* idea of patina.

One reason is that I lived—as an adult—through the 1970s. People who want old houses are trying, consciously or not, to connect with an earlier time. A decade ago, the architect and writer Witold Rybczynski wrote a wonderful book entitled *Home: A Short History of an Idea*. He actually puts dates to the concept of "old"— roughly the period from 1890 to 1930. "If department stores or home-decorating magazines are any indication," he says, "most people's first choice would be to live in rooms that resemble, as much as their budgets permit, those of their grandparents." Rybczynski says old-house people are searching for comfort and security in a world that no longer seems to provide such things.

Ed and Sheri Kramer were old-house people. So were Forrest and Sue Wolfe. So was Rita Grimes; her husband, Roy, wasn't particularly, but he went along with his wife's desires. And if it was connections these old-house people were after, they found more than they bargained for at 501 Holly. In fact, I think the stories of these three families are so interconnected that they have to be told as one.

It begins, for me, in the middle, with a fiercely principled young Jewish man from Brooklyn and a strong-willed young gentile woman from Arkansas falling in love in New York City. The year was 1969. Edward Lovett Kramer was the man, Sheri Mabry the woman. Sheri, a petite, dark-haired beauty whose photographs from the era remind me of Jessica Lange, was twenty-seven at the time of their meeting; Ed, bearded and already receding on top, was only twenty-two.

He was like no one Sheri had ever met before. He was an intellectual, but he wasn't an egghead. Instead, he made her laugh all the time, his own eyebrows dancing like Groucho's behind dark-framed glasses. Ed was a New Yorker, but he had the manners of a Southern gentleman. And he had more talents than any one man should be allowed—he could play the guitar and sing (he might pick out a sensitive rendition of "Don't Think Twice, It's All Right" on his six-string, then segue into a campy tenor version of "Yes Sir, That's My Baby"); he could draw and paint; and he was a writer. He wrote movies. Movies were his life, it seemed. Ed's father had been a doctor, and Ed had grown up with the idea that he would follow in his father's footsteps. But he also loved movies and theater, and he wanted to be a writer, too. He had gone to his father's alma mater, Tulane, but instead of studying medicine he had gotten a master's in screenwriting. Ed now had an actual job creating screenplays for a producer who had a production deal with MGM. None of Ed's scripts had been made yet, but he showed great promise—for a time, a new director named Robert Altman wanted to shoot one of his screenplays, but the timing didn't work out. When Ed wasn't writing movies, he was watching them. He was serious about watching movies. He studied the work of the greats in the business—James Agee, Herman Mankiewicz, Graham Greene—and after he and Sheri got together, they would spend every Friday night, *all* night, in Ed's apartment with the television tuned to the old-movie channel. He introduced her to classic films like *Sergeant York,* starring Gary Cooper.

Ed also loved listening to music of any kind, and in his tiny apartment next door to the Chelsea Hotel, he had a pair of speakers that were nearly as big as his door-top desk. Sheri loved to sing, too, and though she was only five feet tall, she had a big, full voice. She had sung in church in her hometown of Russellville, and then in Conway when her family moved there in Sheri's tenth-grade year. But she had never developed her talent further. Instead, after college, she had studied to become a medical technologist. She and Ed had been introduced shortly after Sheri moved to New York to work.

Now, though, they sang together—Sheri belting out an a cappela "Summertime" hot enough to scorch the downtown streets, or the song she dedicated just to him—"Can't Help Loving That Man of Mine." Ed's favorite group was the Drifters, who sang "Up on the Roof." Sometimes he and Sheri would do just that—go up onto the roof of their apartment building and sing or talk. Sheri thought it was funny that in the midst of this big, dirty city, there was a sign on that roof that commanded DON'T SPIT ON THE FLOOR. During their long conversations, Ed told her about his family and about the houses he had lived in. His father, Aaron Sigmund Kramer, had been part of Gen. George Patton's advance team at the end of the war, and he had been among the first of the Allies to document the horrors that had taken place at Auschwitz. What nobody in the family knew was that Dr. Kramer had heart problems. He died just a few years after finishing up his terrible duties abroad. Ed was eight years old.

Ed's mother, Hazel, moved with her two sons out of their flat on New York Avenue—where Dr. Kramer had had his medical practice in the apartment downstairs—and into her parents' big three-story home in a gracious neighborhood on President Street in Brooklyn. Ed's brother, Lawrence, was eighteen by that time, so he was almost out on his own. But Ed was reared by his grandparents. His grandmother Marjorie Lovett had a great influence on Ed's love of theater. She was an actress and a model, and had done three *Saturday Evening Post* covers for Norman Rockwell. She also performed on television in the early days. Living in the Lovetts' elegant home, with its fine furniture and intricate architectural details, also created an indelible impression on Ed. It was a cultured upbringing. He learned to play the piano on an ornate concert grand that had once belonged to the robber baron Jay Gould. The instrument had been one of five pianos created by Steinway for the five crowned heads of Europe. Gould had acquired this one, and then Ed's grandmother had inherited it from her mother. To keep the family from squabbling over it after she was gone, Marjorie Lovett sold the piano to an anonymous buyer just before she died.

Sheri was mesmerized by this young man's life. She had grown up in an old house, though not a *fine* old house, in Conway, the daughter of a state employee. Ed came from a different world. The two of them listened often to opera, whose achingly beautiful arias seemed to capture the drama they themselves were living. There was one opera they particularly loved, Jules Massenet's *Thaïs*, in which a monk in ancient Egypt tries to reform a beautiful courtesan, only to fall in love with her as she renounces her past and dies a saint. Sheri and Ed found the arias wonderfully sad. Whatever they did, wherever they walked or ate, they tingled with the romance of the city— the big, impersonal, impossible metropolis in which *everything* was possible, including finding each other. When they married, they wanted the city to be part of it: They spoke their vows before a justice of the peace at the picturesque old city hall downtown.

Shortly after their wedding, Sheri learned that her mother back in Arkansas had cancer. It was a particularly serious form, requiring a radical mastectomy. That was disturbing enough, but there were other, even more ominous implications: Sheri's aunt and grandmother—her mother's sister and mother—also were fighting cancer. Sheri decided she needed to go home to help her family. Though he had always liked the South, never in his life had Ed Kramer entertained the notion of living in Arkansas. Manhattan had the kind of life and color you could hardly give up. Ed loved telling the story of walking his dog in front of his apartment, and suddenly the dog darted toward a hydrant and pulled the leash taut, tripping a woman walking by. She was splayed out on the sidewalk, a disaster in floppy hat and purple granny glasses. When Ed went to help her, he realized to his horror that it was Janis Joplin. She looked stunned, but then she smiled up at him. "Far out," she said.

But he was a married man now, and his duty was to his wife. He of all people understood her need to be with her family. Besides, it was a good time to be leaving Manhattan: The economy in 1971 was putting pressure on the movie business in general and on his producer in particular. Ed and Sheri packed their belongings and set out to make a new home.

Her brother found them a small rental house in Little Rock, on Woodlawn Street, about nine blocks from Holly. Even that compact house felt like a mansion compared with the tiny apartment they had lived in in Manhattan. For the move to Arkansas, Ed had taken out of storage several pieces of furniture Sheri had never seen—a fine old table with shapely legs, a comfortable old chair with wooden arms, and other items. These had been left to him by his mother, who had died when he was nineteen, and he was happy to have them in his life again. In fact, except for the illness in Sheri's family, life in Arkansas seemed uncommonly good. Sheri soon got a job doing medical technology work, and within a month Ed landed a plum position as theater director at the Arkansas Arts Center. The job paid $6,500 a year.

It wasn't long before the status quo was changed again. At the end of 1971, Sheri became pregnant. The next August, she gave birth to a son, James Sigmund Kramer, named for both Sheri's and Ed's fathers. The little boy whose name spanned such disparate cultures became known as Siggy, though nobody in Arkansas seemed able to pronounce it. They persisted in calling him Ziggy, after a character in the comic strips.

As Sheri remembers it, in the spring of 1973 she happened to be at the Safeway store in Hillcrest when she ran into an old friend from her Russellville years, the former Rita Rhea—now Rita Grimes. Sheri and Rita had been very close before Sheri's family had moved away—the girls had spent the night at each other's houses, and Sheri had even later been in Rita's wedding. That had been thirteen long years ago, and they hadn't laid eyes on each other since. They were both thrilled to hook up again after so many years. Neither could believe they now lived so close to each other.

Since Sheri wasn't working, she began taking Siggy over to visit at Rita's house. It was a wonderful house with a front porch and a big side yard. Rita's three oldest children were in school, but her youngest, Kristi, who was almost four, was still at home. While their babies crawled and played, Sheri and Rita caught up on each other's lives. At one point, Rita mentioned to Sheri that she and her husband had decided to put their house on the market—that they had a weekend lake place now and wanted to spend more time there.

Sheri began mulling over the idea of buying Rita's house. The rental house she and Ed lived in was cramped, now that they had a baby. Ed also happened to have a small inheritance—enough to afford a down payment on Roy and Rita's asking price of $33,500. Sheri soon arranged for Ed to come see the place, and he fell in love. The porch, the French doors, the den with the floor-to-ceiling bookcases—that would be his study (never an "office"), the place where he would retreat at night to create new movie masterpieces.

Neither Ed nor Sheri had ever bought a house before, but they decided to hold their collective breath and take the plunge. After all, they were young, they were bright, and they'd been blessed time and again. And they were buying from one of Sheri's oldest friends. Didn't the stars seem to be on their side?

Rita and her husband, Roy, didn't know exactly what to make of Ed Kramer. He was a shortish, dark-bearded New Yorker, and he was in the *theater*. Roy was a big old easygoing former high school basketball and football player at Russellville High, and he had gone on to become an up-and-coming civil engineer with a respected Little Rock firm. In fact, it was largely because Roy was an engineer that they had finally decided to put this house on the market in the first place. Had it been up to Rita, they would be staying—but, then, she hadn't been the one to spend all her Saturdays working on the place, trying to patch the walls, prop up the floors, rebuild the windows. After seven years, Roy had just gotten tired of it all—he wanted his weekends back. Rita remembers thinking that if she *had* to give up this house she loved, she was glad it was to a friend.

That, at least, is the way she felt about it at the time.

It's a funny thing how a relationship with a house can be so much like a love affair. At first it's all magic, all rockets in flight. Then, sooner or later, the reality sets in. If it's not going to work, the realization sneaks up on you gradually, moving from the feeling to the knowing, the way the awful need to end a marriage does.

The Grimeses were the first of several families to divorce this house. By that, I mean several families left it not just to go *toward* something better; they left it mainly to get away from this house's incessant misery, its overwhelming neediness. They left it to save themselves. But inevitably, such a break leaves scars on both sides.

Rita was twenty-three and already the mother of three when she and Roy moved to 501 Holly. The year was 1966, the month September. As young as she was, she knew even then that she loved old houses. She thought of the one she had grown up in as "the old home place," imbuing it with a magical quality that transcended mere brick and mortar. In the mid-sixties, however, she had been living with her husband, Roy, and three young children in an 1,100-square-foot house in a new subdivision of houses all pretty much like theirs, all occupied by people pretty much their age. The house had actually been built for them, though—the developer showed them the lots they could choose from and then let them pick from among five or six floor plans. It was the training-wheels version of building a house. The plan Rita and Roy had selected was a three-bedroom ranch. They had moved in in 1963, when Rita was twenty.

By then, they'd been married three years and already had two sons, Scott and Mark. Roy, who was six years older than Rita, was embroiled in his work with the engineering firm of Garver and Garver. It was an exciting time to be an engineer. Little Rock was being virtually encircled by the new interstate highway system, and Roy's company was involved in a major study for part of that. Roy and Rita, who had met and married in their little central Arkansas hometown of Russellville, felt that their future was as limitless as that interstate highway now seemed to be. Rita had studied art for a while and then had switched to engineering herself. Finally, she had dropped out of school to marry Roy. Now she was happy just being a mother and housewife.

After having lived in a succession of apartments, they even found their new house in the subdivision limitless at first. Then Rita got pregnant again. In February 1966, she gave birth to a daughter, Lori. Scott was two and a half, Mark was one and a half, and now they had a new baby. It was amazing how fast that house had shrunk. Rita started watching the want ads, circling and clipping descriptions of houses that seemed promising. One day, she ran across an ad for a house at 501 Holly. It sounded wonderful—a front porch, lots of bedrooms, wall-to-wall carpeting, a big corner lot. Not only that; there was no down payment required—the buyer would just assume the loan. The house was for sale by the owners themselves. That night when Roy came home from work, Rita had already made an appointment with the people, a Mr. and Mrs. Murphree.

Dropping the kids off with Rita's aunt, Roy and Rita drove from the new subdivision into the old tree-lined streets of Hillcrest. It was

*Rita Grimes, second from right, with her two sons and Roy's sisters. Rita loved 501 Holly no matter what calamity came along.*

dark when they got to Holly Street, but the house lights glowed. In the blush of lamplight, the timeless dance ensued: Rita was mesmerized, the way Ruth had been on *her* first day almost twenty years before. Roy and Rita never even saw this house in daylight before buying it. There are times in your life when you don't want to risk having your mind changed.

They told themselves the house was in a spectacular location for a family with young children—the Pulaski Heights school, offering nine grades in one location, was practically at their back doorstep. They told each other that no matter how hard they looked, they wouldn't do better. The Murphrees were asking $24,000. Roy got them to knock fifteen hundred dollars off that. In the end, the Grimeses put $500 down and assumed the mortgage for $22,000.

That September of 1966, 501 Holly's third owners moved in. But it's part of the alchemy of houses that even when a man and wife move into one together, they don't necessarily move into the very same house. There's a photograph of Rita, one of the few snapshots of her taken here, and she's standing in front of the house with three of Roy's four sisters, plus Scott and Mark, who're perched upon one of the brick half columns, as though on a pedestal. Rita, in her bright yellow A-line and sixties bouffant, is only twenty-four in this picture, but her deep-dimpled smile says she's shed her cookie-cutter box in the subdivision and slipped into a unique identity, an identity even older women would have to respect. Rita would love this house, the *idea* of it, the whole time they were here.

There are numerous snapshots of Roy at 501, and many of them catch him, naturally, with a smile on his face. But one picture taken about the same time as the one of Rita captures what I now know to be the worry Roy felt about this place. He's standing in front of the house, with his arm around his mother, and just over his left shoulder is a tree I had never known existed. He says it wasn't much of a tree— it'd been struck by lightning or something, and the top was gone from it. As soon as Roy saw it, he knew he would have to take it down eventually. At this house, even the *trees* needed work. Roy's expression in this photo says *he* had left his new, small, easily managed house in the subdivision and slipped into maintenance quicksand. He would be weary of it long before he would find a way to escape.

They took to calling the living and dining space "the bowling alley." With the sudden absence of Ruth's heavy Victorian furniture, that sprawling expanse of beige carpet now looked incredibly empty. Rita and Roy had no dining room furniture at first, just a dinette set for the kitchen. They placed their small white brocade sofa and a couple of velvet chairs in the living room area, spreading an Oriental-style rug under the side-by-side cocktail tables. Rita arranged a few items—a picture, some sconces, one of those big decorative keys that were popular then—over the mantel and positioned her family knickknacks in the otherwise-empty bookcase by the fireplace. Still, it wasn't exactly cozy. Every time they walked through the front door, they were met by the ringing reminder that this was a *real* house, and they were neophytes.

They did have a piano, though, and a record player with an eight-track cassette deck. Rita put all of those music-related pieces in the room off the living area, which was now officially the music room. The middle room, the one with all those bookcases, became the den. That's where the TV set was. Nineteen sixty-six was the year color television became the norm—the demand for color sets was so great that you had to *wait* to get one because local stores would be out of stock for months at a time. Roy and Rita had just made the switch, buying a big black Magnavox console model, which they placed in front of the bookcases. The years the Grimeses lived in this house spanned the eras from *The Green Hornet* to *Kung Fu*, from *The Milton Berle Show* to *The Sonny and Cher Comedy Hour*. In the evenings, Roy and Rita would settle back in the old green Herculon chair or spread out across the floral-print sofa, while the children sprawled on the floor in front of the TV, their chins in their hands.

The whole family slept upstairs. In the beginning, the two boys shared the big bedroom where Martha Murphree had walked on doorknobs; in the smaller room adjacent, little Lori slumbered in her crib. Rita and Roy, who had a king-size bed, planned to use the big attic room as their master suite. This room does have wonderful potential for that. It's cozy; the ceiling slopes on either side, evoking the romantic aura of a Parisian garret—especially at night, when the shadows from the big elm brush across the walls. Back when the

Murphrees had taken out the first pair of French doors downstairs, they'd knocked out a couple of windows facing the front of the house and installed the French doors here. Now you could open those doors and step out onto the roof of the front porch; in theory, it was like having your own terrace off the master bedroom.

Roy and Rita had big plans—they were eventually going to level the floor, and there was talk of building a bathroom in the big storage closet just inside the door. To get them started, though, Roy covered the bare floor planks with rust-colored linoleum designed to look like a basket-weave pattern of bricks. Thirty years later, that linoleum is still here. There's no bathroom. A marble still rolls to the wall.

Eventually, Roy and Rita traded rooms with the boys, giving them the attic and painting their old room a bold and cheery gold, complemented by a red-and-gold bedspread and curtains, as well as by a bright red piece of carpet that captured the spirit of their Spanish-style furniture. It hadn't taken Rita long to decide the attic wasn't for her. That first arrangement was scrapped after a night when Roy was out of town and Rita was trying to drift off to sleep. Suddenly, a book on the bookshelf fell over. Rita was petrified. *What was that noise?* She was afraid to scream, afraid to do anything. She lay there hugging her pillow all night long.

Old houses, with their creaks and groans and gothic shadows, do have a way of playing tricks on your mind. I once lay awake for hours in our big old house in Hazlehurst, convinced that the hooded figure in the far corner was Death and that, although I could see *him* plainly, I would never again see morning.

All these years later, Roy Grimes can still take a sheet of tattersall drafting paper and sketch out a precise portrait of the malaise that had overtaken the den. He shows me how time, conspiring against joists in the damp darkness beneath the subfloor, eventually succeeded in shifting bricks in full sunlight outside the window, allowing rain to invade the wall. It's a lesson of life, taught by a house: Everything is connected. Joists had rotted, the floor had dropped, and the brick had kicked up. Roy spent a good portion of his first months at 501 Holly crawling on his knees beneath the den, propping up the joists with concrete blocks, firming up the sagging floor as far to the north edge of the house as he could go—which wasn't quite far enough.

He takes out another piece of paper and draws one slanted line, representing the angle of the terrain sloping from right to left—north to south. Then he draws a horizontal line, representing the subfloor of the house. The lines intersect at the far right. He explains that this house was actually built into this hill, and the contractor didn't excavate completely on the north side. There's no room to crawl under there—which means you may have no idea if something *else* is crawling under there. A man had to come out and jack up the corner of the house in order to reset the row of tipped brick.

The garage was obviously on its last legs. Roy was afraid to park his Mustang in it, but more than that, he was afraid for his children's safety. Young boys love to explore musty car sheds, where old tools hang from bared ribs and boxes of potential treasure loom in the half-light. After six months of worrying, Roy came to a decision: The garage had to go. He hired a crew of high school boys, who came over wielding sledgehammers and testosterone. They probably would've paid Roy to *let* them do the job, though he paid them two hundred dollars instead. When it was over, Roy had dirt hauled in to fill the void where the garage had been. With that area built up to the slant of the rest of the backyard, he blocked off the driveway with railroad ties and a section of fence. He did away with the wooden gate between the garage and the back sidewalk. Finally, in the spot where Jessie Armour's servant's quarters had stood, he poured a slab of concrete and put up a white prefab metal shed from Sears.

Had Rita been watching this process from the downstairs back bedroom, she would've been careful not to get too close to the window, which was about to fall out. Obviously, there had been movement in the floor and wall, and the entire window frame was now cocked out at the top. Roy had to jack the windows, horizontally, back into place. Then he went in like a surgeon and reattached the frame to the wooden skeleton inside the wall.

Throughout the house, the story was always the same—the ravages of time, combined with carelessness or neglect. The infrastructure was crumbling. Tile in the upstairs shower had been painted over and was peeling. There was some problem with the plaster in the corner bedroom upstairs—wallpaper wouldn't stick to it, and they papered that room three times in the seven years they were here. The kitchen was covered in what Rita says was "cheap paneling"—even the cabinets were made out of it. There were no built-ins, and the stove was twenty years old. Roy had a carpenter come in and redo the kitchen. The man added cabinets, plus a new stove and dishwasher in that buttery seventies yellow. There's a photograph obviously taken by Rita—it's of her family posed before the new stove and range. Somehow, the aim of the photographer has shifted slightly, so that Roy, Scott, Mark, and Lori are off center to the left, sharing the spotlight with the sparkling new range top.

Rita says the kitchen was *the* big change they made in the appearance of this house. Here in this old place, they indulged in very little of what you might call pure decorating—changes made to please the soul instead of to redress the injustices of age. For a while, Rita's brother lived in the downstairs back bedroom, and he wanted his room red. They bought him the paint and let him do it. Their most ambitious attempt at pure cosmetics was in the living and dining area—the bowling alley. Just before they moved out, they tried a two-tone green motif, lighter on the walls and a tad darker on the squares of decorative molding. Rita felt, after it was all done, that she hadn't quite pulled it off, that the two colors hadn't contrasted enough.

When the days and evenings of work were over, they would retreat to the den and watch television—which increasingly featured news of the Vietnam War or the trial of the Chicago Seven or the search for the Weathermen. Those were unsettling times, and the anxiety of the era was reflected in the house itself. Sitting there in the den at 501 Holly, Roy and Rita could usually hear footsteps skittering in the walls, as if the decay all around them had thousands of legs and could outrun any human effort to overtake it. One night, the footsteps weren't *in* the walls. Roy cornered a huge rat in the music room. He yelled for Rita to bring him a towel, and when the rat tried to get past him, Roy pounced on it with the heavy cloth. He took it outside and beat it until it stopped squealing.

There's such a thing as being out of sync with your surroundings. I haven't said this to Rita and Roy, but I believe that's what happened to them. In one respect, they were ahead of their time; in another, they were too late.

When they moved to Hillcrest, the area at large had become old—both the houses and the people who lived in them. The commercial buildings on Kavanaugh were clearly deteriorating. A neighborhood study showed that the population of Pulaski Heights had dropped 10 percent between 1960 and 1970. In the early 1960s, the Methodist church—the church the Grimeses attended— even considered leaving its location on Woodlawn Street and moving farther west, following the trend. Like the Murphrees, that's where most of the people had gone. Others had simply died. Over the next decade, the restless generation would discover this old neighborhood and move into it, feverishly fixing up the inexpensive houses and trying to connect with a life that had charm and meaning. In those terms, Roy and Rita were practically alone when they came here. They were gentrification pioneers.

Many of their neighbors were elderly. One old lady was on the telephone the *minute* the Grimes family dog, a Pekinese named Pixie, started barking. Others seemed to resent any evidence of fun, especially if it involved music that wasn't by Lawrence Welk. One summer night, Roy and Rita and a few friends had cooked out and then migrated to the front porch. It was only around nine o'clock, and they were swinging and rocking and enjoying themselves when one of the men started everybody singing—Roy doesn't remember the song, only that it was loud. Soon Mr. Grimes was wanted on the phone.

"Are you having a party over there?" said a voice. It was someone from a few houses away.

"Well," said Roy, "kind of."

"Well, this is a decent neighborhood," said the caller, "and we'd appreciate it if you'd get quiet."

Another night, the entire family was spread out on the floor in the bowling alley, playing Monopoly. The children were fidgeting and crawling and trying to pay attention, and Roy and Rita were shaking the dice, dealing the cards, and handling the money. Suddenly, there was a knock on the door. Roy opened it and two policemen stood there. "We have a report that you're gambling in this house," the cop said. Even now, Roy and Rita are incredulous about that episode. They suspect that someone who was canvassing the neighborhood for a charity had come to the door and caught a glimpse of them through the window and then had dashed off to report the further decline of morals in Hillcrest.

In August 1969, Rita went to the hospital to have another baby. It was a girl, Kristi—the second child born to this house. While Rita was gone, Roy stayed home with the children. Scott was seven, Mark six, Lori three and a half. The three males used that time to build a patio in the backyard. Roy spread a bed of sand and ordered a load of bricks to lay in it. He worked for hours on his knees in the hot sun, the boys bringing him brick after brick. He laid them in with-

*The four Grimes children, posed in front of Rita's new stove and range.*

out mortar, two this way and two that, effecting the classic basket weave. When he finished the patio, he poured concrete and installed a gas grill, the latest thing. Scott and Mark etched their initials in the concrete. Everything looked beautiful, except that anyone sitting on the patio would list north to south at about ten degrees. I asked Roy, the civil engineer, why he did it that way. "That's the way the land was," he said. He didn't recall their using the patio very much.

Scott and Mark were both at Pulaski Heights Elementary that fall, Scott in the second grade, Mark in the first. Rita found herself feeling lonely with the boys off at school. Scott, she says, kept the house pretty lively when he was at home, and I can see what she means even in his photographs. There's a sunny kind of cockiness that comes through in the way he angles his head and breaks into his lazy smile. Rita says Scott took great delight in pestering his little brother and Lori, keeping them upset, making them run and tell. Mark was mischievous but sweet, always flashing an engaging, snaggle-toothed grin from having knocked out a tooth in a fall when he was three. The strange thing about Mark was that he was scared to death of rain. Sometimes the family would go sit on the porch in a spring storm, but Mark wouldn't set foot outside the door. Lori, on the other hand, looks like someone the rain wouldn't touch even if she was standing in it. There's a wonderful photo of her—of all the kids—again taken in front of the new stove. Lori, probably age five or six, is wearing nothing but white underpants, and she looks like a golden-haired California girl, one of those suntanned angels glowing with good health and blessed with promise.

In fact, looking at photographs like that one, I have a hard time remembering that not everything was perfect in the Grimes household.

Even though Lori was good company, Rita felt like a bit of a misfit on Holly Street. She yearned to have a conversation during the day with somebody over the age of three. In her old neighborhood, several of the mothers gathered daily with their children and helped one another pass the time. There might've been as many as fifteen kids in tow, all under the age of six. It had been madness, but fun. Here on Holly, Rita was by far the youngest woman on the block. Most of the other wives worked, and the ones who stayed home were old. It was just another way the Grimeses were out of sync.

In 1971, Rita and Roy learned that the Little Rock school district was going to start court-ordered busing. This was one of those wrangles that seemed to have been going on forever—since Central High, at least, which had been fifteen years before. Throughout the sixties, the Little Rock school board had been studying ways of achieving "desegregation," and even in 1966 there had been articles in the newspaper that pointed clearly to busing. Rita says she hadn't noticed them, or hadn't paid attention. Now, suddenly, having nine grades just three blocks from Holly Street was totally moot.

To add the proverbial insult to injury, Scott and Mark didn't qualify to be actually *bused* to school. The rule was, if you lived two miles away from your new school *as the crow flies,* a bus would pick you up and bring you home. By that measurement, Forest Park Elementary was just under two miles from 501 Holly.

Rita's days of boredom were over, replaced with a regimen that kept her on the go. She packed five-year-old Lori and two-year-old Kristi up in the morning so she could take the boys to school. To complicate matters, Lori was starting kindergarten that year. In the afternoons, Rita and Kristi had to drive one place to pick Lori up at noon, then come *back* for Mark and Scott at 3:30. The next year Mark was transferred to a school farther away, so he was bused. That didn't help, since Rita still had to be away from the house morning and afternoon hauling Scott and Lori. Rita remembers one period when she had to make three afternoon pickups—at noon, 2:00, and 3:30.

The truth is, moving to 501 Holly had taken some of the fun out of life for Rita and Roy. Since they'd been here, they hadn't been able to go and do the way they had in the past. Of course, now they had four children—that had something to do with it. But the house itself was expensive to keep up. Before, they had partied at restaurants and clubs. Now, at Holly Street, they tended to invite friends to play cards at home. Occasionally, on fall Saturdays, a group would meet here and they would all walk the nine blocks to War Memorial Stadium for an Arkansas Razorbacks football game. They threw only one major party in this house in seven years, on New Year's Eve 1970. Rita's mother kept the kids, and Roy cleared the furniture out of the bowling alley and everybody danced to the eight-track—to *hell* with the neighbors. Cabin fever had definitely set in. Rita says there's an 8-mm movie of that party, but she refuses to let me see it.

I think it's telling that one of the fondest memories Rita and Roy seem to have of their time in this house didn't happen here. One spring in the early 1970s, they went to New Orleans with their Russellville friends Jim and Lynn Hardin to celebrate both couples' wedding anniversaries. Lynn had introduced Roy to Rita, and Jim and Roy had been friends for ages. On this night in New Orleans, they all had a wonderful time eating and drinking and catching up with what was important in one another's lives. Soon these couples would decide to build a lake house together, an A-frame nestled among the oaks and hickories on Greer's Ferry Lake, two hours north of Little Rock. From the wistful way both Roy and Rita tell me this story, I sense that this joint lake house was an expression of how much they had missed one another, how much they had been missing the good times.

The celebration, the toasts, went on for hours. Before the night was over, these old friends were walking arm in arm together through the ancient streets of the French Quarter, and the song they were singing was "American Pie," an anthem about changing times.

Roy's escape came with a phone call out of the blue. Rita's aunt owned quite a few pieces of property, and she regularly worked with a certain Realtor. One day, this Realtor called Roy and asked if he could come look at their house. Being nice to the man because of Rita's aunt, Roy agreed. The Realtor was interested in seeing everything, so Roy and Rita escorted him around.

A couple of days later, the man called Roy again. He said he could sell this house if Roy was interested. The truth is, Roy and Rita never had openly discussed selling. Rita loved the house despite the problems with the neighborhood, and Roy had repaired the major defects. They'd even bought an antique dining room suite, so the bowling alley was no longer quite so empty. Roy told the man he wasn't interested in selling. The Realtor said to let him know if he changed his mind.

Then, before he hung up, Roy said, "What do you think you could sell it for?" The Realtor threw out a number.

*Weekends at the lake house, the kids water skiing, Roy and Jim reeling in the bass. At the end of the day, there was the party barge— was anything more peaceful than drifting on the glassy lake at sunset, sipping a cocktail, watching the day go orange and slip beyond the water?*

All in all, Roy decided, he'd rather spend his weekends like that, instead of painting and wallpapering and watching for the latest crack in the plaster. He let the Realtor know their decision.

And then Sheri Mabry walked back into Rita's life.

*To Ed Kramer, a boy from Brooklyn, a tree was a precious thing—especially the towering tulip tree, at right in this picture.*

*Chapter Ten*

# Kramer

---

## *1973* 🍂 *1976*

I t rained hard last night. We knew it was coming because the TV
station kept a small boxed picture of the state in the lower left
corner of the screen throughout the evening. All the counties in
Arkansas were shown, and as the storm overtook a county, the color
of that county went from white to red. The rain reached us early, but
not the real storm. That would probably hit while we were sleeping.
Before I went to bed, I walked through the house, checking windows,
securing doors, making sure the skylight was shut tight. I turned out
the lights—and then, for just a moment, I stood in the kitchen in the
dark, looking out at the yard, watching the tree branches sway in
that ominous way they do, like horses sensing snakes.

I couldn't sleep. As I lay there listening to the patter on the
roof, the image of young Mark Grimes came to mind. His childhood fear of rain is fascinating to me. It's almost as though he was
prescient about the lethal mix of houses and water—of how truly
*vulnerable* a house is to nature. We build houses to protect us from
nature's Darwinian ways, and as soon as the house is completed,
the assault begins. Animals probe until they find a weakness. When
they do, I go to my Rolodex and look up the phone number of my
urban trapper, a strange man who comes and captures the beasts

and, whenever possible, takes them back to the wild. He has rid this house of squirrels and raccoons, and at my previous Little Rock house he snared—with peanut butter and vanilla wafers left in a cage—a succession of opossum. Practicing a wilderness art in an urban environment, he comes across as a Hollywood high concept— Natty Bumppo meets Sherlock Holmes. I once went with him up on the roof of this house. He pointed to some slick-looking yellow seeds in the crease where two angles of the roof come together. "Raccoon droppings," he said. I've forgotten what the creatures had been sitting on my roof eating and eliminating, but I was impressed nevertheless. When we reached the spot where the upstairs section of the house meets the original roofline, the trapper squinted his eyes and reached over and picked up a microscopic hair between his thumb and forefinger. He held it up, as though studying it under Sherlock's magnifying glass. Then he cut his eyes at me. "See that?" he said. I nodded.

"Flying squirrel," he said proudly.

Animals are easy, though. At least you can hear them. Water is an opponent from a *Terminator* movie—it slinks and slips and runs and hides. It rises from the earth and falls from the sky. It *morphs*— sometimes as brooding pools dooming joists in the dark, other times as arrogant hail tap-dancing on rooftops. It freezes in pipes and explodes into rooms. Water and houses are a dialogue about uncertainty. In the natural world, water is good—it's the source of life. In the spiritual world, too—at Billie Murphree's Baptist church, once-lost souls were regularly submerged in water to be saved for eternity. But water is death to a house.

The most frightening moments I've ever had in houses have been because of water. In Chicago, my wife and I once came home from a vacation and found our basement flooded. The water was deep and dirty, and I half-expected to find a body floating in it. In Beth's and my early months in this house, we had water problems.

The bathroom floor had to be replaced when we moved in—rotted joists again, just as in the Murphrees' day. And we had a house-guest one rainy night who, at breakfast the next morning, casually mentioned that we might want to check the roof. I went upstairs and there was a huge stain on the bedroom ceiling. Water was dripping from the ceiling fan.

Another time, just after we had spent thousands to have most of the downstairs painted, Beth and I were sitting in the living room having a drink when I suddenly noticed a small bulge in the beautiful terra-cotta paint above the mantel. It soon began to move, a sag on the run, drooping down the wall in a narrow track. Imagine looking in the mirror one morning and seeing a puffiness under your eye and then staring in horror as the puffiness built up and sagged more, gathered steam and ran like a bloated blister all the way to your chin. That's what sitting in the living room watching the paint sag was like for me.

Another rainy night, I heard Beth screaming for me to come upstairs. I got to Blair's room, and Beth pointed me to the large cedar closet. Water was *pouring* in along the line where the wall meets the ceiling. It was a veritable waterfall. We ran and got stacks of towels, and I spent hours holding the towels against the ceiling while Beth carried Blair's clothes into the bedroom and piled them on the bed. Finally, thankfully, the rain let up.

Most of those leaks were in the almost-flat roof in the added-on part of the house, and we've had that roof fixed. The leak over the mantel started around the chimney, for which the remedy was new flashing.

But despite our repairs, I maintain a low-level anxiety about the roof, the way Billie Murphree did about the water under the house. One night about a year ago, I awoke to what I thought was the sound of rain. Rain hadn't been predicted. I got up and looked out the front window—no rain in sight. I went back to bed, but I kept hearing the sound of rain on the driveway: a constant spatter, like bacon frying. By this time, I was a little more awake. I looked out the Geranium Room window—nothing. Then I went into the kitchen. The rain was louder. When I flipped on the light, I saw that the rain was flowing from the ceiling in the back porch/pantry, the area where Jessie Armour had slept during the war years. God, I thought, it's leaking this hard through two floors. For a brief moment, I considered ending my life with a kitchen knife—the homeowner's battle with nature inevitably raises the ancient fight-or-flight dilemma, and after a while you get so *tired*. But the problem turned out not to be another roof leak. The hose on the washing machine had burst and water had been shooting out all over the room, spurting as high as the ceiling. It was a mess, but I was actually relieved.

Then four months ago, the washing machine started dancing during the spin cycle. We found that the floor had rotted—the vertical overflow pipe, or whatever you call it, had become clogged and water was slipping over the top and running invisibly down the pipe to hide in the soft wood. A few more dirty clothes and the washer would've fallen through the porch floor.

All of which is why, on nights when driving rainstorms are predicted, I'm a little nervous. Last night's storm came at 4:30 in the morning. I awoke to the sound of wind howling. But there was an ominous noise inside the house, too—somewhere upstairs, a door or a window was pounding. I got up and went to look. One of the old casement windows in the hall had sprung open. There was water on the floor, and even a few twigs that had slipped in under the screen. Of course, I couldn't find the *thing*—the tool we use to open and close those windows. I lifted the screen and, holding it with my back, manipulated the mechanism on the window and pulled it almost shut. I made another round of the house and then went back to bed. None of my girls had even rolled over.

The storm lasted about an hour. This morning when I took Bret to school, I was shocked at the damage—huge oak trees were down, some snapped in two. A block from our house, an uprooted tree lay across the street. Traffic had to detour. The morning seemed eerily quiet to me—quiet, but not necessarily peaceful: The battle is always joined; nature is always pressing. But water is the most persistent challenger of all. *Water wants in*—that's a basic fact of the life of a house. And once in, water flays open the house to other intruders.

Apparently, that had been happening in this house since the time of the Murphrees.

"I must tell you, I could've killed the Grimeses." Those were very nearly the first words Ed Kramer said to me when I first spoke with him, by phone, a couple of years ago. I hadn't met him at the time, and in fact I wondered later if I would like him. He struck me as a man quick to blame and slow to forget—twenty years after the fact, he still felt passionately that the Grimeses hadn't been forthcoming about the problems with the house. He was also angry at the people who came *after* him, Forrest and Sue Wolfe, because they cut down the tulip poplar tree. "I don't know *what* the hell," Ed grumbled, disgustedly, about the Wolfes. "Their aesthetics are just different from those of anyone I know."

At which point his wife, Sheri, piped in from the other phone: "They had like nine or ten cats, too."

One of the great joys of owning a home is telling horror stories about the former owners—and then, after you've sold the house, driving slowly by and being offended at what the next people have done to it. If you really love a place, you'll feel a pang of possessiveness forever. It's like hearing that an old flame—even one you had grown to hate—has married. You want to feel superior to the new suitor, no matter how many digs you have to get in to do it. Joyce Murphree—now Joyce Stroud—walked through 501 Holly once when the Burneys had the house on the market, but before I bought it. At the time, she hadn't been inside this house in twenty-three years. When I met Joyce, she tried to convey the shock she had felt. "Every room in the house was"—she wrinkled her nose distastefully at this point—"*green.*"

"I *know*," I said, sounding every bit the catty girlfriend.

Since I've been writing this book, I've collected photographs from the various owners, showing how the house looked at different times in the past. At supper, I'll hold each picture up in turn, asking Beth, Blair, and Bret to "name that room." It's amazing how much paint or wallpaper or other people's furnishings can all but obscure these rooms we live in day to day. And of course, no matter how attractive the rooms look in the photographs, we think the way *we've* decorated them is better than the way the other owners did. It would be sad if we didn't feel that way.

But it's best not to let on about it.

It's particularly revealing, I think, that Donna Burney is the only former owner who has refused to meet with me for this book. Although Jack Burney says this is not the case, I suspect it's because when Beth and I bought the house, Donna found out through the Realtor that we weren't going to keep her pretty-but-too-fussy-for-our-taste floral shower curtain, the one that matched the padded floral fabric she had installed on the walls of the pink-and-black bathroom. Donna contacted me through the Realtor and asked if she could have the shower curtain, and I was happy to oblige. Since I wasn't going to be home, I folded it up and left it for her on the front porch. I think now that maybe that seemed insensitive—that if I wasn't going to lie and say I loved it, I could've arranged to hand it to her in person, or at least to have packaged it with a little more respect. That's part of what's fascinating about houses—fascinating in the way that land mines are fascinating. There's nothing about them, not even the blandest beige paint, that isn't wired to a powder keg of ego stored *somewhere.*

Most of that is just the silliness of human nature—we're curious, we're competitive, we're insecure, and we get our feelings hurt. We act like children. We tear others down to build ourselves up.

But there's something more important that we do with houses. Maybe we unwittingly fool ourselves, or maybe—because houses are such a personal reflection of who we are or want to be—we bend memory to corroborate a truth we can live with. Inevitably, a house looked terrible when we moved in, yet looked just fine when we moved out. But take that pattern from one owner to the next, and it doesn't hold up.

Ruth Murphree says this house was in good shape when she and Billie left here; Roy Grimes says he was surprised that the Murphrees could live in a house that looked the way this one did. Roy says he fixed that back-bedroom window that was falling out; the Kramers imply that when they moved in, it was practically hanging by a thread. Forrest and Sue Wolfe say that when they bought, there were huge, fist-size gaps in the living room plaster; the Kramers' mouths drop open at the very suggestion.

I've learned, I hope, not to judge anybody for anything they've done to or in a house. Oh, I'm not so noble: I grouse about them, and I curse them—I think you sell the rights to take your name in vain whenever you sell someone a house. But even as I'm cursing, I *understand*. An old editor friend of mine keeps a needlepoint pillow on the couch in his office: "Life is tough," the saying on it goes, "and then you die." I think the pillow's message might well be amended to read, "Life is tough—and then you become a homeowner." That's why I found Jack Burney's candor so endearing the first time I interviewed him for this book. "I'm not handy," said the man who sold me this house, "and I did everything I could to cut corners and save money."

I refrained from saying that he wasn't telling *me* anything new. I guess I could afford to be magnanimous. Then, as now, I hadn't discovered a hidden disaster the way some past owners had—starting with Ed and Sheri Kramer.

Before Ed Kramer moves into a house, he gets the dimensions of its rooms, and he draws them out on paper. Then he pencils in the furniture, erasing and resketching until he gets the placement just right.

He pooh-poohs any deeper reading of this, saying that it's simply a smart way to handle what otherwise would be a pressured task. "It keeps us from having to decide while the movers stand around waiting," he says.

But I think there's more to it than that. When I was twelve and living in Hazlehurst, Mississippi, I persuaded my parents to buy me my first pair of loafers—cool shoes, as compared with whatever lace-ups I had been wearing. The local department store didn't have my size, so they had to order the shoes. I thought I couldn't *stand* it until those loafers—my new persona—arrived, and every day in Mrs. Smith's sixth-grade class, I drew pictures of the shoes in the margins of my notebook.

Ed is a man who would understand that. He feels deeply about his surroundings, and he attributes that to having seen the worst fears of childhood come true—he lost both his parents early and found himself in a way dispossessed. Heirlooms and mementos and items of personal expression take on special meaning for him. They add up to *home*. "I love the enclosures that I'm in," he says. "I adapt them to myself, and try to make them resonate with me."

He and Sheri generally agree on decor, Ed says, and I don't doubt it: I sense that Sheri has enough strength to be sensitive to his greater need to make rooms his own and that she allows Ed to impress her continually with his talent, his imagination, his wit. For example, when he lived in New York, he built a "piano bar," a visual pun—a bar made from the top of a piano. At Holly Street, he sketched that into the place of honor in the dining room—the east wall, the one you see straight ahead when you walk through the front door. Above the piano bar, he drew in a nice mirror. To separate the living room from the dining room, he penciled in their champagne-colored sofa, with the shapely legged heirloom table at the end by the wall. Across the room, near his precious stereo equipment, he drew in the armchair from his mother.

He took special care sketching in the room that was to be his study. In the bay window, he pictured his massive sawhorse-and-door-top desk, with his typewriter in the center. He envisioned himself working facing the window, his back to the room—to the wall-to-wall bookcase holding his beloved books, to the sprawling beanbag chair that Sheri had made just for him, to the urn of dried flowers she had lovingly placed in the corner by the door.

When they finally moved in in the spring of 1973, Sheri painted Ed's study a deep and moody blue. It's a color he loves. He remembers one night being in his wonderful new study all alone, unpacking his books, and suddenly he couldn't believe that all this space was just for him. "The sense of space made me giddy," he says. "There was so much space that I would get *lonesome*, and I would have to go upstairs where Sheri was unpacking in another room."

Soon after that, he took his seat at his desk and rolled a piece of paper into his typewriter. He placed his fine, gently curving pipe to his lips and fired it up. Sheri says she hardly saw him again the three years they lived here.

During the days, Ed would be at the Arts Center, working with the theater group. At night, after supper—and on evenings when some of the cast didn't come over to plan or rehearse behind closed doors in Ed's study—he would repair to his room and work on a screenplay he was calling *Sweet William,* about a countrified criminal investigator who found himself teamed up on a bizarre case with a hypochondriacal medical examiner. Ed would sit there at his

*Ed and Siggy in the front yard, four months after they moved in.*

typewriter, dreaming about another world, tapping late into the night.

Whenever he needed inspiration, day or night, he would step outside into his yard and walk among the trees, smoking his pipe and absorbing the miraculous strength of this house and land he now owned. He couldn't believe his good fortune. I have a photograph of Ed and Siggy in the front yard of 501 Holly in the fall of 1973. It's one of those sun-dappled days—not just in the neighborhood, but in Ed Kramer's young life. He would've been twenty-six in this picture, and Sig would've been just over a year old. They had been in this house for only four months. On the September day this photo was snapped, Sheri was two months away from giving birth to their second child. It's a moment out of time. Far away from this halcyon spot, the President of the United States was being assailed for sins against the people who had sent him to office. But here in the middle of the country, on this insignificant plot of land, there was still hope in the lasting virtues of home and family.

"To think," Ed says, still amazed, "that I could, at that age, presume to have a house like that, in that neighborhood." He counted the trees, and he would say, over and over to make it sink in, "These are my trees. These are *my* trees." He felt a kinship with each and every one of them. He particularly loved the tulip poplar, which, people had told him, had been designated the number-one tree of its kind in all of Arkansas. It grew straight and tall, towering over the house. It was taller by far than the other trees—the big elm, the maple, the walnut in the side yard, any of them. The tulip tree stood in the front on the edge of the hill, and twice a year it stunned passersby with the beauty of its blossoms.

To a boy from Brooklyn, a tree was a precious thing. This one was simply magnificent.

Rita Grimes visited often in the early days. Sheri still recalls the time Rita and Mark arrived on the front porch, and Mark, who tried to open the front door but found it locked, threw a tantrum—screaming and kicking the door, still not quite grasping that this house he had lived in for so long was no longer his.

At first, Rita enjoyed being back on Holly Street. But it wasn't long before she noticed a change in Sheri's attitude. Sheri herself admits to having a temper, and Rita says Sheri never had any trouble expressing her opinion. That's what began happening during Rita's visits. Before the Kramers had bought the house, Sheri had asked Rita what their real estate taxes were. Rita had given her a number, but now the property had been reassessed and taxes had been increased. Sheri was upset, and she let Rita know it. She began mentioning the taxes every time Rita came over. "She thought we had pulled a fast one on her," Rita says. After a few such visits, Rita stopped going—the situation was just too uncomfortable. Rita says Sheri never once called to see why she'd stopped coming to see her.

Sheri doesn't remember the tax problem, but she does recall an incident about a year after they had lived in the house. Sheri and Ed were at a department store, and suddenly who ambles over to say hello but Roy Grimes. Ed was livid. "Come on," he said to his wife, "I'm not waiting. Let's get out of here." And with that, he stomped away, Sheri following behind.

The anger festering in Ed Kramer had begun with the discovery that the wall and part of the floor of the downstairs bathroom were rotten and would need to be replaced, along with the walls in the back bedroom. "We had a termite inspector go under the house," Ed recalls. "The guy said, 'Right under this bathroom, all this wood is just bad wood. It's going to have to come out.' He told us of various sites on the underframing of the house that looked very bad."

Even now, Ed is adamant in his belief that the Grimeses weren't fully forthcoming during the sale of 501 Holly. Ed admits that he and Sheri were infatuated with the house and so overlooked certain problems—Sheri recalls that the floor seemed to sag between the living room and the former music room, and there were cracks in the plaster, especially going up the stairwell wall. Of course, the trouble in the downstairs back bedroom was obvious, even to buyers blinded by the *worst* case of house fever: The window frames were literally falling out of the wall, Sheri recalls, though no air seemed to be coming in. That room was so bad that, after they bought the house, Ed and Sheri simply shut the door and never went in there. It became a storage room.

"Yes, we saw things that needed to be done," says Ed, "but they were just the tip of the iceberg. When we moved in, we set priori-ties—we'll fix this but we won't worry about that now. We figured it was a lifelong process. I like to live in a house awhile before I go about changing it. You don't know in what way you want to alter the house, or alter yourself *to* the house. You want to give the house a chance to represent itself.

"Then we came to find out there was all this extensive work that was going to need to be done. It absolutely devastated us financially. It stripped our resources entirely."

So that when Ed looked up in the department store and saw a smiling Roy Grimes walking toward him, all the rage that had been bubbling up in him overflowed. "I was so angry, I couldn't even face him," Ed remembers. "I turned away, and I ordered Sheri to come with me. I was not going to stand there and make polite chatter after realizing that this man had just single-handedly demolished all my savings—by not having fessed up from the head end what kinds of expenses we might be incurring."

Roy Grimes, who doesn't remember that incident, says he is astounded by Ed's anger. When I told him about it—told him it was still boiling after all these years—Roy called Adams Pest Control and had them send a copy of the termite protection contract he had taken out on April 20, 1973, in order to sell the house to the Kramers. The Murphrees had given the Grimeses a similar policy, but the company providing it had gone out of business. Apparently, Adams bought out the other company. There's an entry in Adams's 501 Holly file dated October 10, 1971, indicating that the left side of the substructure was "badly damaged," and that the joists and subfloor were "badly damaged." In April 1973, Roy had Adams go under the house to install a four-by-four subsill along the north wall. When that work was completed, Roy received the termite protection contract that he later passed on to the Kramers.

The contract states that Adams would, for a period of one year, protect the property at 501 Holly "against the attack of subterranean termites for the sum of $265.00." The liability of the termite company wasn't to exceed five thousand dollars. Inspections would be conducted at least once a year, and the policy would remain in force for an annual fee of eighteen dollars. Ed Kramer acknowledges having received the termite contract.

A Little Rock Realtor, when I told her this story, said there's hardly any old house in this section of town that doesn't have *some* past termite damage. I told that to Ed. Could it be, I asked, that because this was the first house he'd ever bought, he just didn't know what he was getting into? Could it be that he was, and still is, being unreasonable?

"I don't think so," he says. "I asked them point-blank—I said, 'Is there any termite damage in this house?' and they said no. That's as straightforward as you can make it. I wasn't saying, 'Is this house termite infested?' I was asking if it had any termite *damage*. They said no, it's been looked at, it's been checked. Then to learn otherwise was a cold shock."

He thinks about that for a moment, and then adds this coda: "They had been, ostensibly, Sheri's good friends. I thought that if *anybody* was going to be faithful and straightforward and honest to you, it would be somebody you had known since childhood. I felt that they had betrayed that friendship to us."

Roy Grimes just shakes his head. "If *anything*," he says, "because we were selling to Rita's friends, I wanted to bend over backward to make sure everything was okay. I don't know what to say. I'm sorry he feels that way. It's just not the way I remember it."

Alicia was born in November 1973, months before Ed and Sheri's disillusionment set in. They were still living in a magical world then, and so they gave their daughter the middle name Thaïs, after that opera they had loved when they were courting. Alicia Thaïs Kramer was the third child born to this house.

Looking at the Kramers' scrapbook/photo album from the Holly Street years, I don't see the disillusionment, of course. As with houses, such stresses are usually hidden. What I see instead is a young family enjoying their life and taking pleasure in the memories they were making. Their album itself, an imposing corduroy and leather volume such as banks once used to note their transactions, attests to the importance Ed and Sheri placed on the moments captured within: There are photos of Ed's productions at the Arts Center; news clips from the local press about Ed and the work he was doing; snapshots of everyday family life. Ed made sure these moments were pasted down in appropriate order, and, in his role as official wit of the family, he penned clever captions at the bottom of every photo: "Siggy getting ready to mow the lawn," reads the line accompanying a photo of Sig climbing on the lawn mower.

They kept their memories in other ways, too. On weekends, Ed would turn on the tape recorder in the living room while the family gathered around him on the floor. Picking out something like "Froggy Went A-Courtin'" on his guitar, Ed would try to get Siggy to sing along. One of their tapes has Ed and Sheri coaxing and cajoling, but Siggy won't sing a note. Finally, Sheri begins to sing and Sig immediately throws a tantrum. Next thing you know, he's warbling along with his father on "Yes Sir, That's My Baby," Sig taking the "do-wacka-do-wacka-do" part all by himself.

Sheri says she sang a lot in this house. She loved the way her voice reverberated through the rooms. Today, she protests that she smoked for too many years to sing well now, but on the tapes you can hear her, a crystal-clear coloratura soprano, singing a lilting harmony in the background, all the way from the kitchen maybe, while Ed and Sig croon into the mike in the living room.

But after the episode with the bathroom wall, minor chords began to sound in the singing at 501 Holly. Sheri started noticing herself feeling tired a lot. It was true she had had two C-sections in fifteen months, and now she had two babies to take care of, but this weariness felt somehow elemental. She was exhausted to her core.

The money was a worry, of course, but that wasn't all that was on her mind. She couldn't shake the specter of the cancer that had brought her back home in the first place. Her grandmother had already died, and her aunt would die while Sheri was still in this house. What about her mother?

And what about her *own* inexplicable tiredness?

She was too tired even to sleep. She found herself channeling her worry into an obsession about the house, specifically on the cracks in the stairwell plaster. Late at night, after everyone else had gone to bed, Sheri would set up a stepladder on the stairs, balancing precariously, and she would slather spackling compound into the cracks. They never seemed to get filled. No matter how much compound she knifed in, the house would consume it, and still be ready for more.

One fall, probably their second in the house, Sheri called the gas company to come turn on the gas for the floor furnaces. The man who came out took one look and said he was sorry but that he wouldn't be able to turn on the gas—the exhaust pipe from the floor furnace didn't meet current code, which decreed that such exhaust had to have at least a twelve-foot clearance of the roof. The one at 501 Holly was barely two feet above the roof. That meant, the man said, that carbon monoxide had probably been blowing back into the house for years. Thank God the upstairs windows wouldn't shut completely, Sheri says.

The cost of bringing the twenty-five-year-old floor furnaces up to code was prohibitive, so the only answer was a new central heating system. Sheri and Ed had Sears come out. The man recommended putting the new furnace in the closet in the back bedroom.

It all made Sheri even more weary. She became increasingly angry at Ed, resenting his absence, begrudging his arty little life by day and his selfish retreats at night. They had no money—the repairs had devoured Ed's inheritance the way the wall swallowed spackle—and Ed didn't make enough to save anything.

With Sheri not working, it soon became obvious that Ed would have to give up this job he loved and find one that paid enough money to relieve some of the pressure at home.

For a child, one of the great pleasures of any house is in what my family called "meddling." I did a lot of meddling when I was young. We would go to visit my aunt Gusta and uncle Wib in Tupelo, and, while the grown-ups were talking in the living room, I would wander off into the back of the house, where no one could see me. My aunt and uncle had a fascinating dresser that sat back into an alcove between the hall and their bedroom. This dresser had a few big drawers containing boring clothes, but it also had a number of smaller drawers at the top. Inside those drawers, a meddler could find cuff links, old coins, political buttons, photographs, exotic fountain pens, you name it. That was part of the fun, the imminence of discovery. Not to mention the voyeurism, the private peeking into secret lives.

I eventually got caught, of course, but not in the way you might imagine. I was at my aunt May's and uncle Alex's house in Hazlehurst, and I was old enough to know better—a teenager, as I recall. Upstairs at May's, there's a room that used to be an attic, but which she finished off once she began having grandchildren. That room became known as "the dormitory." There was a chest of drawers up there that I was particularly attracted to. Part of the attraction was a number of small boxes tucked away in the upper drawers. Usually, they contained pieces of May's costume jewelry, and I seem to recall once finding one of my uncle's old fraternity pins. On this particular afternoon, absorbed in my meddling, I picked up a curious little white box. I shook it, then shook it again. Then I slowly lifted off the lid—*only to find my uncle's glass eye staring back at me!* Alex had lost one of his eyes playing tennis back in the twenties, and I guess he kept an extra just in case. But I felt caught, as though that unbound eye had seen right through me.

I always think of that story when I think of Siggy and the pistol.

In late 1975, Ed had made the necessary career change. He had given up his beloved theater to become part of the state bureaucracy—though, for a government job, it did have a degree of glamour. His title was Director of Information and Education for the Governor's Highway Safety Program. With the title came a badge emblazoned OFFICE OF THE GOVERNOR. Ed says he decided that a man with a badge ought to have a gun to go with it. Sheri hastens to add that he's joking—that a series of rapes had Hillcrest homeowners nervous—but I sense that he isn't entirely facetious. "I was fraternizing with people who carry guns," Ed recalls, "so I bought one, too. It was a Smith & Wesson .38 Chief Special."

Siggy was three years old when the gun episode occurred. Ed and Sheri were downstairs in the living room, and they thought both Alicia and Sig were asleep upstairs. Suddenly, Ed heard a noise. When he got up to look, he found Siggy at the top of the stairs in his little back-flap pajamas, and he was laughing and waving Ed's loaded pistol like a drunken cowboy.

Ed always kept the pistol in its holster on top of an armoire in his and Sheri's bedroom upstairs. Either Sig had known the gun was on the armoire or he had been meddling and found it. How he climbed up to get it, Ed couldn't fathom, but that wasn't the most important problem at the moment. For the next five minutes or so, Ed played the role of police negotiator, gently trying to persuade his son to give up his weapon. "What you got, honey?" Ed cooed. "Show Daddy what you have in your hand." Sig, enjoying the spotlight, played his own role to the hilt, doing everything but calling for the media.

In the end, Ed managed to close the distance between them without startling his son, and what could've been the worst episode of their time at 501 Holly was averted. As it turned out, that honor was reserved for something that happened not at the top of the stairs but at the bottom.

Ed was standing in the dining room, looking into the mirror over the piano bar, tying his tie for work. In his peripheral vision, he saw Sheri come downstairs and turn left to go to the kitchen. She was angry. He heard a door slam on the other side of the wall—he *saw* the slam, shaking his very image in the mirror. But the moment the door slammed, that sound was drowned out by a bloodcurdling scream that wouldn't stop.

Dashing into the hall, Ed found Siggy on the floor, wailing and holding his right hand, which was covered with blood. Sheri threw open the kitchen door and was in tears herself as she and Ed tried to get Siggy to let them see. When they finally got a glimpse of his hand, they saw that the end of his little finger was missing.

Ed had the presence of mind to find the finger and wrap it in ice before running to the car and speeding Siggy to the hospital. The doctors sewed the tip of the finger back on, but it didn't take. Six weeks later, the finger was turning black.

Soon afterward, they decided to move—accepting, finally, that the longer they stayed here, the less whole this house would leave them.

*Forrest and Sue Wolfe rescued 501 Holly, but they also paid the price—years of living like this. They scraped ten layers of paint off this den woodwork.*

# Chapter Eleven

# Wolfe

## 1976 🍂 1980

Afriend of mine says his idea of home is a place where the only hand tool he needs is a telephone. The older I get, the more I agree with him.

And yet, here I am, living in a seventy-two-year-old house in which things break or rot or give or snap or wear out all the time. It's happening somewhere around me right this minute, and I don't even know it. All I know is that if your manhood is tied to being handy, a house will show you no mercy. One of the first times I cried as an adult was the result of trying to fix a bathroom leak. Even after that shameful moment—for *years* after it, in fact—I maintained the facade, even to myself. Now, for various reasons, I feel close to uttering the words the house so obviously wants to hear: I'm not handy. I'm so unhandy that even my *toolbox* is broken.

It's part of the perversity of these old houses that they have the power to attract people like me—or like Ed Kramer, for that matter. Old houses *look* like home to us. They appeal not to our practical side but to whatever romantic part of us traffics in hopes and dreams, or wallows in nostalgia. They're flirts, old houses. They get painted up real pretty—the way this house was when I first saw it—and they show off a lot of front porch and invite you in for a little

French dooring, and the next thing you know, they've snared another sucker. Of all the men who've lived here, probably Roy Grimes knew the most about fulfilling the requirements of a house like this. Or maybe Forrest Wolfe.

Me, I'm just a sugar daddy: I write checks.

Over the years, I've thought a lot about this business of being handy. I've come to believe it's as much a matter of attitude as aptitude. I used to think I had both, and to a certain extent, I did. In my lifetime in houses, I've wallpapered, painted (both inside and out), laid linoleum, put down tile, grouted, stripped layers of paint off a staircase and mantel, installed rheostats, built shelves, put on a new roof, built a driveway, stripped wallpaper, ripped up layers of flooring, used an auger to dig postholes for a new fence, put up a cork wall, installed a bathroom vanity, packed faucets to repair leaks, fixed shutters, reglazed windows, planted bushes and trees, and, of course, mowed hundreds of miles of lawns. I'm sure there are jobs I've forgotten—I've spackled and plastic wooded, screwed and drilled and hammered. Some jobs I did better than others, but all of them I felt reasonably competent to do. After all, was I not my father's son?

The shadows of our parents fall long across our houses. My father could seemingly do anything when I was growing up. One Saturday morning in Miami, he rousted me out of bed—my Saturdays before noon always belonged to *him*—and as I was trying to clear the sleep from my head, he said, "Get up, Jim—we're going to put a new roof on your room today." Sure enough, in an hour or so I could stand in my bedroom and see the sky. On this particular Saturday, my dad and I ripped out and replaced the rotten beams, hammered down new wood, and then covered the once-afflicted spot with the requisite layers of heavy rolled tar paper and great gobs of tar.

Another time, my father decided he needed to repair the ceiling in the living room. This was one time I thought he wouldn't pull it off—Mother was due to have a bridge party, but something like that never stopped Dad. When he got it in his mind to do something, he just did it. While Mother was nervously planning her table seatings, Dad was on a ladder, knocking great chunks of the ceiling down onto the living room carpet. To the best of my memory, he managed to slap plaster in the hole and give it a few decorative twists with the trowel before Mother's guests arrived. Of course, the huge spot on the ceiling was wet and unpainted and couldn't be missed by anyone stepping inside the door. Why would my father have chosen that moment to take on that job? I've pondered that a lot. Maybe he felt that a mess of *commission* reflected better on him than a mess of *omission.* I've caught myself thinking that way. Company coming is one of the most powerful incentives to getting house chores done.

But when it came to being handy, there was something antithetically out of control in my father. I sense that whatever caused it in him has caused it in me, too.

I don't read directions, and I can't imagine that he did, either. He was impetuous. He would come home from church and, getting out of the car in his suit, he would notice something that needed fixing. Next thing you knew, he was tackling that job, still in his Sunday best. He often mowed the lawn in his good shoes. He spent a large portion of his life at the hardware store, and he had what seemed like hundreds of tools. And yet he would often pick up whatever was at hand and go at the job with that, rather than taking the time to get the right tool. I do that, too. The other day, I spent five minutes trying to loosen a Phillips-head screw with the palette knife from my art table, instead of walking downstairs and getting my Phillips screwdriver.

But my father—who as a teenager ran away from his family farm and his fifteen siblings, and who put himself through high school, college, and graduate school—had a stronger innate sense of house than of home, and in the glorious moment of improvisation he would sometimes overstep himself. Once I came home and found that he had used the metal playing field from my electric football game to dredge dirt from under the house. This was my favorite game—I had sat hunched over it for hours at a time. You had football players on metal foot plates, and when you turned on the juice, the men would vibrate across the green chalk-marked playing field toward the end zone. My father, needing to make more crawl space under the house, drilled holes in the corners of the metal field and ran small pieces of rope through the holes. Then he lay on his back and tossed the game board into the nethermost reaches of the crawl space. When he pulled the board toward him, he also pulled great mounds of soft dirt. He had turned my frivolous toy into hardware.

Hardware was a theme in my relationship with my father, which means it's been a theme in my life. One of the biggest fights Dad and I ever had was over hardware—a hardware store, to be exact. He obviously found solace in hardware stores—found some kind of peace from rubbing the cool steel of the levels and fiddling with the symmetrical bolts of the turnbuckles. The summer before I went to college, he got me a job in a hardware store—one of those dark, primeval, plank-floored places with a twenty-foot pressed-tin ceiling and fans turning lazily overhead. One entire wall was taken with shelves of screws stacked floor to ceiling, and my job for the summer was to take inventory—*count* those screws. Being an arrogant teenager, I resigned after the first numbing afternoon. My father was furious. To get me out of his sight, my mother sent me to spend the rest of the summer in Hazlehurst, at my aunt May's house, that illusive home where everything appeared to run smoothly and the sound of hammering—of things being fixed—was seldom heard.

Throughout my early years in houses, pure attitude propelled my illusion of handymanliness. I wanted to do right—was determined to put into practice those lessons my father had tried to teach me about tools and hardware. For most jobs, it never occurred to me to call anyone else. I had the good sense to be scared of electricity, but even plumbing was something I thought I ought to do on my own. That tearful session with the leaky faucet took place twenty years ago in my house in Minnesota. The leak was in the small half bath on the first floor. I had to go down into the basement to turn the water off, come back upstairs to work on the leak, go back downstairs to turn the water back on, and then come back upstairs to see if the faucet was still leaking. I followed that routine for maybe three hours, and every single time I came upstairs, the leak was waiting for me. Finally, I just put my head down on the vanity and sobbed in frustration. But of course the frustration wasn't just about the *leak*.

It's only recently—since I've lived at 501 Holly—that I've admitted to myself how little I actually learned from my father: just enough to make me feel guilty hiring someone to come fix whatever's broken. That wasn't my father's fault; it was mine. I didn't pay attention, and now I seem to have forgotten everything he told me. Oh, some things come back whenever I practice the skills: Last weekend, I was sawing, and I remembered how he used to say not to saw straight across but, rather, to saw *down* at the same time, using the arc to cut deeper. Hammering a nail last Saturday, I remembered how he told me to grip the hammer at the bottom of the handle and really pound the nail, instead of tapping tentatively.

But I don't practice those skills much these days. In apology for hiring out the big jobs around this house, I generally tell people that I just got to a point where I couldn't meet my own standards—which is true enough—or that, working for yourself, you don't have the luxury of a salary to allow you to take valuable hours for ambitious household projects. I think that's true, too, at least at this stage of my writing career. Mainly, though, I've just lost the attitude, and the aptitude has vanished with it. I don't *want* to have to fix things around a house anymore.

I tell this by way of introduction to the story of Forrest and Sue Wolfe, who moved to 501 Holly in 1976, the year my father died. On the surface, their story was all about hardware and hardware stores. But there was something more. Their life in this house began during the Bicentennial summer. You remember that: tall ships, firecrackers, a celebration of who we were. It was a looking outward and a looking inward, a quest for both our future *and* our past.

No theme could describe the Wolfes' time here better.

We often receive the things we need at the moment we need them most. That's what happened to this house when the Wolfes bought it.

Forrest and Sue will be embarrassed by this, but, to my mind, it was almost as though they had been sent to offset the corrosion begun half a century earlier during the era of Elizabeth Armor.

On the other hand, maybe they just came for comic relief.

Not that their life here was particularly funny. It was, in fact, an almost unbelievable grind—a grim and perpetual battle against decadence and degradation. But Forrest and Sue are funny telling about it, whether they mean to be or not. They have no children, and by now they've been married almost thirty years. Their conversation is a kind of ongoing jointly told story, a sentence and an echo, reflecting all the hours they've spent, alone, in each other's company:

SUE: Every *inch* of the woodwork in these rooms—the paint was all removed . . .
FORREST: All down to the bare wood . . .
SUE: We used plastic *playing* cards. We bought—
FORREST: Bought paint remover in five-gallon cans . . .
SUE: And we did *every* inch of this . . .
FORREST: Did it ourselves . . .
SUE: We had no money. We couldn't *afford* this house . . .
FORREST: The plaster was all cracked. We finished the den first, so we would have a haven . . .

SUE: Oh, it was awful. It was *horrible* . . .

FORREST: It was horrible . . .

SUE: It almost *killed* us, almost broke up our marriage, almost bankrupted us . . .

FORREST: Well, it didn't almost break up our marriage . . .

SUE: But we made a *lot* of money off it . . .

Until they moved to Holly Street, Forrest and Sue had lived in a small, newer house in southwest Little Rock. Nothing wrong with southwest Little Rock, but it wasn't quaint; it didn't have character—it lacked the patina of age. The Wolfes had friends who lived in an old house on Lee Street, right across from 501 Holly. "We *loved* their house," Sue says, "and we wanted an old house, too." For many couples, dreams like that get lost in life's shuffle—children, careers, just keeping heads above water. But couples without children have more resources for nurturing their dreams.

At the time they moved to Holly Street, Sue, thirty-five, was a high school teacher, and Forrest, thirty-eight, worked for the State of Arkansas administering the burgeoning Medicaid program. The Wolfes had been married ten years, during which they had become used to a certain amount of freedom. They liked to travel, liked to go out to eat, liked to spend Saturdays poking around antique shops. Sue had a desire to become an interior decorator, so she and Forrest signed up for an upholstery class. Otherwise, they were homebodies. To them, their house was a refuge. In their evenings at home, just the two of them and their cats, they enjoyed long, leisurely cocktail hours. Forrest was a Jack Daniel's man. Sue was partial to manhattans. It was their time to dream.

Their friends on Lee had learned the Kramers were selling, and they immediately called Forrest and Sue, who phoned the listing Realtor. They walked through this house just once, and never looked at another. They fell in love with the front porch.

It's no wonder Ed Kramer feels a bit hemmed in between the Grimeses and the Wolfes. Not only had the dry rot cost Ed his inheritance but that injury had been compounded by an insulting loss on the sale, too. Forrest and Sue Wolfe bought this house for $32,500, a thousand dollars less than Ed and Sheri had paid just three years before.

Despite all that, Ed continued to love this place, even as he was forced to leave it. Two decades later, looking back over his family photos of their brief time on Holly Street, he can still summon a hint of the softness he felt at the beginning. "It's got great street appeal," he says, holding up a view of the house with the tulip poplar in the foreground. "The house is just an embracing, warm, generous-feeling kind of a place. A big, open, happy space—the best I've seen for a writer to work in."

He smiles in my direction—a bit wistfully, it seems to me. I think he's finished talking, but then he continues. "Just as married people tend to grow to look alike as time goes by, so, too, do houses seem to attract the same kind of people—I really think that. If I had gotten to know Rita and Roy better, there probably would've been a lot better feeling there."

In the summer of our Bicentennial year, though, Ed Kramer wasn't inclined toward such mellowness. As firecrackers popped like corks in the distance, as neighbors draped red, white, and blue from homey front porches, as all over the country grills filled the air with the very scent of the American dream, Ed and Sheri packed their belongings into cardboard boxes bound for a smaller house a few blocks away.

Meanwhile, out in southwest Little Rock, Forrest and Sue loaded their few pieces of furniture, and their beloved cats, for a move up in the world.

\* \* \*

*Before Forrest repaired it, their three cats came and went through a hole in the closet floor.*

It wasn't *really* nine or ten cats, the image that Sheri Kramer has harbored, out of emotional self-defense, for twenty long years. "Three cats," says Sue flatly. "Well, at one time we had eight here—but it was just because we couldn't leave one, and she had a litter of kittens. But we got rid of all of them."

During Forrest and Sue's era, 501 Holly was a pretty good house to live in—*if* you were a cat. The den closet had a hole in the floor—all the way down to the close dark ground—and the Wolfes' cats found they could come and go through that hole at will. Forrest says that after they repaired the hole in the closet, whenever he and Sue were away, the cats came and went through the unclosable gaps in the upstairs windows.

Not that he and Sue traveled much in those years. They hadn't lived here long before they realized the enormity of their situation. Fortunately for this house, they decided to meet it head-on. They were what 501 Holly had been waiting for—a couple with good jobs and no children, with the will to use all their time and money to reclaim this house from its rush to dust. Not only that; they also had the know-how—Forrest's father, a carpenter in Mississippi, had taught his son well. Sue's parents had redone a house in Pine Bluff, and Sue had absorbed many of the skills required. Others she had simply been born with:

SUE: I'm a Virgo, and Virgos—

FORREST: Make lists . . .

SUE: Make *lists.* For months, I would wake up on Saturday morning and I would say, Okay, we get up at seven-thirty, bathe at eight. Eight-fifteen to eight-thirty, we—

FORREST: Eat breakfast and read the paper . . .

SUE: Eat breakfast and read the paper, eight-thirty to nine—I would have every *minute* of the day planned. And I have a mother who is, um . . .

FORREST: Compulsive . . .

SUE: *Compulsive.* My mother makes *me* look laid-back. And she would come in, and one of the things she'd always say was, "Now, Sudie, all you need to do is . . ." And I swear, I could've *killed* her. That's how I put myself to sleep at night, thinking of torturous ways to get *rid* of that old woman. . . .

The first thing they did was establish their limits. For phase one, they planned to focus on the large living/dining area, the front room, which they called the solarium, and the den. In those rooms, their goal was to repair the plaster in walls and ceilings and to strip the half-century worth of paint back down to the bare wood. Like the

Kramers, they shut off the downstairs back bedroom, using it for storage. They planned to do no work in the kitchen, even though they hated how it looked. Other than what the Grimeses had taken away, the kitchen was still covered—walls and cabinets alike—in the paneling Ruth Murphree had installed after the fire in 1958. Upstairs, only the shower was part of their plan—though, once they really delved into that bathroom, they had to revise their thinking. They also planned to take up the rotting wall-to-wall carpet, remove the floor furnaces and reweave the floors, and then sand, stain, and refinish the hardwood throughout the downstairs.

And those were the fun jobs. It was time, Forrest knew, to redo the fifty-three-year-old plumbing in this house. He hired a plumber who worked with his brother-in-law, and those men crawled around under the subfloor for weeks. "I tell you," the plumber would say to them time and again when he came up for air, "this old house will be here after we're all dead and gone." In the fume-filled den, stripping back this house's past to find its future, Forrest and Sue thought the plumber might well have a point.

Until they got the den done, there were few places of real refuge. Their bedroom—the big one upstairs, with the cedar closet—wasn't comfortable in any way. They hated the hot gold walls and red carpet left from the Grimes era, but that was just the start of it. In the summer, the room was too hot; in the winter, it was freezing. "The windows fit so poorly," Sue says, "that at night we had to pin the curtains down to keep them from billowing."

The only place they could go to hide from their troubles was the front porch. They bought a swing, and Forrest hung it on the south end of the porch, just where it begins to jut east around the house. It was an unexpectedly private place—hidden, high on that hill, by the west corner of the porch, and by the immense shadow of the tulip poplar tree just to the west. The porch swing became a favorite spot, a haven more rewarding than the den would ever be.

A few months after the Wolfes moved to 501 Holly, the singer Jimmy Buffett came out with his hit song "Margaritaville." That's what Forrest and Sue began calling their cocktail hours, which dragged on long after the sun had set. Surrounded by their cats and relaxed by the drinks, they would swing on the porch for hours. When the moon on the trees made the shadows just right, Forrest would tease Sue that he could see the faces of a man and a woman in the brick columns of the house. "Watch 'em, Sue!" he would say, spooking her. And then they would swing awhile more, giggling like children in the dark.

If you're the type who'll fool yourself into thinking you have a life when you don't, a house will all too gladly be a partner in your self-deception.

When I lived on Chicago's North Shore, my then wife and I spent a solid year working on our old house. I painstakingly stripped sixty years' worth of paint off a walnut staircase and mantel. We supervised the replastering and painting of entire walls and ceilings. I sanded and refinished the floor of the front porch. We shopped for and ordered wallpaper and expensive Berber carpeting. We bought new furniture—very, *very* costly pieces. We bought antique Japanese prints and had them framed to museum specifications. We planned out a room at a time and checked the items off our list—beds, lamps, bedspreads, miniblinds. One night, after our own stint in Margaritaville, I went to the basement and came back with a crowbar, which I used to rip up layers of kitchen linoleum. As I recall, the strata ran six deep. At the bottom was hardwood, a combination of oak and cherry, which we had bleached and sealed.

On the surface, it *seemed* like a life. It was certainly full-time. But it wasn't a life at all. Instead, it was an escape from life.

For close to nine months, no one but my wife and I and the various workmen walked through the door of our house. We didn't see our few friends—the house wasn't *ready*—and I invited none of my colleagues from work. But one of these days, I told myself, we would have all those couples over for an elegant dinner, and boy, weren't they going to be impressed. First, though, there was that upstairs bedroom that needed papering.

In Witold Rybczynski's book *Home: A Short History of an Idea,* he traces the way people have lived in houses since the Middle Ages. He shows that, slowly and over a long period of time, *home*—as opposed to the relatively cold concept of *house*—has come to be equated with the word *comfort. Comfort* is a word whose definition certainly requires an entire book. Its meaning can be as simple as having everything you need close at hand—in my daydreams of Aunt May's house, there's always that image of me reading a book in an easy chair, with the afternoon sun streaming through the ceiling-high windows, filtered by the sheers. But comfort can also mean something as complex as being at home in your own skin. You can decorate and decorate and *decorate* a house and yet never achieve that.

We're all works in progress, if we're continuing to live and grow. Our houses are works in progress, too. Yet some people postpone life to devote themselves to their houses. They spend all their time decorating and redecorating and fixing and fussing, as if fidgeting on a grand scale. Have you ever received a newspaper or magazine in which the printing is slightly out of register? People who work on their houses to the exclusion of everything else remind me of that: They keep tinkering with the second image in the vain hope that it'll blend with the first, giving them that feeling of wholeness, completeness—comfort.

I wasn't happy with my life during that period in Chicago, so I spent all my time working on my house. I invited nobody in. I can just imagine what old Dr. Jung would say about that. A house can be a refuge in ways we don't even realize. Home *is* where the heart is. But as the Eagles used to say, every form of refuge has its price.

I'm not saying the Wolfes wanted to hide from life during their time at 501 Holly. The house needed the work, and it is certainly the better for their having lived here. But the regimen they set for themselves was all-consuming. Even if the intent wasn't there, the effect was the same. Forrest woke up on Saturday mornings and Sue's lists were his marching orders. First, he had to tend to the lawn—had to push that infernal mower up what he had labeled "Heart Attack Hill." After that, he came back inside, only to find that no job on the list was simple or freestanding. It was like with Uncle Remus's Tar Baby—every time Forrest poked at one problem, he ended up mired in another. Once, hooking up a new washing machine, he discovered that the floor in the back porch area was rotten. "I actually saw a live termite," he says. They called Adams and had the house checked and sprayed. But no matter—the new washing machine now couldn't be installed until Forrest built a new floor to set it on.

It was the same with the upstairs bath. Forrest and Sue especially wanted to save the old white shower tiles that had languished for decades beneath increasing layers of paint. The tiles had once been beautiful, back in 1926 when Charlie Armour had built the upstairs addition, but now they were eaten up with mold. Still, Sue tried to clean them—only to find that the shower pan was rusted out and would have to be replaced. To get to the pan, the workmen had to tear out the tiles. Forrest and Sue replaced the white tiles with a soft but undistinguished yellow, then went on to the next job.

That turned out to be near at hand. While working in the shower, they discovered that the three windows in the upstairs bathroom were completely rotten. Forrest had never installed windows, but he decided to give it a try. He and Sue splurged on Pella, instead of settling for a cheap brand. "We dreamed of putting Pella windows in," says Sue. *Dreamed of Pella windows*—how profoundly sad, I sometimes think. Often I catch myself daydreaming about laying black-and-white tile on the kitchen floor, or of installing central air downstairs. A house can steal your youth if you don't watch out. Some days I have to remind myself that I still lust for a Porsche.

For Forrest and Sue, there were times when Margaritaville blended so with what passed for real life that it was hard to tell where one ended and the other began. Forrest repapered the hall—the small room with seven doorways—while he was drinking Jack Daniel's:

FORREST: You talk about something that's hard to paper . . .
SUE: There's not *one* complete wall . . .
FORREST: When I papered this, Sue was sick . . .
SUE: Lying on the couch . . .
FORREST: And I was inebriated. I wasn't normal when I did this. If I'd been normal, it probably would've turned out pretty. . . .

When I try to put myself in the Wolfes' shoes, I inevitably think of that famous stress chart from the seventies, the one that applied a numerical value to various life events—divorce, death in the family, a job change, a change in financial situation. When you added them up, you had an indication of your stress level.

Forrest and Sue's were probably at the top of the chart during their time on Holly Street. Besides the constant grind of the house and the major expense involved, each of the Wolfes changed jobs twice in the four years they lived here. As Medicare and Medicaid boomed in the mid-seventies, Forrest found himself well positioned to take advantage of the growth. In his job as state administrator for Medicaid, he had made valuable contacts. One was with a California company called Optimum Systems, Inc., or OSI, which had the contract with Arkansas Blue Cross and Blue Shield for Medicare software. Forrest left the state to go with OSI, working in the Blue Cross building downtown. After a while, Blue Cross itself, which had contracts with Medicaid for both drug and physician claims, made him a better offer. Forrest joined Blue Cross as manager for the drug-claims division.

Even though Sue still liked teaching, she wanted to go into business for herself. A woman she knew was opening a gift shop in an old house in Hillcrest, and Sue thought that might be just the opportunity she'd been looking for. It wasn't. She joined the other woman as a partner, but after six months it was obvious that they weren't compatible. Besides, there wasn't enough volume to support two people out of that little shop, which added to the conflicts. Sue left and went into sales for the Du Pont Corporation.

So much change put great pressure on the two of them, and when they turned to their usual refuge—their home—it failed to provide comfort. On the downstairs woodwork and walls, they counted some ten layers of paint. The house was a living photograph album. The colors of times past were frozen moments for them to study. Then they would peel them away and move on.

With their own lives on hold, Forrest and Sue found themselves taking refuge in their *neighbors'* lives. They didn't say that, but that's my interpretation. When the Wolfes first told me about their time in this house, the neighbors across the street figured prominently in their story. It makes sense, of course: In our hearts, we all know that the national pastime isn't baseball; it's watching and speculating about our neighbors. That's especially true when we're trying to avoid the turmoil within our own walls.

Besides, Forrest and Sue didn't have just *any* neighbors. They had the Treadways.

I first heard about the Treadways approximately half a day after I moved here six years ago. Since I've been working on this book, numerous people have raised the Treadway name. The presence of this unique couple, who owned the bungalow directly across Holly Street from 1968 to 1978, obviously enriched the experience of living at 501 Holly for the Grimeses, the Kramers, and the Wolfes. Of all of them, though, Forrest and Sue seem to have been the closest to the legendary couple.

The Treadways' names were Bill and Jimmie. He owned an electric-supply company, and she ran a beauty college. But that wasn't what made them such compelling neighbors. What did it was their strange obsession. Forrest and Sue are practically uncontainable on the subject:

SUE: We could tell you stories about them *all . . . day . . . long . . .*

FORREST: They were fire freaks. They had an antique fire truck in the front yard. They also had matching fire outfits. And any fire—they had seventeen or eighteen scanners in their house, all of them going—any fire in town, at any time, you could look over there and here they came, going to the fire. He was considered some kind of expert, and he could get in with the firemen.

SUE: They had *one million* fire things in their house. Lamps were made out of fire extinguishers. They had all kinds of little fire hydrants sitting around—every kind of thing you could imagine. They collected old Cadillacs, too—fire-engine red. *Everything* had to be red. We loved taking care of their house. We'd take care of the cats and dogs whenever, and the *minute* they left we'd get that key and we'd go through that house. . . .

FORREST: The funniest thing I've ever known, they left here and built a big house over in the Heights. They were very wealthy people. And they had a dog they loved, so they built a doghouse out there in the backyard. They heated it. And it *caught fire!*

One Saturday morning, Sue noticed that something was wrong with Forrest. He was glum. She detected signs of crankiness. "What's the matter?" Sue said, glancing at her schedule to make sure they weren't falling behind.

"Those lists," Forrest said. "I hate those damned lists." He said it with such pent-up conviction that she knew another change was headed her way.

"We had to come to an understanding," Sue says. The understanding was that they would take back their life.

Their final year here was the best. By that time, they had finished most of the messy work and could focus on the enjoyable task of decorating. Having taken the upholstery class, they began keeping an eye out for old pieces of furniture they could pick up for practically nothing. One such piece was a French Provincial sofa, which they covered in a chocolate brown suede trimmed out in white. It was pure seventies—and they decorated the entire living and dining rooms around it.

The walls became a rich chocolaty brown, with the wood trim painted a dazzling white. The floors, which Forrest's dad had rewoven after removing the furnaces, had also been refinished a dark brown. "Mediterranean," says Sue. "That was in then." In photos from the time, the living and dining areas look like rooms from a gingerbread house. Forrest and Sue's dining table was glass and chrome, and it stood on an imitation Oriental rug. Bentwood chairs, whose seats had been upholstered in a pale plaid in tones of tan and white, completed the tableau. There was a shag rug in the conversation area of the living room. Above the mantel, Sue hung a beveled mirror on the bias, the way a decorator would've done.

They painted the den a rich blue and the solarium a soft yellow-green, almost a chartreuse. Sue took great delight in wallpapering the closet in that front room, knowing full well that such radical creativity would baffle her friends. When the women of Sue's book club first came to 501 Holly for a meeting, they were indeed amazed. "They had no idea how people lived in houses like this,"

Sue says. "They were used to the suburban three-bedroom ranch-style, with the fireplace in the corner and all the paneling around. *We* were the wild ones." When the other women went home to their houses with hollow doors, Sue sat back and smiled.

Toward the end, they did more porch sitting and felt less guilt about it—even on Saturdays, which had once been ruled by the tyranny of Sue's lists. On one such day, Forrest and Sue were swinging on the porch, watching a violent thunderstorm. It was the middle of the afternoon. The rain was coming down in sheets, and the thunder was crashing as though the gods were making a point. Lightning slashed the sky. Suddenly, there was a tremendous noise, the front yard turned white, and the tulip poplar tree split right down the middle.

SUE: You could see where the lightning went. It dug a ditch up and down . . .

FORREST: It went under the house, went into the electricity, came up in the den and ruined my stereo. It was very frightening. . . .

The first time I spoke with Ed Kramer, I told him the Wolfes had *had* to cut down the tulip poplar tree. It didn't seem to register. Then when I met him and he was railing about what kinds of people would level a tree like that, I explained it to him again. This time he seemed to understand—and even to feel better.

I didn't tell him everything, though. I just couldn't bring myself to mention that, because the tree was on the arboreal equivalent of the Historical Register, the Wolfes got to take a huge tax write-off that year.

*Myke and Sue Landers in St. Louis in November 1979—the night they announced to family and friends that they were moving to Little Rock to seek their fortune.*

*Chapter Twelve*

# Landers

*May 1980* ❧ *March 1981*

T he 1980s, as we know them, actually began at the end of the previous decade. I remember assigning a magazine article in early 1979 about the new trend in condominiums. The writer turned in a prescient piece, perfectly capturing the fever of the go-go market in which buyers were paying ever-higher prices to own a part of— well, a part of whatever condominiums were. The condo craze didn't seem to be about home; it was about money. I remember our illustration showed a skyscraper puffing up like a giant balloon, just waiting for the inevitable pinprick.

That article reflected the Chicago influence on me—my image of home had always been a single-family house, and I was fascinated by this other way of living. As it turned out, though, the writer's words had resonance beyond the metropolitan centers. The fever that had infected urban condo buyers was also boiling up in home seekers across the country. I guess it was a confluence of factors. The so-called sixties generation had reached their mid-thirties; they had jobs and money and fancy cars, and the next puzzle piece in their self-image was a place of their own. Plus, the steady climb in interest rates sparked some kind of wild landgrab spirit in them—*get in before the rates rise.* I've often wondered what the social fallout from that time has been. I mean in terms of expectations, fears, and disappointments. For a lot of people, this was their first house-buying experience.

The market was moving so fast in the late seventies and early eighties that strange, mutant chains were created. People were making deals to get into houses any way they could, and sellers were carrying notes for buyers. That meant that when time came for the buyers to move, the former sellers were still involved—sometimes many years later—in the process.

To me, it's always intriguing to step back and observe how the stars fell into place, or didn't. One second later on this end, a moment earlier on that end—it's a meditation on chance, fate, the bittersweet mystery of what might have been, especially after the rhythm of life, so steady in the Armour and Murphree years, had become a staccato beat.

For example, one day, with no discussion beforehand, Sue Wolfe simply got into her car and drove off to look at other houses. Later, when she told Forrest about it, he realized he was ready. He had a no-nonsense criterion for their next house: "I wanted a place," he says, "where I could vacuum the entire house without unplugging the vacuum."

The Wolfes were beneficiaries of the real estate fever. In just four years, the market had changed to the point that they could ask double what they had paid for their house. They had invested plenty in it, of course, but that wasn't the determining factor. Markets speak louder than sweat and tears. Forrest and Sue had rolled up their sleeves in the Bicentennial spirit of renewal; now, in the prevailing mood of commerce, they were due a payday.

And the stars presented Myron Landers, a man who never would've bought this house had it not been for a peculiar series of events that led to this moment.

Myron goes by the name of Myke, with a *y*. By the time Myke found his way to Little Rock, in the waning months of 1979, he was a thirty-year-old man who had labored in his wife's family scrap business in St. Louis for seven years. Now, finally, he was striking out on his own. He and two partners had selected Little Rock as the place to launch their recycling company. They were pros; they had done their homework. On paper, everything looked great. No wonder Myke was excited. Arriving in town a couple of months before his wife and two young daughters, he shared an apartment in west Little Rock with one of the partners and buried himself in the exhilarating details of creating something from scratch. In his head, he harbored the visions that every young entrepreneur has—of achieving independence, of gaining respect, of being his own man.

But when his wife, Sue, came down for the whirlwind weekend home search, she brought along visions of her own. It's possible that her visions were more complicated than Myke's, or at least more embellished—looping forward and back, outward and inward, from childhood to adulthood, from fantasy to fact. In any case, I think it's safe to say that his visions were influenced more by hers than the other way around.

Sue says this house *called* her. The way she says it brings to mind images from the realm of myth—*a ship on a journey, choppy waters, a young woman at the bow, hair trailing in the wind, gown flowing, her hand shielding her eyes as she scans the horizon for her destiny. Then, from the porch at 501 Holly, the siren song.*

The Landerses bought the house from the Wolfes for $72,500. Sue Wolfe remembers they seemed in a rush, and that they got in just as interest rates were edging into double digits. They took a mortgage with Savers Federal Savings & Loan. But they were still a little short, so Forrest and Sue agreed to a bit of creative financing, carrying a note for a second mortgage. That in turn left the Wolfes a little short, so the people whose house they were buying also had to carry a note for *them*.

It wasn't as clean as everybody would've liked, but that was the new way. You had to join the chain if you wanted to break free.

There is a photograph, as there almost always is. Once again, those who know the subjects look at this frozen moment and invest it with whatever truth they wanted it to capture. To Myke and Sue, born three months apart in the same Jewish hospital, this is a picture of the two of them celebrating their joint thirtieth birthday with a cake made to look like a football field. The month is November, the year 1979. It's also the night they announced to their family and friends that they were leaving St. Louis to seek their fortune in Little Rock.

I took an oil-painting course a few years ago, the first such course I'd taken since high school. The instructor talked about how most of us don't really see things. We look, and we see what we expect to see. But we don't see the nuances, the interactions, the gradations. I've tried to train myself to see better. Looking now at this photograph of Myke and Sue, I can't say for certain what I would see if I didn't already know their story. But where Sue, even today, sees a happy moment, I see a heavyset man and a thin woman on either side of a table, a man in jeans and western shirt and a woman in disco clothes, and a cake in the shape of a contest.

Myke would leave for Little Rock soon after this photograph was taken, and Sue would follow five months later. Now, after fifteen years and all they've been through, when they each sit down to tell the story of what they thought they were doing in Little Rock, the result is two stories, two agendas. It's hard to know exactly which feelings existed then and which have been clarified by the filter of time. But what's obvious is that these stories, intersecting at points and then veering this way and that in wildly different directions, form a diagram of a marriage. Maybe houses, like airports and office buildings, should be rigged with an X ray at the door, with a glowing monitor that tracks the shape and weight of the baggage being carried over the threshold.

For Sue, her brief time at 501 Holly—ten months—was a turning point in her life. Even as she was living it, she had an inkling that it might be. The problem was, she could feel her plan moving in the wrong direction. Sue fully admits she married a concept, not a man. I suppose it's not unusual for a young woman to look for a husband who reminds her of her father; it does seem rare, however, to recognize that fact so clearly and still push ahead with such resolve. Sue's dad always said he'd gone about as far as a poor Jewish boy could go. He'd been raised in a rural area outside St. Louis. Trained as a lawyer, he'd become an assistant prosecuting attorney in his early days. But at the time he reminisced to his five children about his upbringing, he was a wealthy, successful businessman, having gone to work for his father-in-law in the scrap-paper industry. The company had prospered, becoming a multimillion-dollar international firm. Now Sue's dad was a leader in the community, the first Jewish president of the city's athletic club. He was popular, a man's man. "He was a great gin rummy player, a great golfer," Sue recalls. "He had all the right attributes."

Sue and Myke had met at the University of Missouri in Columbia and had started courting after her sophomore year. Myke's background was totally different from hers. He was adopted. His folks had wanted him to become a doctor, but then a high school biology teacher had told him—wrongly—that he didn't have the aptitude for science. "Then you can be a lawyer," his parents said. When Sue met him, that's what Myke planned to be.

Sue felt herself at odds with some of her female classmates in the late sixties. Major changes were coming, they all said. They had choices now. But Sue's choice was what it had always been: "One of my driving forces, being the middle child, was, I wanted attention," she says. "I wanted affection. My older brother and sister had moved away and were living kind of hippie lifestyles, so I decided, if I was *normal*—if I stayed in St. Louis, married to a *normal* guy, having children gradually . . . As a freshman in college, I started doing all these things that got me the attention and affection I had been craving, so I went on this pattern." Her internal plan called for her to be engaged by her senior year, then to get married right after school, then maybe work for a few years before settling down and becoming, essentially, her mother. That meant her husband had to be her dad. Myke looked like a good candidate to fit the dream.

She graduated, they got married, and she began working as a nurse. She figured three years. Meanwhile, Myke, a year behind her, was getting ready for law school. He took the boards, made his applications. Sue made Myke her pet project. "I saw him as a diamond in the rough, and I was the rescuer," she says. "I spent a lot of energy trying to change him. He was kind of on the chunky side, and I came from a skinny family. I spent a *lot* of energy." She liked dancing—disco especially. "That outfit I'm wearing in the photograph, it's a Danskin leotard with a matching skirt. It was really hot. I had these wild three-inch burgundy heels with gold." Myke was less interested in dancing, but he tried.

One Sunday, after a weekend trip home to St. Louis, he told her that her father had mentioned his joining the family business. It was an idea he obviously liked. When Sue asked about law school, Myke said he was having doubts about it. He wasn't sure the law was for him.

Sue was enjoying her nursing even more than she'd expected, and Myke's going home to work in St. Louis meant she would have to give that up. But the idea of Myke's joining the family business had its appeal. Sue decided the move would work for her—even though today she remembers a tiny voice inside her head: Something doesn't feel right. Her mother, of course, was thrilled with the news.

Myke worked for Sue's father for most of the seventies. They started a family. Sue gave birth to two daughters, Tracy, in 1975, and Michelle, in 1977. She found motherhood incredibly hard—

overwhelming, in fact. That brought her new respect for her mother's accomplishments. "I was amazed that any woman could be a mother and still function and keep her sanity," Sue says. The difficulties were offset by the fact that Myke and Sue were "on the upward socioeconomic momentum." They'd even built a house.

When Myke began complaining about his job, Sue wasn't shocked. All her life, she'd heard her father grousing about butting heads with his brother-in-law. That's the nature of a family business. But Myke wanted to leave. Through business, he'd met a man in New York. I'll call him Tom. Myke and Tom wanted to start their own recycling company. "Well, gee, if you're unhappy . . ." said Sue.

Myke began working up a business plan. He and Sue traveled to New York several times to get to know Tom and his wife. Myke and Tom had considered a handful of cities and their criteria pointed to Little Rock. There was another man there who would become a partner. The two couples visited, and Sue liked what they saw. She'd even begun to warm to the idea of going into business. "For me, there was this underlying thing," she says. "Not only did I want to have affection from my parents but I also wondered if maybe I could do better than they had. This was an opportunity for us to do better. I remember telling a friend, 'We're going to make a lot of money.'"

Which brings us, inexorably, back to the photograph of the happy couple and the gridiron cake. Everyone was shocked that night when they dropped the bomb about their new venture. Sue has always kept a diary, in which she outlines her dreams and names her fantasies. After her announcement that night, when she'd met her mother's eye, this is what she entered in her book: "I felt like I had stabbed my mother in the heart."

Myke knew exactly what kind of man Sue wanted. "I tried to be like her father," he says. "But then, as I got older, I realized you can't be somebody else. You have to be yourself."

As himself, Myke Landers was a far cry from Sue's dad. Despite his engaging laugh, he's introverted, not particularly social. He was a marketing and history major in college, but in real life he found that he didn't like to sell. He's an intellectual. He says he reads five hundred pages a week—biographies, spy novels, military history. Myke loves military history. One of his great pleasures is watching war movies on TV. He even attends World War II reunions to talk with the old warriors firsthand. "I love the army," Myke says.

He joined the Army Reserves in the mid-sixties as an E-1—buck private. Twenty years later, he retired with the rank of major. In Little Rock, he commanded a smoke-generating company, which is part of the Chemical Corps. In battle, smoke companies use diesel fuel to generate a smoke screen for advancing armor and infantry units. For Myke, the army provided things you didn't get in, say, a family business. "I like a disciplined environment," he says. "You have structure. You know what you're going to do, and what everybody else is going to do." The part he liked least was the internal politics, just as in the business world. In St. Louis, the politics drained him. "If I said, 'It ought to be *this* way,' or 'Why don't you give me credit,' they'd say, 'Be quiet so you don't upset so-and-so.' And I would say, 'Yes, but so-and-so isn't pulling his weight, and I am.' 'Yes,' they would say, 'but it'll all come out in the wash.' After awhile, you get tired of waiting for the wash."

It wasn't like that in the military. It was clean. You had rank, privilege, camaraderie, perks. You had the respect your position and performance deserved. "For me," Myke says, "the military is a comfort zone."

Sue's dad retired as a major, too. She grew up loving to hear him tell his war stories. Maybe if they'd simply skipped Little Rock and gone into the army, things wouldn't have turned out the way they did.

\* \* \*

Myke's partner Tom and his wife rented a place, and Tom suggested the Landerses do likewise. But Myke felt that Sue needed a house of her own. Having grown up in a small ranch-style tract house, Myke wasn't an old-house guy himself. "I've always had reservations about older homes," he says. "You don't know what you're getting. The one guarantee is that it's going to take time and money to make it livable." But at this point, he was still trying to live Sue's dream, even as he was trying to break away from it. He wanted her to feel at home, and the house her parents lived in was big and rambling and old.

From Sue's diary, written, as a catch-up, in July 1980:

> *In May, I picked out a big older home in Little Rock in an area called Hillcrest. I saw at least 20 homes in one day. We decided on a large older home done in dramatic colors. It needs a lot of work. My only reservation is it is on a busy street on one side.*
>
> *We bought it peeling paint and all.*

Myke doesn't remember much about that first summer—that *only* summer—sixteen years ago. He was too busy at work. The recycling business was located in a warehouse district on the edge of downtown Little Rock, close to where Charlie Armour's Nu Grape plant had stood six decades before. Myke recalls that one of his daughters played with some children on the corner of Holly and Woodlawn, and that those people invited them all to the country club that Fourth of July to see the fireworks. He remembers pouring concrete to anchor the green jungle gym/swing set they'd brought from their house in St. Louis. He remembers mowing the lawn. He remembers occasionally sitting on the front porch, especially that fall, when things started to unravel. Otherwise, 501 Holly hardly exists for him.

Sue, thanks to her diary, can summon more:

*I was so supersexed the summer of 1979. This year, I have been dead. I have had so few fantasies. I have been depressed this summer of 1980. More on that later.*

Sue's diary is, by her admission, a candid record of a young woman's battle against low self-esteem. She needed to be seen as pretty, as desirable. She needed for her internal plans to be working in the real world. It seems that when she felt comfortable with herself, her fantasy life was full and vibrant; when her real life was out of kilter, that's the only thing she was left with.

Her diary entries for the summer of 1980 mostly concerned the events of the spring. That fall, she would spell out the extent to which her plans had gone off track so soon. In the meantime, from the outside looking in, there were few hints that all wasn't well at 501 Holly.

One of the reasons this house had appealed to Sue was that it was so perfectly laid out for entertaining. She had planned a lot of parties in St. Louis. Now she loved how her antique dining room furniture looked against the chocolate brown walls. And yet, the only parties she had here were for the children. She and Myke didn't know many people, and besides, Myke was never at home anyway. When he was, he was upstairs in his study or watching late-night war movies on TV. Sue occupied her time working with her plants. She filled the small green front room with ferns and scheffleras and called it the "plant room." She hung her Indian prints on the blue walls in the den, and she liked walking by and catching a glimpse of how finished that room looked, with the curtains, the pictures, the couch she'd covered in blue denim. The kids, especially, spent a lot of time in that room watching TV. Children from the neighborhood were in and out. One of the girls' greatest thrills was to get their pillows and ride them down the steep stairs into a laughing pile at the bottom.

There were other projects Sue eventually wanted to tackle—the kitchen needed to have all that old paneling ripped off—but she wasn't in any hurry. "I thought we were going to live in this house forever," she says. That was at the beginning of the summer.

She was friendly, outgoing. She was on speaking terms with the Chapins, an older couple who lived catty-cornered across the street. Ruth Chapin had been Ruth Ream, and she had played with Carolee Armour as a girl in the twenties. The Chapins told Sue stories about the house—how, years before, the garage had been consumed by termites; how Forrest Wolfe had put in those great Pella windows.

Not all the neighbors were as approachable. Shortly after she arrived in Little Rock, Sue thought she detected anti-Semitism from a woman who lived in the house behind 501 Holly. "I sensed something different, a kind of coolness," she says. The Landerses weren't what you would call Orthodox—in St. Louis, the girls had had Christmas trees and Easter bunnies. Now, though, they were the only Jewish family in the neighborhood. When fall came, Tracy was the only Jewish child at school. It was an awakening for Sue. "I felt a kind of commitment. Whenever I had the opportunity to volunteer, to be the mother in charge, if there was a chance to present some aspect of Judaism—which I knew very little about—I would try to work it in." Tracy and Michelle remember 1980 mainly as the year they stopped getting to have a Christmas tree.

They were too young, of course, to know how much was actually happening. In September, Sue needed a new volume for her diary entries. She found exactly what she was looking for at a store on Kavanaugh Street. Late at night, she would sit alone in the den and make her notations. Sometimes, as in this passage, she used her diary as a way of focusing the increasing bitterness that was bubbling up in her.

From Sue's diary, September 6, 1980:

*Dear Diary,*

*This book is very special. I have bought it at a time when money does not come easily. Upon seeing this book with lovely cover and light pages, I was seized by the desire I must have it, and I deserve it, for times have been difficult.*

*Myke has been drawing no income. He has been stabbed in the back by so-called best friend [Tom]. Myke and I have been through much anger and depression in the last two months. . . . Supposedly [Tom] is stabbing Myke to get him out of the company for whatever greedy reasons he may have. The whole thing has been heartbreaking. Myke spent so many hours, months setting this up. I have gone through a period of self-pity. I have seen my dreams shattered at least temporarily. We really extended ourselves. We owe so much money in house loans and car loans. I am working part-time. It is not enough to meet the bills.*

Sue cashed in some stocks. She began teaching private aerobics classes, as well as signing up for temporary work as a nurse. Eventually, she found a full-time job at the VA Hospital in North Little Rock. She worked in the Chronic Organic Brain Syndrome Unit. She joined a women's soccer team, then quit when the coach didn't let her play. She took clog dancing.

From Sue's diary, September 8, 1980:

*Poor Myke suffers daily. The children are jewels of light.*

She began working the night shift at the hospital. It depressed her to take care of the old people, and then she felt like a zombie during the day. But on those long nights away from her family, she had time to think about her dreams, her marriage, and herself. When good news finally came, she reflected on that.

From Sue's diary, September 30, 1980:

> *A ray of hope and joy. Myke has a job offer selling insur-*
> *ance. It sounds fairly good. It will bring in more income*
> *than I make now. . . .*
>
> *I have seen a bit more of the kids. They are getting used*
> *to Daddy caring for them. I do like the excuse of not doing*
> *the daily work of bathing and feeding them. . . . I guess this*
> *experience has taught us to work together. Also I need to take*
> *charge of my life . . .*

In early October, they went to a football game at the University of Missouri. After the game, they planned to spend the weekend at Sue's family farm a couple of hours outside St. Louis. It was a home to her, the place where she had spent so many happy times as a child.

From Sue's diary:

> *I'm going to plant my yellow tulip bulbs there. I don't*
> *want to plant them in Little Rock. I probably won't be here*
> *next spring to see them.*

Myke says he and his business partners had philosophical differences. Eventually, they offered to buy him out, and he accepted. He used his time that fall to organize a door-to-door campaign for Ronald Reagan. He also worked to defeat Bill Clinton, who was in an uphill battle for reelection as governor of Arkansas. During the few months Myke was with the recycling company, he'd been in meetings attended by attorney Hillary Clinton, and he had taken an intense dislike to her. "We were there as part of opposing interests," he says. "Even sitting over on the side, she was radiating, I am the governor's wife, and this is what I'd really like to see happen. I took great delight in seeing Clinton lose that election."

Reagan's success brought Myke an opportunity, he says. "Under Nixon, our chemical capability had gone to pot. Nixon, of course, was goaded into that by the liberals—he had his back against the wall because of Watergate. So when Reagan came in, he said, We've got to fix this pretty fast. So they activated lots of chemical officers."

Myke recalls that the army "started breathing down my neck in October. Everybody could see that Reagan was coming." At one Reserve meeting, a man approached him and several other chemical captains and told them the army was going to start calling them up. The man said that if they would volunteer, they would at least get to choose their first assignment.

There's nothing in Sue's diary about that, but Sue doesn't believe it happened that way. "I don't recall any pressure from the army," she says. "I recall that he was looking for employment, and this was an opportunity for him." Myke admits that the army, his comfort zone, came back into his life at a time when he certainly needed comforting. He decided to go in for a three-year tour of duty.

So as the air turned crisp and the leaves began to fall, Myke began the process of getting himself back in shape. Countless times a day he would run up Holly Street toward Woodlawn—up the hill, up the hill, as they say in the army—then come down and do it all over again. It was hard work, shedding all he'd been carrying. But he was a happy man. Home was on the horizon.

Meanwhile, next door, John and Linda Burnett noticed something they thought was very odd. They remember seeing Sue Landers out in her driveway a lot that fall, standing alone near the bay window with a trowel in her hand and a tub of strange red mortar at her feet. She spent hours there, the dead leaves blowing around her, as she knifed that bizarre filling into the cracks in her house.

From Sue's diary, October 7, 1980:

> *This week I tuck-pointed for the first time. . . . There is*
> *so much to do, but I'm getting the hang of it. It does me proud*

*to teach myself a new skill. I do enjoy being outdoors. I'm still not tired of raking up leaves. There are many here.*

*Myke wants to put this house on the market. I am sad to do that: I do like this house. I did, then I didn't. Now that we will lose it (sell it), of course I've become more attached to it. Everything becomes dear to me when I have to leave it behind.*

And so we come, at last, to the roller-skating transvestite hippies. It strikes me as a particularly cruel joke that their brief fling here took place during the ownership of Sue and Myke Landers. Sue, who always wanted to be so "normal."

Myke left for Fort McClellan, in Anniston, Alabama, in early February 1981. Sue and the girls packed up and followed at the end of March. They put the house on the market and continued to make payments, but they wanted to sell as fast as possible. No one involved admits renting out the house, but obviously someone did. My guess is that it was the Realtor, Janet Jones. Janet remembers nothing about a rental and says she has no paperwork on it. But she admits it sometimes happens that a Realtor will rent out a sale house, following the conventional wisdom that prospective buyers can visualize *home* more easily in a house that has people living in it. In theory, the conventional wisdom holds true. I'll never forget the lightning-bolt effect of that one red lipstick print the day I first saw this house.

By all accounts, there were plenty of lipstick prints around 501 Holly during the few months of its rental.

I have to confess, right here, that I don't know the names of the roller-skating transvestite hippies. Owners' lives are splayed open like bodies on an operating table, but the renters still glide—giddily, in my mind—down shadowy corridors. I feel them taunting me. I suppose I should be impressed that this house hasn't given up all its secrets so readily.

Their time here was just four months, from April through July 1981. If you lived in the neighborhood, you noticed the difference—especially late at night. John Burnett recalls the first time he heard the red car. Fifteen years ago, throbbing automobile stereos weren't as pervasive a fact of life as they are today. Most people listened to their radios or their cassette decks without feeling the need to share their pleasure with the world. Today, music lovers are more thoughtful.

John was sleeping. Suddenly, his bedroom was invaded by a noise that sounded as if all the drummers in all the rock bands in all the world had been captured inside a metal container and were trying to beat their way out. But they were pounding in unison, *boom-boomba-boom-boomba-boom*, keeping it going, steady, endless. John looked at the clock. It was 2:00 A.M. He went to the window. The car was a Firebird, and it was shaking. The driver, whom he couldn't see, was sitting there listening to a song at top volume on the car stereo. John couldn't hear the music, but the bass notes throbbed down through the metal and into the molecules of the spring night, pounding the bruised air into the bricks of John's foundation, from which the noise vibrated up the wall, passed through his headboard, and rattled his spine. This began to happen every night.

For a long time, I thought I had a suspect. Maribeth, the woman who cleans our house, told me she knew a man who said he'd once lived here. I'm going to call him Bob. And in fact I *did* call him. He said he had sublet from someone whose name he couldn't remember. Bob denied having ever roller-skated here, much less in a dress, but he described the inside of this house with enough accuracy that I wanted to meet with him. His spot was a water bed in the attic. He told me that another renter, a poet, had slept in a closet across the room—the very closet, I was guessing, where Beth and I now keep our supplies.

I made a date for Bob to come walk through the house with me. He stood me up. I called again, and again he stood me up. I called again. Each time, he was maddeningly blasé. Something had always come up at the last minute. I tried to get other names out of him, but he couldn't remember any. And then, just as I was ready to write him off, he would recall some juicy tidbit—a woman with the "Rainbow" name of May Apple, who didn't live at the house but grew opium poppies in planters here. I would make a date to see him, and he wouldn't show. This would go on for weeks at a time, and then I would get busy with some other aspect of the story and put Bob aside until later.

I placed a classified ad in the local paper, asking anybody who'd ever known *anyone* who lived at this address to contact me. The Grimeses' old paperboy responded. A woman called and said, yes, she had lost her husband while she lived in this house. I was on the line with another caller at the time, and when I phoned her back, I found the number she'd given me was that of the local police department. Another woman left a message on the answering machine: "Call Mary Ann at three-seven-two–HORE."

One afternoon, I heard from a man who said, "I know some things about that house. Weird things. *Supernatural* things." "Such as?" I asked. "My former girlfriend lived there for a while," he said, "and sometimes, even on hot days, you'd be walking through the living room and suddenly a gust of cold, cold air would hit you. It seemed to come up through the floor." The man promised to put me in touch with the old girlfriend, though there was some reason he couldn't do it at that precise moment. He was going to call me back. When he didn't, I called him. He wasn't at that number.

I could just hear the roller-skating transvestite hippies shrieking with bent delight.

From Sue's diary, Anniston, June 11, 1981, 1:30 A.M.:

*Still financial trouble looms. 2 houses vacant—the situation has to change. We can't go on like this one more month. We won't make it. I don't trust Myke with money matters at all. It's been almost disastrous for our marriage.*

On that summer night in 1992 when I'd had supper at the Burnetts' house, they said the person who had actually seen the roller-skating transvestite hippies *in action* was Judith Long, who lives at the head of the block, where Holly runs into Woodlawn. I called Judith and told her who I was and what I was doing. Then I asked her about the incident.

"No, it wasn't me," she said. "I think it was Toni Cullum." She gave me the number. The Cullums had lived on Woodlawn for years but had moved to a bigger house over in the Heights.

I called the Cullums. A woman answered. Yes, this was Toni Cullum. She had a refined Southern accent, soft like gardenias, and there was caution in her voice. When I mentioned roller-skating hippie males in dresses, there was utter silence on the other end of the line.

Finally, she said, "I think you must be mistaken." I apologized and got off the phone as fast as possible. It was dawning on me that the story that had spawned this entire book might be apocryphal.

But late that afternoon, Beth came upstairs bearing a small, heavy buff envelope. While she'd been on the phone in her office, a woman had stopped in front of our house and had run up and dropped this note in our mailbox. It was from Toni Cullum. She hadn't gotten my name, but she'd called her husband after she'd hung up with me. He remembered the story vividly. It *was* Toni. She'd obviously repressed the memory.

Toni is from Alabama. She's younger than I am, but she reminds me of Southern belles I knew in college—khaki shorts, Weejuns, madras. That's not the way she was dressed when I met her, but that's the *manner* in which she was dressed. I thought of her as very traditional—which made her encounter with the hippies all the more amusing.

"First of all," she told me, as we sat in her spacious sunroom, "they weren't hippies." She'd asked her husband, Skip, to come home at lunch to sit in on our meeting. It occurred to me that she considered it improper otherwise.

"Not hippies?" I said.

"No," she said, her eyebrows lifting slightly and her head moving ever so perceptibly closer to mine. "They were *transvestites*." I was thrilled. I'd been afraid that part was an embellishment. Like a sorority sister dishing dirt, I asked her to tell me the story.

"I'd made a cake to welcome the new neighbors," she said. "In this neighborhood, there were a lot of people who stayed home at that time. You kind of noticed when people came and went."

It happened at maybe three o'clock on a weekday afternoon. "I made the cake and took it down and rang the doorbell. And there I stood with my little cake in my hands. A person answered the door, and it was a very large—*person*. In women's clothing. With a blonde Barbra Streisand wig, and makeup, and long white fingernails. There was no furniture in the house, and they were all on roller skates, in fifties dresses. There was music. I think they were making a circle through the house. I can't remember how many there were, but there were *quite a few*."

The very thought still has the power to produce a blush.

"Everybody was a little uncomfortable. There was a lot of looking back and forth and that kind of thing. And there they were in shoe skates on those hardwood floors. I can't remember any of the conversation or anything, except that I just tried to stumble through my 'Welcome to the neighborhood'—you know—'We're so glad to have you.' And I handed the cake over and *left*."

She has a nervous laugh when flustered or embarrassed. I'd bet the Holly Street Streisand heard that very laugh as he shut the door.

"The thing that stands out most in my mind," said Toni, looking off into some twilight zone beyond the window, "are those big male hands, with those long white artificial nails. It was the last time I ever took a cake to a family."

At the end of June, the Landerses got word they had an offer on the house. That, as they say, was the good news. The bad news was that the offer was for only $67,500—five thousand dollars less than the Landerses had paid scarcely a year before. "I was looking for a house with a lot of possibilities," Jack Burney says today, "but that I could buy right." He means at the right price. At 501, the owners had moved; the house was being abused by renters. It looked like Jack had found the perfect place.

On the contract, his Realtor had made the following notation: "Offer is further conditional on buyer having the floors inspected within two weeks and approving the cost of repairs." Jack says the living room floor was buckled in the center. He shows me, putting his fingers together into a point the way Billie Murphree did when he had a tough decision to make.

Neither Jack nor his Realtor, his friend John Witherspoon, ever met any of the people who were living in the house. But they saw evidence of them. "The house was in horrible shape," Jack says. "The renters had kept dogs upstairs, and it smelled. They had let them go to the bathroom on the floor, and it was still up there." John Witherspoon tried to dissuade Jack from buying this house, but it was the wrong time—Jack wasn't rational. He was a man in love.

At the time he first saw 501 Holly, Jack Burney was a fun-loving forty-six-year-old entrepreneur who had been divorced for four years. He was close with his family. Every weekend, he saw his two young sons and one daughter, who lived in Little Rock with his ex-wife. He also made sure he stayed in touch with his elderly parents, who were very religious and didn't approve of his lifestyle. What they didn't know was that Jack had decided to get married again.

Which is why he needed a house. And why, instead of focusing on the problems with the place, he was seduced by its homey charms. You can fix floors. You can clean up dog doo. "I loved the porch," Jack says with a sheepish grin.

Jack's floor man told him that to take out the buckle would require going underneath the house and putting in new sills, then jacking up the floor. That didn't mean much to Jack—he knew what a windowsill was, but the rest of it was just so much blather. The floor man explained that sills are the horizontal pieces that hold up the vertical parts of a frame. It's all connected—when one piece settles, or rots, then whatever is resting on it will sink, too. If it doesn't sink uniformly, but only on one end, then the other end will kick up—causing, for example, a buckled floor to appear inside the living room. The now-buckled floors were, of course, the very hardwoods the Wolfes had refinished to such elegance just a couple of years before. Obviously, the weight of large roller-skating men in dresses had been enough to tip the floors into a full-scale Billie Murphree steeple.

Jack's man figured the cost of repairs, and that became part of the negotiation—part of the rationale for offering so much less than the Landerses had paid. Myke and Sue weren't in a position to argue. They were apart for much of that summer. Myke had been transferred to Fort Hood, Texas, and it had made financial sense for Sue and the girls to stay with her parents in St. Louis until Myke could get situated. For Sue, it was a summer of worry, and of reassessment. To occupy her time, she'd signed up for a modern-dance class at Washington University. It felt good to exercise, to move her body. The instructor kept telling the students to "use the music, use the music." They could move any way they wanted, act out any fantasies they chose. For Sue, it was a kind of salvation.

She and Myke said yes to Jack Burney. The closing was set for July 31.

The elusive Bob continued true to form. I would call, offer to buy him lunch, and he would accept. He would meet me, he'd say. I would know him by his red car, he told me. He'd already said that everybody who lived here liked their music loud. Now he revealed an interesting preference in car colors. I took it to be a sign.

But he never would show. I would call again, and we would have a long conversation on the phone, during which he would recall playing a lot of chess in this house, as well as doing his share of drugs. "Maybe I was having a bad acid stomach," he would say, explaining why he couldn't seem to remember this or that. But "this or that" amounted to amazingly huge gaps in his brain. He couldn't recall the name of anyone who had lived here with him. He vaguely remembered renting from someone who "worked at a head shop on Kavanaugh." A head shop in the early eighties? I suppose. But that was another problem: Bob felt certain he had lived here in the early *seventies*.

I felt certain he wasn't certain.

Not long ago, I was complaining about Bob to the woman who cuts what's left of my hair. Kelly Marlowe is her name, and we've been friends for years. Her shop is in Hillcrest, about four blocks from Holly Street. Kelly was trying to concentrate, and I was haranguing about this Bob. I wasn't even sure she was listening. Then I used his full name. "Bob?" she said, her comb and scissors dropping to her side. "*Bob?* I know Bob. I cut his hair!" Then she fell into a spasm of laughter—inspired, I assumed, by the wondrous smallness of the world we live in. She couldn't even speak. She was shaking her head and laughing, doubling over, holding her side. Then she managed to get a few words out: "He is," she said, "*the* most obnoxious person I've ever met in my life." I realized she was laughing because Bob was my only lead.

After she regained her composure, she told me an amazing thing—that Bob was due to get his hair cut three weeks from that day, at eleven o'clock. "Why don't you surprise him," she said, her eyes dancing.

I rescheduled a trip around it.

On the appointed day, at five to eleven, my phone rang. It was Kelly. *"He's here,"* she whispered. I gave them another five minutes. I wanted Bob sitting in the chair with that cloth snapped tightly around his neck, a pair of razor-sharp scissors pointed at his head.

I walked in carrying my briefcase. Kelly feigned surprise. "Hi, Kel," I said. "I'm on my way to an interview, but I can't remember what time I'm supposed to get my hair cut tomorrow." I nodded, by way of saying, Pardon me, at the guy in the chair. He looked pleasant enough. He was a big fellow, with a long, wet ponytail hanging down the back of the chair. I wondered how he would look in a Streisand wig. Most of him was covered. All I could see were his Birkenstock sandals (how had I known?), with no socks.

Kelly pretended to check the schedule; then we made small talk for a few seconds. Finally, Kelly said, "Oh, I'm sorry, do you guys know each other? Jim, this is Bob. Bob, Jim." She used our first and last names.

I acted astounded. My mouth dropped; my eyes got wide. Maybe I even slapped my forehead. I pointed to him with both hands. "Bob!" I said. "I can't *believe* this! You're the guy who's been standing me up for two years!" There was a slightly sick look on his face. He was nailed and he knew it. Kelly pretended to be absolutely amazed.

"Hey," I said, "as long as we're finally in the same place, do you mind if I ask you a few questions?" He said he didn't. I pulled out my tape recorder and turned it on. Then I handed him a picture of 501 Holly. "Is this the house you lived in?"

A huge hand (I glanced at the fingernails) came out from beneath the cloth. He took the photo and studied it. "Yeah," he said. "There aren't many porches that look like that one." After which, we made a headlong run toward our usual impasse—the man at the head shop, the water bed on the floor, sleeping atop the front porch at night. "I don't even roller-skate," he said, referring to the story I had told him on the phone.

"Ever wear a dress?" I asked, laughing.

"Not since last Halloween," he said.

He insisted that he was married and living out of state in the spring of 1981. "Well, how," I said, "do you reconcile the fact that you know this house, that you've identified it from a photograph, and yet you couldn't have lived here when you said you did?" He had no answer.

We left it like this: I would go right home (completely abandoning my story of being on the way to an interview), and when he finished his haircut, he would come over. "I'll just retrace my steps—just 'go home' like I used to," he said. I expected never to see him again. Kelly called, laughing, to say he had left, and I went to the door to watch for his red car.

In a minute or two, I saw him rounding the corner. This time, I really *couldn't* believe it. From the upstairs French doors I watched him slow down and look at the house—and then pass on by. He turned left at Lee and I lost him behind the trees. I had no idea how to read that.

A few minutes later, Beth came home with a trunkful of groceries. Just as I had nestled two heavy bags into my arms, the red car pulled up at the curb. Bob got out, and I guess he could see from my expression that I hadn't expected him. "It was *Ridgeway*," he said, referring to a street about six blocks down Lee Street. He ambled on up the sidewalk as I stood there on the porch—"holding the bag," was the phrase that came to mind. Two years I had chased this man. He explained that the house looked a lot like this one.

And then the funny thing was, he wouldn't leave. This was what Kelly had said about him. He was a big old goofy guy who invaded your space. Now he wanted to talk about books. He followed me in so I could put down the groceries. He commented on our art. He asked for my card. He wanted to give me all the time in the world, now that I couldn't think of him as a roller-skating transvestite. "I've got a joint in the car," he said.

Later that day, I drove down to Ridgeway. The house is bigger than ours, with natural stone columns. It has a porch, but that's about the only similarity. It doesn't even face in the same direction. I suppose it's possible, if you've had enough bad acid stomachs, to confuse the two.

But you'll pardon me if I cling to a scintilla of doubt.

After all but crossing Bob off my list, I had no choice but to turn to other sources. And I *have*, as it turns out, other sources. I once read that many transvestites actually aren't gay; but some are. We happen to be friends with several gay men, one of whom—call him Gene—particularly likes to lip-synch in drag. I haven't seen him do it, but I've seen him on video. He's a very funny man, in women's clothes or not. At parties, after a few drinks, he affects that laconic, just this side of bitchy tone gay men do so well, and he says things like, "Let's all get drunk and rearrange the furniture." Gene and another gay man—Rick—came to a Monet lunch Beth and I gave last year in the garden. It was on a Sunday afternoon—*all* Sunday afternoon. After several bottles of wine, Rick was mincing around that perilous sloping patio in one of the women guest's turquoise high heels. I remember wondering, if he broke a heel and hurt himself, would our umbrella policy pay?

After the party, Rick—still in heels—and Gene drove several of us around in Rick's recently deceased mother's big boat of a Cadillac. I suppose we might've been carrying a bottle of champagne or two. Every time we passed a male jogger, Rick and Gene would roll down the windows and shout in prissy unison, "Show us your dick! Show us your dick!"

Gene and Rick are now on the case of the roller-skating transvestites.

Early on the morning of July 31, 1981, Jack Burney received a call at home from the floor man. Jack figures it must've been around 8:00 A.M. The real estate closing wasn't scheduled until one o'clock that afternoon, but the man had had a cancellation on another job and asked Jack if he couldn't just get started at 501 Holly. Since nobody was in the house, Jack said fine, go ahead.

The Landerses weren't going to be at the closing. Myke was in the army at Fort Hood, and Sue was still in St. Louis. All their paperwork had been handled by their agent, Janet Jones. Sue had been instructed to call in at a certain time that afternoon to check the status of the deal. Sue could hardly wait—at last, *one* major financial burden off their shoulders.

The other interested party was the Wolfes. For a year, they had been carrying a note for the Landerses in the amount of $22,500. Forrest and Sue were ready to get their money and put the Holly Street chapter of their lives behind them.

By 9:00 A.M. on that hot summer Friday, Jack was at his office getting ready for his day. The phone rang, and it was John Witherspoon on the line. "I'm at Holly Street," he said. Jack remembers that there was a definite note of urgency in John's voice. "You better get your ass out here."

When Jack did, he found his Realtor and his house leveler looking like greeters at a funeral home. The floor man broke the bad news: "Every time I try to jack up a sill, the jack goes right through it. You've got some real problems here."

Jack called off the closing—called off the deal itself. When Janet Jones heard about it, she was furious that Jack had let the floor man in before the closing. "She tried to force Jack to close anyway," John Witherspoon says, though Jones doesn't recall that. John says he told her no way. There were frantic and angry phone calls to the abstract company, to Adams Pest Control, to the floor leveler, and back and forth between the agents.

Meanwhile, far away in St. Louis, Sue Landers was blithely enjoying her day. Myke was in Texas, the girls were at her mother's, and Sue was free to do whatever she wanted. Besides, it was her last day of indentured servitude to that disaster in Little Rock. She drove to her modern-dance class feeling lighter than air.

Years later, one of Sue's most vivid memories of that dance class was how the hardwood floors shone so. They seemed so well taken care of, so resilient, so solid. She and the other women in the class were moving to the music—swaying, feeling, interpreting, being. The day's assignment was to "just get in your own little space and do what you want to with the music." The cheery instructor was *psyched* about this group's energy.

At the appointed time, Sue excused herself from the class and went to use the phone in the hall. By now, she thought, it should be a done deal. She dialed, waited, finally heard Janet Jones's voice on the other end. It's another scene I think of as from a movie: *Sue's face dropping, her hand clasping her mouth, her head shaking in disbelief.*

Back inside the studio, the instructor watched Sue rejoin the class. There was a slight slump to her shoulders now, evidence of an invisible burden she had brought into the room. Attitude, feeling, interpretation. Sue began swaying to the music, began trying to dance, but she just couldn't do it. She collapsed on the floor, curled into a fetal ball, and began writhing wildly.

The instructor watched, fascinated, for a moment, then came and stood over her pupil. "Boy," she said to Sue, "you really use that music *well.*"

*Donna and Jack Burney on their wedding day in September 1981.*

*Chapter Thirteen*

# Burney

---

*1981* ❧ *1989*

S tudy one house over time, and it'll tell you all you need to know of life and death, of dreams and disappointments, of vanity, desperation, duplicity, denial.

Sue Wolfe remembers receiving a call from Sue Landers in the wee hours of the morning following the aborted closing. "She was hysterical, shrieking. She said they'd found that termites had eaten out the entire floor and that it was going to cost them seven thousand dollars to fix it. She said they thought we had cheated them."

Sue Landers says this house was the beginning of the end for her marriage. She and Myke never actually laid eyes on the grave site, which was just inches below the floor of the space that Sue had called her plant room. In hindsight, how appropriate, all those potted plants marking the spot.

The damage wasn't as extensive, or as costly, as Sue had first thought. But it was bad enough. I found a diagram of the problem in the files of Adams Pest Control: The damage stretched across the front beneath the living room and along the side into the den, but it looks as though the problem *centered* under that front room just off the living room—the room that had caused Billie Murphree so much worry about water, the room in which Martha Murphree had seen the floor furnace float. Apparently, because of how the house was built into the hill, there had never been enough room to get under that part to check adequately. For almost sixty years, time had been taking its silent toll. And now that that substructure was known to be rotten, there wasn't room to go under the house and do the work required.

So they had to tear out the floor from inside the room. Neighbors who peered through the windows during construction describe the scene as though describing an open grave—a dark hole in the surface, surrounded by that which once had covered it and soon would be put back in place, thankfully resealing the sight from human eyes.

The work took only a couple of days. The Landerses credited Jack Burney $3,800 for the repairs. The Wolfes discounted by two thousand dollars the note they were holding for the Landerses. The closing was rescheduled for August 14. At the end of the day, the Landerses—who, with Sue's father's help, had put down $20,000 on this house the year before—walked away with $8,334.93.

The repair work wasn't begun until after the closing. Before it was started, much less finished, the Landerses were trying to find someone to blame. When they finally took a good look at their termite contract from Adams Pest Control, they discovered that, as with most insurance policies, it came with a caveat: "Note: Existing damage to front sill & joists, center sill & joists, and left & rear sills and joists not to be replaced." If they looked further, they might've found a letter sent from Glynn Adams to Landmark Abstract/Title at the time they bought the house from the Wolfes:

*May 6, 1980*

*Gentlemen:*

*You will please be informed that we have inspected the above-captioned property and are pleased to report to you that our inspection revealed no evidence of active termites. However, there is evidence of past infestation and existing damage.*

*Our original treatment was performed on this structure April 20, 1973. The owners have maintained a Termite Protection Contract on the structure since that time. The coverage is effective through April 20, 1981. Attached is our Termite Protection Contract reflecting that the existing damage is excluded from coverage.*

*It is evident that such areas as finished floors, studding, sheathing, interior trim and others could not be visibly inspected for possible damage; therefore, all future claims or adjustments, if any, will be based on actual infestation at the time damage is found.*

*This letter is not to be considered a letter of clearance. It is merely a transfer of an existing Termite Protection Contract which has an exclusion of existing damage.*

Of course, there *wasn't* actual infestation—just old, sad bones that'd returned to dust.

The Landerses hired an attorney, who contacted the Realtor with whom they'd worked when they bought the house. The Realtor, whose company had since gone out of business, steadfastly denied any liability or responsibility for the "oversight" of allowing the termite contract to be transferred, instead of requiring a standard letter of clearance. The attorney recommended filing a complaint with the Arkansas Real Estate Commission; if that brought no relief, then they could sue the Realtor for damages.

Myke and Sue decided they'd had enough. They dropped the effort to find an external scapegoat and instead went on with their lives.

I sometimes think of that gash in the floor in 1981 as the physical equivalent of Ruth Murphree's emotional cave-in when Pat eloped twenty-two years before. Each in its way marked the end of something and the start of something else. Not, as you'll see, that the problems with rot were entirely over. But the gash in Sue and Myke Landers's plant room seemed to mark, literally and finally, a bottoming out—a culmination of the long, painful slide that had been taking place since the end of the Murphree years.

It had been a period during which existence of the house had overshadowed existence *in* it.

Now that's changed. With Jack and Donna Burney, and later with Beth and me, this house has seen parties again—more, it seems, than at any time since the Armour years. There's another similarity, and probably you could make a connection between the two. For both the Burneys and the Morgans, 501 Holly represented a new beginning—the first home of a newly blended family.

Shortly before Jack closed on this house, he brought his parents over to see it. The floor was buckled, of course, and the place looked the way Jack has described it. His father wandered around, taking it all in. "Boy," he finally told his son, "I think you've bitten off a lot here." Jack's mother didn't say a word the entire time.

A couple of weeks later, Jack went to see his parents. He sat them down and told them he had something to say. "I'm going to get married again," he said, "and I just wanted to let you know about it." He gave them all the details about Donna, who lived in Dallas but who would be coming to Little Rock the very next weekend. He promised to take her over to meet them.

Jack's mother was beside herself. "Oh, Jackie," she said, "I'm *so* happy. I was just so afraid you were going to buy that house and move some girl in there and *live* with her."

He did, for a few weeks. He and Donna wouldn't marry until late September, but they had to move in at the beginning of the month. They wanted to get the floor work going, but that wasn't the main reason. The real reason was that Jack had a tradition to uphold.

On the day in 1993 when I finally met Jack, I had a sense that I had known him somewhere before. I liked him, found him to be an affable, easygoing sort of fellow. I could imagine having a beer with him. As he told stories about his time in this house, I watched his face and listened to the way he talked—the way he tacked on the phrase "that type of deal" to other things he was saying, such as in "I had eight people working for me, and that type of deal." It was involuntary, a nervous filler; or it was just good-old-boy imprecision. *That* type of deal. Then it came to me: Even at age fifty-eight, Jack Burney reminded me of several guys I'd known in college.

The aura of college surrounds Jack like—well, I was going to say like *ivy,* but that gives the wrong message. The aura Jack projects reads more like pep rallies, panty raids, frat cats, and beer busts. He's a product of the rah-rah fifties, before the world changed so, and he admits that in his mind he's never really gotten out of college. He went to the University of Arkansas in Fayetteville. After he left that day, I thought of Updike's Rabbit Angstrom. Jack probably wouldn't have been a basketball star, but he gives off a sense of having found the old days golden. Until recently, he was president of the local Sigma Chi alumni group. He even looks the way I imagine Rabbit to look: the boyish shock of hair gone to gray; the collegiate khakis and fraternity-boy blazers in a middle-age size.

No, the reason Jack had to be in this house early that September was because of his annual first game Razorback party.

He and Donna and her twelve-year-old daughter Andi moved in—without furniture—and slept upstairs on a mattress while saws buzzed and clouds of dust filled the downstairs. The important things were the pigs. Jack has a collection of red concrete razorback hogs, the Arkansas mascot, and he positioned them around the side yard like garden ornaments from a Martha Stewart nightmare. He set up his kegs and his buffet tables and that was it. He and Donna invited fifty couples. Jack and his guests dressed in red and white and drew themselves a few cool ones, no doubt celebrating a new season not just for the Hogs but for good old Jack—husband, homeowner, host.

An hour before game time, they flung open the French doors to the kitchen and the men simply picked up the tables, food and all, and set them inside. Then as many as could fit piled into Jack's car and rode the few blocks to the stadium, which was designed by the same architect who had designed Jack's house, and parked in Jack's special close-in parking space before pouring themselves out into the wider sea of red. After the game, they returned to 501 Holly and carried the groaning buffet tables back out to the yard, and they picked up again right where they'd left off. Jack's new neighbors could tell that a whole new era had been ushered in. "Wooooooooooooo PIG!" went the cheer that, time and again, pierced the soft fall night. *"Sooieee!"*

Though the fifties tugged gently on Jack's blazer sleeve, the life he and his family lived here strikes me as more representative of their time than any family since the Murphrees. The Burneys were pure eighties. There were three reasons for that: one, their work; two, their materialism; and three, their family.

Jack was then and still is a salesman. When he moved here, he and a partner owned a wholesale distributorship for appliances and electronics. They had Gibson ranges and air conditioners, Sharp microwaves, televisions, and VCRs, plus various car radios and stereos. They were the middlemen, selling to dealers throughout Arkansas, north Louisiana, and east Texas. The public had a passion for the latest in electronics, and Jack reaped the profits from that passion. Meanwhile, Donna, who in Texas had worked for a construction firm, found a good job as executive secretary to the comptroller of Fairfield Communities, a company riding another eighties wave—time-sharing.

Their house reflected their taste and times. When I first walked through here, I remember thinking that I had never seen so many television sets and sofas in one house in all my life. There was one of each in almost every room. A big-screen TV stood right where Jessica Armour had lovingly placed her Empire sideboard; where her guests had dined at a table for twelve, the Burneys lolled on a sectional sofa. In other words, they didn't use their dining room *as* a dining room; it became instead a kind of shrine to the god of electronics, with the remote as a much-fingered rosary. The downstairs back bedroom—our Geranium Room—was where they placed their dining room table.

I'm slightly surprised that Jack bought this house. I guess, after four years of his being single, it said *home* to him in a way that a new house in the suburbs couldn't quite manage. Or maybe it was Donna who liked old houses. Her decorating was certainly fussier than the family's apparent lifestyle.

A vivacious blonde twelve years Jack's junior, Donna was bold and outgoing in her touch: They ripped out the old kitchen (finally!) and started over, and when it was done the kitchen was green, with green paisley wallpaper on the walls and ceiling. Donna covered the downstairs bathroom in a pink floral-print fabric, and it was padded. The shower curtain was made of the same material. The upstairs bath was padded fabric, too, as was the big bedroom across the hall. Green, lots of green. My stepdaughter Blair remembers that one downstairs room had green shamrock wallpaper, which Blair wanted to keep because her birthday is March 17.

Jack doesn't spend a lot of time pondering the finer points of decorating. "I don't really care," he says. "That was Donna's deal. Donna has two sisters, and all three are into decorating. They really work the flea markets hard. The sisters are into what color is in now, and what's out. Donna got into greens. And our house was green."

Burglars seemed to see it that way, too. I don't know how thieves choose a target, but maybe it has something to do with telltale electronics boxes stacked by the curb—and access, of course. The Burneys provided both. They were cleaned out twice—burglarized, looted, once while they were out buying even *more* things. It was just before Christmas that first year. They came home from shopping to find all the Christmas gifts gone, as well as the TVs and stereos and VCRs. Another time, after a weekend at their condo in Hot Springs, they returned to the same sickening scene. There was no tall fence around the backyard in those days, and thieves could kick in the back door and empty the house under cover of a thick tangle of trees. After the second burglary, Jack had a wooden fence built, with a heavy wooden gate. That stopped the problem.

And so the party roared on. Throughout the eighties, the Burney house was a magnet for people. Maybe the energy emanated from all those electronic gadgets, but whatever its source, the result was palpable—LaughMan, EatMan, DrinkMan, DanceMan, *Party*Man. Donna had causes—one year she was president of the Advocates for Battered Women ("Had nothing to do with me," Jack says with a salesman's nudge), and they held fund-raisers here. Donna, who loved to cook, invited her company's executive staff for elegant Christmas fetes.

This house was the after-school hub for most of daughter Andi's friends, and even though Jack's children—Butch, Brad, and Bitsi—didn't live with their dad, when Brad ran for president of his senior class, Jack and Donna threw banner-painting parties here several nights a week. Andi and Bitsi were the same age and in the same grade, and all their friends were invited here to breakfast after their senior prom. The breakfast was supposed to be outside, but that night it rained. About 1:00 A.M., hundreds of inebriated teenagers showed up, and Jack and Donna took them in. The kids sprawled all over the house in their hot pink taffeta and pastel tuxes, wet mud caking their *peau de soie* heels and rented patent-leather pumps, not to mention the house itself. The house was a wreck the next day, but everybody had a good time—including Jack and Donna.

There was even a wedding here once. In January 1982, four months after the Burneys moved in, Jack's old roommate during his bachelor days decided he was going to get married. He asked if he could say his vows in this homey house, in the living room, in front of the fireplace.

It's very hard to find home alone. When Jack married Donna, he'd become weary of the single life. He likes marriage, he says. But then you get the other side of the coin: Marriage requires putting up with other people. Remarriage means even *more* people who fall into that category. Next thing you know, married people start thinking they'd feel at home if only they were single.

Jack says that if he and his first wife had had three sons, there wouldn't have been a problem. As it was, they had two sons and a daughter. In junior high, Bitsi and Andi didn't go to the same school. But by the fall of 1984, both were tenth graders at Central High. The way Jack tells it, the girls competed for everything, and their mothers monitored the contest like a pair of peckish hens. You can guess where Jack stood in all of this.

"The two mothers were the problems," Jack tells me. "Not the daughters. You understand that?"

"Yeah," I say, "I do."

If one daughter made cheerleader, the other had to make it, or there was hell to pay. If Jack bought one daughter a car, he had to buy the other a car, too—and it had to be just as *good* a car, or there was hell to pay. If Jack gave one daughter a credit card—as he did— then he had to give the other one a credit card, and that was *really* hell to pay.

Cotillion was vitally important to the girls' mothers. The lady who ran the program in those days, a Mrs. Butts, ruled with an iron hand. You had to pass muster to get in. Boys hated it; girls and their mothers loved it. One way for a girl to get in was to have an older brother who'd been in cotillion. So Jack forced Brad to pave the way for Bitsi. Bitsi got in, but when they submitted an application for Andi, she was turned down. "Donna wasn't happy about that," Jack says.

One day, Jack was flying home after doing business in Atlanta, and a woman sat down in the seat next to him. She looked to be in her sixties. When the flight attendants pushed out the beverage cart, Jack asked the lady if he could buy her a drink. She accepted a glass of wine and he ordered a beer. They talked awhile, and Jack bought her another drink, and they talked awhile longer.

Finally, he introduced himself. The lady turned out to be Mrs. Butts. "Mrs. *Butts,*" Jack said, "I'm so glad to get to visit with you. I've got a real problem." When he got home, they resubmitted Andi's application. Donna was very pleased with the outcome.

The porch was where Jack usually went to work out his problems. He recalls sitting out there a lot, especially during the mideighties. He sold his half of his business to his partner about then, and for a while he didn't do anything. "It was the most boring time in my life," he recalls.

One day, he was just sitting on the porch, pondering his life, when he was interrupted from his reveries by a voice. There was a man standing down by the curb. Jack didn't know him. "Would you mind," the man was saying, "if I came up and sat on that porch with you?" Jack said no, come on. So the man did. They talked for a long time. "I've been walking past this house for years," the man said, "and I've *always* wanted to sit on this front porch."

The problem for Jack is, the porch became synonymous with trouble, with bad times. I should have brass plaques made up: *This is where Siggy lost his finger,* on the door to the kitchen. *This is where Ruth's heart was broken,* in the middle room. *This is where*

*Sue and Myke's marriage is buried,* on the front room floor. For Jack, I would affix the plaque to the porch: *This is where a Burney tradition ended.*

It was on the porch that Brad told his father he wasn't pledging Sigma Chi.

You may think this is frivolous, but Jack Burney is a man for whom such things still matter deeply. His older son, Butch—Jack junior—had decided not to go to college. Butch, in his father's words, was "a holy terror" as a child. "You name it, he did it," Jack says. In Butch's young teenage days, the Vietnam War was still going on. "It was the era of the hawks and the chickens," Jack recalls. "He was into the long hair and everything. I was a hawk. I couldn't believe anybody didn't want to go to Vietnam. I've changed a lot since then. But Butch would fight everything I believed in. He did a lot just to aggravate me."

Butch was so notorious that when the younger kids got to Central and people asked if they were kin to Butch Burney, it was just easier to lie.

He was a musician, an artist, and after high school he decided he wanted to go to Hollywood and become an actor. Jack pulled strings and got him into Lee Strasberg's acting school. So Butch went west. He appeared in one episode of *Happy Days* and in a few plays, but, says Jack, he was just so immature that he didn't take advantage of the opportunity.

"So he came home and worked for me. For a few years, he gave me lessons five hours a day. He preached to me. Then he got married, and his life changed."

With Butch, Jack hadn't had the chance to pass along the tradition. Brad, on the other hand, was the perfect son—never got in trouble, made good grades, was class president. Jack refers to Brad as "Mr. Do-Right," and it was only after listening to the tape later that I got the feeling there was a slight jab inherent in that nickname.

"I was a Sigma Chi," Jack says again. "President of the Sigma Chi alums. True-blue Sigma Chi. Donna, not growing up here and not going to the university, she really didn't understand that. And so when Brad went through rush, I stayed out of it. He knew how I felt, but I stayed out of it. He came and talked to Donna about it, and she told him, 'You do what you think is best. Your father will understand.' But it's a guy thing. And so he came and told me one day that he had accepted Phi Delt. It was a real disappointment. Took me a year to get over it.

"It happened right out here on the porch."

The house itself was hard on Jack. And to be perfectly honest, he was a little hard on it, too.

He's the first to admit he's not a handyman. Two or three times, he fell down the Lee Street hill while mowing the lawn. That in itself doesn't make a person unhandy, though you might have a hard time convincing anyone who was watching. But Jack's problem seemed to be this: As a handyman, he was a salesman. He wanted the best deal, not the best job. "I'm always trying to find somebody to do something," he says, "always cutting corners on it, and it's always the wrong thing to do type deal."

There was a time in this house's life when all the upstairs windows rolled open and every window had a screen. When Beth and I moved in, we had ten of the window frames repaired and repainted and new screens put in; I think that job cost two thousand dollars. We no longer have that kind of money for such details, so even today there are several windows upstairs that have no screens. Fortunately, most of them don't open, either, since Jack's antidote to Andi's and Bitsi's nocturnal adventuring was to paint the windows shut and cut the tree they would shimmy down.

But when the Burneys were first here, the windows would open, and they had screens. The problem was, the windows needed

*Jack and his two sons, Butch and Brad. The Burneys threw a
lot of Razorback parties in that side yard.*

painting. Real painters cost a lot of money, so Jack came up with a
better way. "I had these two friends of mine, guys I had met at the
Instant Replay, where I used to hang out before I got married. Big
group of us would go down there on Thursday nights and we'd pick

the high school football games. These two friends were kind of halfway unemployed most of the time. Good beer drinkers, worked part-time."

Jack hired these two fellows to paint his house.

On the back porch, where Jessie Armour slept during the war years, Jack had a refrigerator that was only for beer. He doesn't drink anything else, but he *loves* beer, and he makes certain that he never runs out. That's why he kept this refrigerator. Like a separate telephone line for the fax, this was a dedicated fridge.

On the day the two painters showed up to start the job, Jack began a certain ritual. Every morning before he left for the office, he would take four to six beers out of the beer refrigerator and put them in the regular kitchen refrigerator. "Boys," he told his buddies that first day, "there's some beer in the refrigerator. Whenever you get through each day, go on in there and get you a beer."

One day he forgot. When Andi got home from school, the painters were upset. "Andi," they said, "your daddy doesn't have any beer in here today. He forgot to buy beer."

"No way," said Andi. "He's *always* got beer." And she showed them the stash, which they proceeded to clean out.

Jack didn't see them for several days after that. When they came back, he forgave them. Soon they progressed to the point of taking the screen frames off and removing the screens. They were going to repaint the frames and rescreen them. But in the middle of that job, they came to Jack saying they needed money to buy new screens. On the way to get them, they stopped off to pick up a little beer. Then the police pulled them over and ticketed them for DWI. Jack never saw the screens and never got his money back. And that was the end of his drinking buddies' painting, because Donna fired them.

He tells me that story by way of explaining all those empty frames stacked up in my shed.

The Burneys actually had to finish the job of painting the house themselves. When it came time to sell, they decided the house looked too dark sitting up on this hill half hidden by trees. It looked like a place Boo Radley might live in. What if we painted it? they thought. Not just the woodwork but the brick, too?

One day when they were out in the yard, looking at the house, a young black man stopped by. He painted houses, he said, and he would love to paint theirs. He told Jack he'd painted houses all over Hillcrest. "If you'll take me in your car, I'll show you," the man said. So Jack did. They drove all around the area. "If you'll stop," the man said, "we'll go up to the door and talk to the people." But Jack felt funny about things like that. He said he would take the man's word.

Jack had to provide the ladders, the air compressors, and gas money so the painter could get to the job. Jack felt like a cash machine. Sometimes he would give the man money, and then the man wouldn't show up for days. Donna was on Jack to get the job done. They limped along like that until the man had done all but one side and the chimney.

Then the painter pushed Jack over the brink. "He came to my office one day and he needed money," Jack recalls. "We had a screaming thing, and I gave him money and told him, 'This is what I think I owe you for what you've done. Now go, begone, I don't ever want to see or hear from you again.'"

"Oh no, sir," the painter said, "I'm going to finish the job."

"No you're not," Jack said. "You're *through.*" Jack went home and told Donna he had fired the painter.

So they had to finish the job together. As fate would have it, Jack was afraid of heights, so he stood in the yard, working the compressor, while Donna got up on the ladder and painted the house—all but the chimney, which was still unpainted when I bought the place.

Jack didn't know the coda to that story, but I told him. For at least our first year in this house, I would occasionally be interrupted in my office by a knock on the door. I used the downstairs front room then. I would go to the door and a young black man would be standing there. I could see behind him that another person was waiting in a car. The young man would introduce himself as the one who had painted this house. He'd brought someone over to see it, and would I mind?

I figured I shouldn't if *he* didn't. Once, I heard him and his potential client standing just outside my office window discussing the quality of the job. The other man was older, and he didn't look pleased. His brow was furrowed and his lips were tight. He pointed to a section of alligatored woodwork that obviously hadn't even been sanded before the new gray paint was brushed on.

"I would want a better job than that," the man said.

Toward the end, Jack began to sense that he was a dinosaur. After selling his own business and doing nothing for a while, he'd bought another company that was similar. It had been owned by a friend of his. One morning, the man had gone out to get in his car to leave on a business trip and his estranged wife walked up and shot him in the head. Killed him. Since Jack was available, he was asked to manage that company for a time. Eventually, he bought it.

And business remained good until about a year after he and Donna moved from this house, at the end of the eighties. But even before they left, Jack saw the writing on the wall. "Sam's and Wal-Mart took care of that business," he says. "There are no wholesale distributors anymore. Everybody's direct."

The time-sharing business was feeling shaky, too. Combine that with the fact that Andi had graduated from high school in 1988, and it was enough of a sea change to make them want to get out from under this old house.

And so they painted. And on a bright Sunday morning in late August of 1989, I walked through this house, marveling at the TV sets and the couches and the padded walls and the relentless shades of *green*. Then, outside the kitchen door, I spied a coffee cup, still steaming, and it bore a fresh red lip print that made my heart leap into my throat.

*Jim and Beth Morgan in the living room, 1991. The mirror in the background hangs in the spot where Jessie Armour had her Empire sideboard decades before.*

*Chapter Fourteen*

# Morgan

*1989* 🍂 *1992*

I have a thing about light. My sensitivity to it isn't physical; it's emotional—visceral, even. Our next-door neighbors sit in their living room or their den with the overhead light on. As much as I like and enjoy being with John and Linda, I can't understand how anybody can do something like that. It's not a subject I would ask them about—you either have a thing about light or you don't.

The first thing I do every morning is turn on the fluorescent light over the sink. Beth would leave it off all day and be perfectly happy. But if I go into the kitchen and that light isn't on, I feel a nagging worry, like one of those vague concerns that floats across your mind just when you're sitting down to enjoy yourself, as at a movie. So I turn that light on and leave it on all day. The next thing I do is switch on the small lamp behind the coffeepot, creating shadow figures in that otherwise-dark corner.

On the other hand, when we sit on the porch at night, I have to have the floor lamp inside the living room window turned off. I like the porch best when it's dark—so dark that all you see is the occasional glow of a cigarette lighting up like a red firefly, then fading back into the unseen sounds of tinkling ice cubes and creaking rockers.

In my house, I know the times of day that produce the light I like best. The Geranium Room takes on a rosy glow at precisely 8:30 on spring mornings. I'm seldom in that room at that hour, but the effect is more pronounced from the hall, anyway. As busy as our mornings are, I usually make a point of stopping for a moment to stare in wonder at the light bouncing off the walls and blending with the east sun. The result is a pink mist thick enough to disappear into.

The kitchen is warmest at 11:30 in the morning, when the sun finds the windows and cuts across the pine table like a Hopper painting. My office catches an intriguing sliver of west sun late in the day, after 4:00 P.M. It beams in through the French doors and warms the wall over my oil paints, turning it golden.

I also know the time of day whose light I like least. I adjust the living room miniblinds slightly upward at 6:30 on summer evenings, especially if we're having someone over. Otherwise, the sun's rays will spray the floor and wall and dining room mirror, ricocheting through the room like a drive-by shooting. Such an onslaught inevitably exposes a thin film of dust—no matter how often we vacuum—on the hardwood floors between the dining room and hall.

Since I've been writing this book, I've become especially conscious of my feelings about light. I like rooms moody, indirect. I like candles on the dinner table. I don't like track lights, though we have a vestigial row of the things left on our living room ceiling, a legacy of the Burneys. I don't know what I was thinking.

Mainly, I don't like a spotlight on me. Now it occurs that I should've thought of that before I started writing this book.

When I began, I had no idea how much my illuminating the secrets of my house might also require spotlighting secrets of my own. If our houses are us, then we are our houses. Now I find I'm obliged—by the saga of which I'm a part—to reveal glimpses of my own faulty wiring, cracks in my own foundation.

It's easier just to shut the blinds.

But I began this story as a search, and much of that search had to do with me. I suppose I'll survive the glare. We're all houses. We all have our histories and secrets, our losses, our damaged hearts. No wonder we don't like looking into the black broken places inside our closets. No wonder we cringe at the thought of crawl spaces, or feel a chill about dank basements or skeletal attics. We go through our lives not knowing those we love, the places we live in, or even ourselves. We stand, separately, row after row of us on street after street all over the world—all houses. But in spite of ourselves, we yearn to be homes.

Beth and I came to 501 Holly packing separate pasts, looking for a house understanding enough to accommodate those and our uncertain future, too.

For me, the handful of days that led up to Holly Street were *the* pivotal moments in my life to that point, both personally and professionally. By that I mean, I actually made a conscious decision on both fronts. I know how ridiculous that sounds. I also know that well-adjusted, mature people who don't confuse themselves with a rich inner life probably won't understand. But since I'd always lived most satisfyingly inside my head, I'd made conscious decisions only about my work. The personal side, in a way, had just come along for the ride. I'd allowed decisions to be made for me, or allowed time to take its course. This includes the subject of marriage, which goes a long way toward explaining why I now have two ex-wives.

At the end of August 1989, after our magazine had been sold and our staff replaced, I turned down an offer for the top job at a big-city magazine—consciously deciding to step off base as a day-to-day, salary-drawing magazine editor and instead to accept a part-time consulting deal so I could write. I called an old boss of mine, and he told me, "The only risks I've ever regretted were the ones I didn't take." The ramifications were frightening but exhilarating. They became even more adrenaline-producing when you added my decision, one day later, to ask Beth to marry me. My plan was for us to stay in Arkansas and write, to live together and work at home. She accepted, and the next morning I called my Realtor to look for a house.

I believe Beth made a measured decision, too. She's endured much pain in her life. Her father was killed when she was fifteen, and in many ways her family splintered after that. Right after college, she married her first husband—one of a brood of ten children—trying to find a family to fit into. A home. She learned, of course, that home isn't a quantitative thing. Just before she and I met, she'd been told that her beloved brother and ally Brent, an interior decorator in New York, had been diagnosed with HIV. That had been the most devastating blow of all.

I first saw her in 1986, at a meeting for the new magazine we were starting in Little Rock. A writer, she had come to hear some of us talk about staffing and other subjects. I spotted her in the crowd. She looked like someone who had peered into the black broken places. As I watched her that day, I thought of a *New Yorker* cartoon that had always amused me about my own well-known moodiness. I'd kept it pinned to my office wall for the longest time; then I moved again, of course, and lost it. It showed a man and woman at one of those trendy Manhattan parties. In the background, you could see that the apartment was abuzz with smart talk. In the foreground, however, a young man sat alone on the terrace. A woman had just approached him. "You're not having much fun, are you?" she said. "I like that in a man."

Beth didn't seem to be having much fun.

I was right about her and I was wrong. Wrong, in that she has a relentless spirit, an irrepressible *fun* about her that won't be quashed. This is the woman who introduced me to martinis. But I was right about her, too. It would be a long time before she and I married, but the sadness I saw in her that day would color our first three years on Holly Street.

* * *

Like the Burneys, we moved in three weeks before our wedding. We asked for and received special dispensation from Beth's ex to let his young daughters sleep under the same roof with a man and woman who were living in sin.

Blair was eight, Bret five when we came to Holly Street. I remember the day we brought the girls over to see the house for the first time. We'd decided that Bret would have the smaller room at the top of the stairs, and Blair the larger bedroom adjoining. Both girls were aghast when they saw the fabric walls in Blair's room and the two baths. I told the girls that's how I had known this was the perfect house for our crazy new family—the place came complete with padded walls.

I decided that if Beth and I didn't call off the wedding in those first few weeks, we would have no problem lasting forever. We'd tried to get the painters scheduled before we moved in, but the Burneys were already being pressed. Looking over my house file six years later, I almost get sick summoning back that frantic time. I've never enjoyed the business of buying a house. I don't know how you buy a place in which you're going to live without wanting it so much that you might as well not even negotiate. Many— most—houses don't speak to me with any poetry whatsoever, and so the ones that do are almost too special. Then there's the eternal question of whether I'll be able to afford it once I'm in. No matter how many times I go through this damnable dance, there are always nights when I lie in bed in the dark, staring toward the ceiling, turning numbers over in my head. Suddenly, I'll remember two thousand dollars I had forgotten, and I'll either rise in a cold sweat or I'll doze off to sleep—depending in whose favor my addled brain had temporarily failed.

I bought this house myself, alone, for reasons I will explain in due time. My wrangling with the Burneys took place over just a couple of days, but the tension lasted a month, from the beginning of September 1989 to the first of October. And longer, I guess, since Donna won't talk with me. They had listed the house for $129,900. On September 1, I offered $110,000 and stipulated that they were to finish painting the house and porch and to scrape the paint drippings off the windows. I wrote in that I wanted all ceiling fans, all window air conditioners, and the fireplace screen. I asked for a response by 1:00 P.M. September 2.

They countered to $126,500—with an increase in earnest money— and stipulated that "3 green balloon shades in MBR will not stay." They demanded an answer by 8:00 P.M. that same day.

I went to $117,000, agreeing to deliver the increased earnest money upon acceptance of the offer. The shades were no problem. I imposed a 10:00 P.M. deadline. I seem to recall that I went to $120,000 at one point, but I find no record of that. I also think they once called off the whole negotiation, but I can't be sure.

The last counter for which I have paperwork was for $122,000. I agreed to deliver the earnest money "1 day after acceptance." Looking back, I don't know if that was just balm to ease the bruise of giving in, or because the day of deadline was a Sunday. With that final offer, I also listed another requirement on their part—besides the normal termite contract, I specified "a satisfactory structural report to be included." My agent had known about the Landers episode and thus suggested this move. The Burneys had to respond by 7:00 P.M. September 3.

I don't know what I would've done if they hadn't taken the offer. A buyer was looming for my house in west Little Rock, the house I owned with my now ex-wife back in Chicago and which I had been trying to sell for a solid year. I didn't want to lose that sale—even if it was for the same amount we had paid three years before.

But more than that, I needed that sale to end one chapter of my life and this one to begin another.

Jack and Donna accepted. And then the really unpleasant part began. They had more stuff crammed into one house than any couple I had ever seen (until we started unloading *our* blended histories). My west Little Rock buyers wanted to be in by October 1 at the latest, which meant I had to have the Burneys gone a day or so before that. Playing both ends against the middle, I eventually worked out a grueling closing date of September 28 for both houses, with possession for both on September 29. For three and a half weeks that month, in four dwellings in Little Rock, four groups packed boxes. At the head of the chain, the Burneys, I feel certain, cursed us all.

Before the closing took place, we discovered that the floor beneath our downstairs bathroom was rotten and would have to be replaced. I frankly don't remember paying much attention to any of this, which is sobering to me now, having just spent a year observing how blinding a house's charms can be—and to what devastating effect. Fortunately, I had a tough Realtor, Georgia Sells, on my side. The Burneys wanted to pass us the standard Adams letter, with its exclusions. Georgia recommended that I not accept that. We refused to close, and held off a day. In the end, the Burneys had to pay a different pest control company, Terminix, to repair the damage underneath, and a floor man to repair the inside. The Burneys escrowed $1,981 for Terminix, and $1,519 for the inside floor work. And I received a letter of clearance. Georgia says that deal reflects the new covenant between buyer and seller, an understanding that's become more prevalent over the past five years. "It used to be 'Buyer beware,'" she says. "Now it's 'Seller beware.'"

The painters arrived a day after we moved in. For the first couple of weeks, our furniture stood in a pile in the center of the living and dining room, covered by a drop cloth. The workmen sanded and spackled and primed and painted, while Beth and I planned a wedding and I wrote a magazine article. At night, after the girls had finally gone to bed, we would walk around the house with drinks in hand, moving boxes to make paths, and we would marvel at the transformation that was taking place. Gradually, the green Burney rooms receded into the house's history, and the colors Beth and I chose together went on the walls for all to see.

We married on a Saturday the third week of October. Two days before that, the men came to fix the bathroom floor. On the same day, Brent flew in from New York, and my sons, David and Matt, came from their home in Connecticut. David brought his girlfriend. My mother arrived from Mississippi. That night, we had a festive dinner, the first in our dining room. I was nervous—another beginning—but toasts and speeches were called for. Beth, who once considered following in her family line of lawyers, does these things better. I presented Blair and Bret rings with their birthstones, and Beth gave David and Matt sterling key rings. On each one, she had attached a key to 501 Holly.

Our wedding took place downtown, in a wonderfully ornate vintage building where Beth and I had gone to dances. All four of our children took part in the ceremony. Afterward, there was a party back at our new old house. Our friends were impressed, we could tell. I had the lights just right to cast a glow off the terra-cotta walls. There were no cardboard boxes in sight. Instead, the living room sparkled with the matching blue leather recamiers, the black lacquer bar, the Biedermeier mirror, the fifties lamp and forties table, the deep red Sarouk rug. The dining room chairs ringed that room as guests served themselves from a buffet adorning the old claw-and-ball table, which stood atop a blue Chinese rug older even than this house itself.

Our friends filled their plates and wandered through our rooms. They pushed open the French doors from the living room to my office and stood in clusters, nibbling and sipping, studying the Arts and Crafts desk and the old lawyer's bookcase and the European sofa and the frayed Oriental rugs and the fifties table and especially the then-revolutionary fax machine, which, from the moment I had heard about it, I had seen as a sign from God that, yes, I *could* live anywhere—even here—and still be plugged into the world. Guests drifted onward into the bedroom, murmuring about the black lacquer bed and the bird's-eye maple dressing table and the thirties rattan chairs. And then they followed the inevitable path into the Geranium Room, shocking in its audacity.

We danced some that night—pushed back the furniture the way Charlie and Jessie Armour had done so many decades before, when this house was unscathed, though we knew nothing of the Armours then and, in fact, wouldn't have paid them much mind if we had. They were the past, and our dance was all about the future. We shimmied and shook, and then, as the guests dwindled and our day slipped away, we swayed to Sinatra singing "Someone to Watch Over Me."

The next morning early, I heard, even through my champagne stupor, a steady creaking on the stairs. It was just light outside. I had no idea who was up. My sons and mother and stepdaughters were sleeping upstairs, and maybe Beth's mother, too. Whoever it was, I heard him thumping into furniture on the other side of the wall, and then total silence. I got up and put on my robe. In the living room, I found Blair sitting on one of the recamiers in her pajamas, and she was glaring out the window at the hazy gray light. Her arms were folded tightly across her body. I went over to her, the concerned stepdad, and sat down in a chair next to her. She didn't even look at me.

"What's the matter?" I said.

Even today, I remember the way she looked at me, which was with hatred, and the way she spoke, which was a hiss. "What's the matter?" I said again.

She turned my way. "I should have *never* let you marry my mother."

* * *

We lived our first years in this house electrified by undercurrents. One was the sputtering connection of old failed marriages. Another was jealousy. Still another was the total shutdown power of grief.

Divorce doesn't make the search for home any easier. It makes it possible sometimes, but never easier. The common term for families who've been visited by divorce is *broken homes*. It's an apt description. Divorce, once experienced, can infect the next house, and the next, and the next after that. It can undermine foundations, weaken roofs, compromise the sanctity of the walls themselves. Once you know, it's hard to forget. If you know twice, it's almost impossible.

Beth and I have been married for six years now, and we're still working on blending, blending, blending. Blair and Bret, naturally, being children, have played the usual cards—"I hate Jim. I want to live with Dad"—and by now I think we've gotten past most, though not all, of that. For the first couple of years, when Blair would sulk and say she was "mad" at me, I would smile and say, "So what else is new?" It became a running joke between us, and eventually her anger—at least her anger toward me—seemed to dissipate.

But it's not just those who are children, chronologically, who get caught up in the insidious power of past divorce. What happens is this: After you've been burned, you tend to guard against being burned the next time. The problem is, with your guard so high, you can't see that you're almost guaranteeing a repeat of the thing you dread most.

I had no sense of any of this until my first wife called me at work one Minnesota winter day and said she wanted to meet me for a drink. Over a cocktail table, she told me that after eleven years she was unhappy and wanted a divorce. There was no one else, she said. I'd been able to shut away the alien socks, but I couldn't deny this. I had no idea at the time how profoundly divorce would affect me. I was the last person in the world I ever expected to be *divorced*. It

*Jim, Blair, and Bret celebrating Snapp's third birthday, December 1994.*

went against all I'd grown up knowing. Even though we had moved a lot, we were always together. Always a family. I was old—thirty-two—to be learning this, but learn it I did: There's no such thing as security. There's no such thing as permanence. You can know it in your head, but until you've experienced it, you don't know it at all.

We agreed to stay together for six more months, until David finished first grade. Somewhere, deep in a trunk in the darkest corner of our attic, there's a notebook in which I kept a journal of those excruciating months in that house in Minnesota. It's been twenty years, and I still don't want to look at it. I do remember thinking that time had stopped. We could no longer plan together, so we floated through the days and nights, untethered to anything—to the past we were giving up, to the future we no longer had in common. We just treaded water. At least that's what *I* did.

Then on the weekend of David's seventh birthday, two moving vans came. Hers arrived first, and when they were finished, I said good-bye to my wife and my boys and they drove off, bound for Miami. All of us were trying to be brave through our tears, except for Matt, who was eight months old and didn't understand a thing. He laughed the whole time.

When my van was loaded, I took one more walk through the house, through David's red-white-and-blue room, through Matt's yellow-green garden of a nursery, through the icy blue living and dining rooms that now showed nail holes. When I was ready, I locked the door and slid the key through the mail slot. Then I got into my car and went to meet the movers at my new apartment. Three months later I got the letter from my ex-wife telling me she had remarried.

So when Blair said what she said to me that morning after the wedding, I understood. By then, I understood many things about the way divorce affects our life in houses. For that very reason, I declined to have the girls call me Dad, as my ex-wife instructed my sons to address her new husband.

But I'm not a hero in this cause. In addition to the decision to marry Beth and give up magazine editing, I had made another decision in the summer of 1989: Never again did I want to have to move from a house because of a divorce. Never again did I want to give up things that were dear to me. I had done it twice. I could've stayed in the houses, of course, had I been able to raise the money to pay my wives for their share. But in the first instance, I wasn't earning enough to do that. In the second, there was too much equity involved.

So with 501 Holly, I decided to buy it myself. There was a bad moment with Beth, I remember, just as I was leaving her to meet with the real estate woman. Beth asked if the house was going to be in both our names, and I said I didn't know, that I would ask the advice of the agent. But I knew already. This had nothing to do with my love for Beth. This had to do with that thing I mentioned at the beginning—my bone-deep knowledge of the way life bears on living things.

So I bought this house on my own. And during one early fight with Beth, I spoke the unspeakable: "Well," I blurted, "after all, this is *my* house." To which she responded, "Well, in the state of Arkansas, a wife owns half of a husband's property." It was true, and I knew it, even at the time I bought the house. But I didn't want to hear it. I wanted, somehow, if only in my own mind, to be protected from being forced to leave my house again.

That instinct filters down to the lowest levels. The other day, while I was cleaning out some junk that had piled up on our back porch and pantry, I ran across a red plastic case that I didn't recognize at first. When I opened it, I realized it was Beth's toolbox. I have a toolbox, too, but mine isn't nearly so pristine. In fact, it's a junky bunch of hammers and levels and pliers and loose screws tossed into a small wooden chest that belonged to my second wife.

Seeing Beth's nice toolbox gave me an idea. "How about we combine these toolboxes?" I said. "I'll weed mine out and put my stuff in with yours."

She looked doubtful. She bounced her head from side to side and clicked her mouth in that way that could've either meant, I'm thinking about it, or, No, but I don't want to hurt your feelings. It was the latter. "Oh, let's don't," she said. "That was Brent's toolbox."

"Fine," I said, and it *was* fine. Marriage has to be a careful balance of you, me, and us. But it made me think of how secretly territorial we all are, how we try to protect ourselves, and how that affects the life we lead within these walls.

Marriage is hard enough without having to set up housekeeping together. I guess the trick is for one party to care and the other not to. The Burneys were that way. We're not so fortunate. Beth and I both care a great deal about our surroundings, but she's always held the trump card—her brother the New York decorator.

When I refer to decorating in this context, I don't mean one of those Talbot-suited Junior Leaguers who dresses out your rooms in trendy matching tones of green and mauve. I mean international high style—poufs, leopard-skin beds, port-toned velvet with gold church symbols, obelisks, giant prints of Voltaire, period wallpaper, *vahses*. Soon after we moved in, a no-nonsense friend who'd worked with us at the magazine came over to visit. I asked what he thought of the living room. "It's a mishmash," he said. "Nothing goes together."

*That's* the kind of decorating I refer to here.

I like it. I like antiques. I like eclectic. I like the layered textures of silk and challis and taffeta. I like the Vuillard blend of patterns, and the Matisse burst of color. But I also don't want to lose myself in it.

When we moved into 501 Holly, Beth and I, combined, had a lot of furniture. (We have more now, but that's a story for later.) Even in this big old house, it wasn't long before we started running out of room. Almost inevitably, if something had to be stored or sold, it would be something of *mine*. Even though I often preferred Beth's things—generally, Brent had sent them or helped her pick them out—the trend was disturbing. In the back of my head was that old scene of starting over in another apartment. As Beth and I sparred over furnishings, I began to keep silent score: *my* rugs, *my* dining room table, *my* lacquer bed, *my* European sofas, *my* rattan chairs.

And then: *her* recamiers, *her* fifties lamp, *her* forties table, *her* Arts and Crafts desk, *her* fifties swivel chairs, *her* lacquer bar, *her* lawyer's bookcases, *her* iron bed, *her* trestle table, *her* sideboard, *her . . . her . . . her. . . .*

\* \* \*

We have a set of matching side chairs in our living room. They're small, and they have no arms. They're covered in silk. The pattern is a plaid, actually, but not in the way you're thinking. On this silk, red checks fade toward white, with a stop at dove gray. The gray blocks linger like an echo.

Often, when I look at these chairs, I wonder which one Beth sat in while her brother died.

This is Beth's story to tell, which I know she'll do in due time. I'm going to relate it only in terms of how it changed our lives at 501 Holly. Brent phoned one day in March of 1990. Beth wasn't home, so I answered. He told me he'd been to the doctor that day, and the doctor had diagnosed a particularly virulent strain of lymphoma. We didn't discuss a time frame; that wasn't Brent's way. But it was *cancer,* a bad kind. Doctors Beth later consulted gave him only a matter of months.

Beth came home in a while. I heard her in the kitchen, and so I summoned my courage and went in there. Moments like this change a house forever for me. Mundane backdrops become players in a drama. I remember, in our house in Jackson, watching my mother carried out in the middle of the night by paramedics. She'd had an attack of appendicitis, and the ambulance had arrived in the dark, its eerie red lights flashing across all the familiar things in our living room. The red was like a stain in my mind. Another time, in Tupelo, my brother managed to slip his body through the bars of his baby bed. I heard my mother screaming, and when I got there—I was five—she was holding him up so he wouldn't hang. She dispatched me to get my cousin around the block, but by the time we got back, Phil had been freed by a neighbor who'd heard Mother's screams. I never walked into that room—even years later, as a grown-up, when my aunt Gusta lived in that house—that I didn't replay that scene in my head.

Beth was unloading groceries—was standing by the drawer where we keep the mixer beaters and the barbecue brushes and the rubber spatulas. She saw the look on my face and stopped what she was doing. "Brent called," I said.

Over the next few months, Beth traveled back and forth between Little Rock and New York eight times. She was gone, in total, for ten or twelve weeks. To try to please her, I had our bedroom painted once while she was away—periwinkle, a shade of blue that Brent had picked. At night I would call her and we would talk for a few minutes. Then she would say she had to get off.

I was jealous. I liked Brent enormously, but this wasn't about Brent. I occupied myself by straightening the rusted doors of the shed out back. Then I sanded and primed the shed and painted it blue. As sheds went, it was now okay. I liked looking at it through the Geranium Room windows—my cool blue shed framed in the heat of Brent's perfect red.

Brent died that November, amid plans for a gala Thanksgiving party at his loft. Beth and I had flown up to help. She was cooking, making pies, planning menus, and I was doing whatever she needed me to do. Brent was all but confined to his bed, and he had a full-time nurse. He was concerned about getting his hallway papered before his guests came, and on Monday, the paperhanger stayed late into the night. The nurse and I helped Brent up at one point to inspect the work.

A few hours later, he took a turn for the worse. Beth talked with the doctor, who told her it was time. We pulled up chairs next to his bed, and Beth held his hand while I held hers. He died at about seven the next morning. She sat in one of the silk plaid chairs with the red that fades into gray.

A couple of months later, a moving van from New York pulled up in front of 501 Holly in Little Rock. In preparation for its arrival, we'd moved my big European sofa from the Geranium Room to the attic, which was then called "the playroom." We'd put my black lacquer bed and dresser and tables into storage. What poured out of that van was a procession of pieces the likes of which most of us never see except in magazines—a table shaped like a cannon, a bed upholstered in faux leopard skin, a massive, manly chifforobe, giant lamps with striped shades and fringe, a pouf upholstered in silk and velvet, a pair of red plaid chairs, a canvas screen—firm-breasted Greek maidens and strong young men with penises like jalapeños— that once belonged to Andy Warhol. Overnight, our house was transformed. And in some ways, so were we.

We now lived in one of the many, many houses in the world that had been touched by AIDS, and Brent's furniture was a daily reminder. Beth was both comforted and grief-stricken, in the way I imagine Jessie Armour was when she came back to this house and its familiar surroundings after the death of Charlie. Beth cried a lot. We were trying to write a screenplay together, and we fought constantly. Beth withdrew more and more. She couldn't work. I tried to comfort her, but I didn't do a good job of it. I didn't know how. Once, when I received an assignment from the *Atlantic Monthly*, I was thrilled and went to tell Beth about it. "Brent did that," she said. "Brent made that happen for you." She meant Brent the angel. I should've let it go, but I didn't. We pushed further apart. Another time, she told me our entire house had become a shrine to Brent. I began spending more time in the playroom, hiding away like Billie Murphree had, placing my drink on *my* Middle Eastern table and reading in *my* club chairs that I had bought with my first wife, back in Kansas City in 1968.

Then in the summer of 1991, Beth went to Mexico to a spa called Rancha La Puerta. She came home better. Not a hundred percent, but with a noticeable interest in moving forward. She wrote a wonderful magazine piece about her experience there, and the very act of writing helped her be ready to write more.

That fall, we finished the screenplay, and she began taking on magazine assignments. The next summer, she went to another spa, the Golden Door. While she was gone, I had dinner at my neighbors' house, where I heard the story of the roller-skating transvestite hippies. The story made me think more deeply about this house in which our own lives were being buffeted so. It made me think more deeply about our *lives*. I wanted to dig in, to hang on, not to let go this time. I made a conscious decision to hold the center. My way of doing it was to go back and find the roots in these rooms, and to connect myself—and us—to them.

That fall, I made contact with the first characters in the saga that would become this book. That fall, we also renegotiated the mortgage on this house, to lock in a lower rate. Beth and I both went. We both signed the papers.

# Epilogue

The grass, here in mid-July, is slow-growing in the heat, but it gets ragged and needs mowing nevertheless. There comes a point when the Bermuda on the slope of the front hill begins to sprout a tendril, whose top in turn pops a four-pronged extension. It's like a fireworks display out of the earth.

I've noticed a disturbing thing this summer—the area of bare dirt under the maple tree seems to be growing. Rocks are coming to the surface. A crisscross pattern of small roots is now visible, looking like a railroad switchyard viewed from on high. I don't know why this is happening. When I'm mowing like this, *seeing* it, it worries me. It's moving toward the house. I sometimes wonder if the land is starting the process of reclaiming itself, dust to dust, from the man-made world upon it.

I often look back at the very first photograph I have of this house, taken on a fine fall day in 1923. The house was new then. Its roof was sturdy, its masonry tight. Its walls were as unblemished as a promise. The second story hadn't been added yet. That would come three years later, with the cold wind that brought Elizabeth Armor to this place. I wonder what the house and its future would've been like had she never come. Her arrival was the end of the innocence. And yet I don't wish otherwise. It's possible that the loss she inflicted gives the house the very appeal that's attracted some of us to it.

Of all the houses I've lived in, I feel the most kinship with this one. Could be, that's partly a function of my age—now, as I stare at myself in the bathroom mirror, I can empathize with what I know of the house's slow nod to gravity. It's important to feel that you're a true part of your surroundings.

But I've felt myself gravitating toward this house, this life, for years. I feel at home writing and hope I can continue to do it. I also feel at home with Beth, despite the fact that we fight like cats and dogs. We're often at odds about our ideas of living in this house. I like more open spaces, but she leans, at least now with Brent's things, toward clutter. We have to rearrange the furniture to build a fire. Also, I like doors closed, so I can read without hearing the commotion. Beth likes doors open, likes three TVs and the stereo going at the same time. She lives her life that way—noisy, busy, doing many things at once. I try to focus, to lose myself in whatever I'm doing. I suspect there's something in the tension between us that keeps us alive. A house provides a couple an endless playing field.

We have traditions here now—Blair's ballet recital the first of every June, our Most Bizarre Pumpkin and Easter Egg contests in the fall and spring (I did a Judge Ito Egg last year), baking cookies at Christmas, having the neighbors over for our special eggnog. More than that, we have the comfort of routines and rituals—Bret and Snapp and I bound for school every morning, Bret trying to avoid finishing the milk she got up too late to drink at home; the girls setting the table and me doing the dishes; Beth and I going to the gym every morning to keep ourselves sane.

I think Jessie Armour would approve of most of the parties her house now hosts. They haven't all been as wine-soaked as that Monet lunch in the garden. We've also had rollicking croquet parties on the side lawn, like the Murphrees did so many years before. We've had elegant dinners and Mexican suppers and catfish fries and torch-light garden toasts to returning friends. When we first moved here, we sometimes came home and found our neighbors sitting on our porch, waiting for us, drink in hand. The porch has been our island. We eat supper there sometimes. We go there to get away from life, and we go there to celebrate life. And sometimes we go there just to *be* there. Beth and I have bundled up at midnight in the dead of January and carried cups of coffee to the hammock at the end of the porch, where we've lain like Eskimos, watching our breath blend with the coffee's steam, the wind chimes ringing like crystal in the cold, crisp air.

Left to my own devices, I wouldn't have a life like this. I know that, so I'm glad, mostly, not to be left to my own devices. This old house, with its flawed past and its walls gone to gray, will always be identified in my memory as the place where I knocked and they let me in.

But *memory* is the key word. Martha Murphree says she grieved when her parents sold 501 Holly. Whenever she would come to town for a visit, she would drive her car over to the old neighborhood, and she would park across the street and up the hill. From there, she had a perfect view of the house she'd grown up in. She was a wife and mother and a wife again, but home for her hadn't been any of the places she had lived as an adult.

That's why nostalgia is so strong a force on us. The very word is compounded from the Greek *nostos,* meaning "a return home," and *algos,* "pain." To me, it captures perfectly that bittersweet yearning to go back to a place where life felt secure, peaceful, controlled. The pain comes from knowing that no such place really exists.

Home, I think, is a moment, and that's what attracts us to houses. We search for home in houses because houses stand still. They seem rooted in a place. We want to stop time, like in a photograph.

But we know—don't we?—that even houses are changing constantly. Once the photograph is taken, what you have left is memory.

Outside the frame of the picture, time moves on. Jessie Armour lived in her apartment at the state hospital for the rest of her life. She traveled some. In 1952, her son, Charles, had a heart attack while walking along a street in Little Rock, and there was nobody to help him. He survived that attack as he had survived the war camp—barely. As Charles and Millie got to know each other better, he gradually told her about the war—*his* war. Late at night, lying next to her, he told her he *had* been on the Bataan Death March—the last half of it—and that the horrors had only increased from there.

Jessie died of cancer in 1952, and Charles had a final heart attack the next year. He and Millie had had a child in 1947, but the baby was premature and died in the hospital. Millie remembers being handed the child and weeping, the bundle in her arms reminding her of a porcelain doll she'd had as a girl, and which she had dropped and broken. Two years before Charles died, Millie gave birth to a son, Charles Webster Leverton Armour III—Jessie took it upon herself to name her grandson, and Millie didn't dare object. He's now a Methodist minister in Fort Smith, Arkansas, and his mother lives nearby. Millie never remarried. She hasn't spoken with her sister-in-law Jane in forty years. There was some problem with Jessie's will, and Jane let it be known that she wanted to have no more to do with Millie.

Jane's husband, Pem, had a radio business and later worked for the state forestry commission. Years ago, they moved to Pem's family plantation out in the community of Scott. Jane and Pem's widowed daughter, Janesy, lives in a house on the plantation, and Anne lives with her second husband in Little Rock. But back in the seventies, the McRaes' son, John Pem, was killed in a car wreck. Jane didn't tell me that—Millie did. She said she read it in the newspaper.

At Billie Murphree's funeral, his three daughters wore his

favorite color—red. The choir sang "The Old Rugged Cross," and he was buried with his Bible, duct tape and all. Later, Ruth was diagnosed with lymphoma. At first, her daughters thought she was imagining it, but it turned out to be real. All three girls are proud of the way she's coped. Joyce, the "perfect" daughter, lives in Little Rock with her husband of twenty-three years, and she checks on her mother regularly.

Pat's runaway marriage lasted about as long as Martha's church marriage, but in 1979 she and Larry called it quits. Billie helped her finish school, and now she's remarried and living in Atlanta. Some things don't change, however—she still seems alienated from her sisters, especially from Martha, whose marriage to Jerry lasted two decades, during which she lived mostly in wild and crazy California. She's now remarried. She and her second husband recited their vows in their Florida swimming pool. Since I began this book, they've sold their house and are now living on their boat.

After Roy and Rita Grimes raised their children, Rita went back to college and got a degree in accounting. They stayed in Little Rock, in the house they moved to from Holly Street. Roy left Garver and Garver and went into business on his own. Mark works with him. Scott is in sales with IBM. Kristi, a physical therapist, has moved to Virginia to fulfill a pact she'd made with her sister—they were both planning to live near the ocean. But Lori died in a fire in 1992, on her twenty-sixth birthday. She was with her boyfriend in his mobile home, and they fell asleep with a cigarette burning. Rita got a letter from Sheri Kramer after that. It was the first time they'd communicated in almost twenty years, since the problem with the house.

When I first met Roy and Rita, a year after Lori's death, they were together. But who really knows what's going on inside anyone's house? In 1995, they separated, after thirty-five years of marriage.

Ed and Sheri Kramer stayed in Little Rock for another nine years. In his thirties, Ed decided he wanted to become a doctor. He received his degree at age forty-one. Now he's a neurologist in Fort Worth, Texas. Alicia is finishing her senior year at Vassar. Siggy has managed nicely without the tip of his finger—he's taught himself to play guitar, and he recently had a small part in a movie, *The Road to Wellville,* with Anthony Hopkins. Sheri did have cancer, the cause of her lethargy while she was on Holly Street. The doctors removed the tumor shortly after she and Ed moved, and she's been fine ever since. She stays home now, tending her plants and Ed. Together, they collect ideas for the house they want to build someday.

Forrest and Sue Wolfe still live in the little house they moved to in the Heights, the one they can vacuum without unplugging the vacuum cleaner. Sue is teaching again, and Forrest is still with Blue Cross. They're beginning to plan for retirement—"herbs, goats, and a bed-and-breakfast," says Sue. The last I heard from them, they were getting into their car for a spontaneous trip to Memphis. There was a show at a museum they wanted to see.

Myke and Sue Landers's divorce, finalized in 1986, has been acrimonious from that day to this. They've both gone back to St. Louis, where Myke has tried his hand at several jobs. He's now a chiropractor, and he spends much of his time in legal wrangling with Sue, who has taken back her father's name—Goodman. She travels for a health-care company and lives with her younger daughter, Michelle, in the house she and Myke built together in 1977. Tracy is living with her boyfriend and is going to school.

Jack and Donna separated just around Christmastime in 1991. When I met Jack, he was trying his hand drilling gas wells. I guess they didn't come in, since he's now selling real estate for the very company that represented him in the purchase of this house. Jack doesn't know what Donna is doing now. Andi has moved to Missouri, where she works in real estate. Jack's daughter, Bitsi, lives in Houston and has a job in the cellular-phone industry. His boys live in Little Rock. Butch is a partner in a bond business, and Brad handles wholesale mortgages for the Bank of Boston. Butch, the onetime terror, now has presented Jack with his first grandchild, and Jack is amazed at Butch's patience with that baby.

After this litany, could anyone possibly believe that home is a physical place you can actually go to?

I spent a couple of weeks in Mississippi trying to finish this book. I stayed, alone, at my aunt May's house. She had been dead two years, but her daughter, my cousin Augusta, lives next door and keeps the house the way it was. This was the longest time I'd spent there since I was a teenager fleeing from my father's wrath. Wandering around through May's rooms, I discovered something: The way my aunt's house is situated, it's *impossible* to sit by the floor-to-ceiling windows reading a book, with the afternoon sun streaming in, filtered by the sheers.

"Memory," said Vladimir Nabokov, "is the only real estate." And a vision of the future affects the quality of today, which becomes the memory of tomorrow. You have to live not just in a house but in all the dimensions in which it exists.

You have to become a citizen of time.

When we moved here, this place stood like a sphinx—silent, stoic, mysterious. At night when we slept, I heard only creaks. All its spirits were still unseen. Then I started digging. During my research, it occurred to me to wonder how I was going to feel knowing so much about this place—whether there was such a thing as too much knowledge, and whether it would take away the attraction. It hasn't. For one thing, I know 501 Holly still has secrets. Some things, we just don't tell. Rick and Gene haven't found the roller-skating transvestite hippies, and sometimes when I'm sitting quietly, I think I feel something sailing past my chair like a ghost breeze.

But it's not just that the house didn't reveal everything it knows. For me, what it did reveal is plenty. Through the experience of writing this book, I've connected to something. I've placed myself, and my new family, into a continuum. That it turns out to be a continuum of search instead of discovery is beside the point. Now when I hear creaks in the night, they have voices. It's as though this were the house I grew up in.

One thing is different from my expectations, though. With many of my past houses, I harbored a secret hope that maybe that would be the place I stopped, the place where I lived out my days, the way my aunt May did in her house. Strangely, I don't feel like that anymore—at least not right now. Digging in here has freed me in some way. I feel renewed, not resigned.

Now I'm more interested in knowing what legacy we'll leave for the next people, if we ever choose to move from this place. Mowing this lawn, I can't help noticing how much the house needs painting. I've had the tuck pointing done, though that's a constant battle when you reach a certain age. Skin spots, melanoma. With any luck, we'll paint this fall. We've installed central heat and air upstairs, and I hope to add air downstairs soon. Middle-age dreams. We put the skylight in the playroom, now my office. By my count, that's the fifty-sixth window in this house. No wonder it's seen so much of life.

And I guess *that's* the legacy I've got in mind. Not the things, the improvements, though they're certainly an integral part of inhabiting this house over time. More than inhabiting it, living up to its history. I don't want to fail at that. I pray there won't be debilitating decay or bloodcurdling calamity, but if there are, I hope we rise to those challenges, too. The legacy I'm talking about, though, has little to do with brick and wood and plaster and glass. It concerns instead that space in the middle, that charged air in which we act out our daily lives. At night before I doze, I like closing my eyes and drifting until the music comes, the tinny nasal Victrola that summons Jessie and Charlie from wherever they are, with their rugs rolled back and the soft slide of the fox-trot on the hardwood just beyond this wall. I like hearing

Elvis, back when he was bad, and imagining Martha in the music room doing the dirty bop. I like hearing the tinkle of Jessie's dinner parties and the click of Ruth's cards.

I want our chapter to ring with the sounds of life in our time. I want us to make good stories. Because someday, somebody like me may need to hear them.

And the walls have ears.

*Acknowledgments*

Home is supposed to be the place where your privacy is sacrosanct. For that reason, I owe a great debt of thanks to all those former residents of 501 Holly who allowed me to probe into the lives they lived within these walls. I won't name them again, since they *are* the story. But I want them to know that I approached this project without judgment, and I end it the same way. For all homeowners, in this house and elsewhere, all I feel is a deep and abiding tenderness, and I hope that comes through in the book. Life is a struggle, and our relationships with our houses capture that struggle to a remarkable degree.

Many others also helped me over the three years of this project. Since it would be impossible in this short space to spell out the specifics of every contribution, I'll simply list the names and trust that each knows the degree of my gratitude: John and Linda Burnett, Patti Kymer and B. J. Davis, Don and Ruth Chapin, Annabelle Ritter, Susan Sims Smith, Guy Amsler Jr., Georgia and Bob Sells, Toni and Skip Cullum, Tina Poe, Maribeth Magby, Peg Smith, Mary Worthen, Kelly Marlowe, Tom Murphree, C. W. L. Armour III, Judith Long, John Witherspoon, Janet Jones, Lisa Matthews, Joe Kuonen, George Bilheimer, Jerry Russell, Jack Trotter, Linda Overton, Bill and Jennifer Rector, Max Brantley, Alan Leveritt, Olivia Farrell, Debbie Speck, Sandy McMath, Augusta Day, David

Sanders, Lu and Dave Richards, Bliss Thomas and John Gerke, Richard Woodley, Steve Edwards, Betty O'Pry, "Gene" and "Rick," Jan Emberton and the reference staff of the Little Rock Public Library, the staff at the Arkansas History Commission, Linda Green of the Bankruptcy Court, the helpful people at Beach Abstract and at the Pulaski County Clerk's Office, Barbara Lindsey-Allen and Robin Baldwin of the Arkansas Historic Preservation Program, and my agent, Joseph Vallely.

In addition, many people whom I've never met or spoken with helped immeasurably by their writings, and I want to mention them in addition to those works I've already cited in the text: Cheryl Griffith Nichols for a paper called "The Development of Pulaski Heights," plus many other works about the background of this area; James W. Bell for his *Little Rock Handbook*; Jim and Judy Lester for their book *Greater Little Rock;* F. Hampton Roy for his *How We Lived: Little Rock as an American City*. Alan Gurganus for his wonderful essay in the collection *Home*; Joseph Mitchell for *Up in the Old Hotel*; the film *The Wisdom of the Dream*, part two, on which you can hear Carl Jung's description of the pivotal house dream. Also, though I mentioned Robert Grudin's work, I didn't give the title of his book, which I found so useful—*Time and the Art of Living*.

I want to single out the contributions of my editor, Jamie Raab, and her then-assistant, Rob McQuilkin. They loved the idea of this book from the beginning, and they never failed to let me know it. No *wonder* both of them have been promoted since we began this project. Jamie proved to be an astute and insightful editor, both in the big picture and in the small details, and I count myself lucky to have been able to work with her.

Finally, I want to thank my family, beginning with my mother and father and brother, with whom I shared so many houses. For this book, my mother, Pat, refreshed my memory with her wonderful stories. My brother, Phil, a writer himself, read portions of the manuscript and offered insights of his own. My late father, Leger, simply loomed over the whole project, as he seems to loom over so many things I write, no matter how much I try to escape it. My own sons, David and Matthew, with whom I've shared so few houses, encouraged me to pursue this quest even when it looked like the longest of long shots.

As for the current residents of 501 Holly—Beth, Blair, and Bret—I'm grateful to them all, not just for being such an important part of my story, but for their love and forbearance during my telling of it. Especially Beth, who knows right where I live.